A Black Woman's Journey
from Cotton Picking to College Professor

"All gain from reading this book about the life of Dr. Mildred Pratt. There are few fields of scholarly inquiry or general interests that are not at least touched upon in these pages. Here is, ultimately, an important commentary on race and rights, class and status, gender, and Jim and Jane Crow. The world was made better by Dr. Mildred Pratt having been a part of it. Others will be left better for having read this story of her life."

—Stephanie Shaw, Professor of History, Ohio State University

"Dr. Mildred Sirls Pratt's story is one of the genesis, rise, and remarkable triumph of an extraordinary individual overcoming herculean odds. Her remarkable feats—despite successive setbacks—as she navigated a career as a tenure track professor without a blueprint is a story of legend. Her life is an amazing journey from sharecropping to the academy. Her memoir is an insightful window into what it means to be Black in America, individually and collectively."

—James Anderson, Dean, College of Education,
University of Illinois at Urbana-Champaign

"This enormously important volume documents the first generation of African American women professors at predominantly White academic institutions in the wake of the modern civil rights movement. It will make a splendid contribution to women's history, gender studies, and to African American life and history. It will inspire African American women in the academy to chronicle their own lives and contributions to the intellectual and historical record."

—Darlene Clark Hine, Professor of African American Studies
and Professor of History, Northwestern University

"*A Black Woman's Journey from Cotton Picking to College Professor* is a wonderful and special journey. I encourage others to explore this amazing life story. I'm sure they will enjoy it as much as I did."

—Nikki Giovanni, University Distinguished Professor
of English, Virginia Tech

A Black Woman's Journey
from Cotton Picking
to College Professor

Rochelle Brock and Cynthia Dillard
Executive Editors

Vol. 107

The Black Studies and Critical Thinking series
is part of the Peter Lang Education list.
Every volume is peer reviewed and meets
the highest quality standards for content and production.

PETER LANG
New York • Bern • Berlin
Brussels • Vienna • Oxford • Warsaw

Menah Pratt-Clarke

A Black Woman's Journey from Cotton Picking to College Professor

Lessons about Race, Class, and Gender in America

PETER LANG
New York • Bern • Berlin
Brussels • Vienna • Oxford • Warsaw

Library of Congress Cataloging-in-Publication Data

Names: Pratt-Clarke, Menah A. E., author.
Title: A black woman's journey from cotton picking to college professor:
lessons about race, class, and gender in America / Menah Pratt-Clarke.
Description: New York: Peter Lang, 2018.
Series: Black studies and critical thinking; Volume 107 | ISSN 1947-5985
Includes bibliographical references and index.
Identifiers: LCCN 2017036940 | ISBN 978-1-4331-4973-3 (hardback: alk. paper)
ISBN 978-1-4331-4974-0 (pbk.: alk. paper)
ISBN 978-1-4331-4970-2 (ebook pdf) | ISBN 978-1-4331-4971-9 (epub)
ISBN 978-1-4331-4972-6 (mobi)
Subjects: LCSH: Pratt, Mildred, 1928–2012. | African Americans—Social
Conditions—20th century. | African American sociologists—Biography. |
African American women college teachers—Biography. | Race
Discrimination—United States—History—20th century. | Race
Relations—United States—History—20th century. | Civil rights
Movements—United States—History—20th century. | African
Americans—Civil rights—History—20th century. | Sociologists—United
States—Biography. | Women college teachers—Biography.
Classification: LCC E185 .P73 | DDC 301.092 [B] —dc23
LC record available at https://lccn.loc.gov/2017036940
DOI 10.3726/b11827

Bibliographic information published by **Die Deutsche Nationalbibliothek.**
Die Deutsche Nationalbibliothek lists this publication in the "Deutsche
Nationalbibliografie"; detailed bibliographic data are available
on the Internet at http://dnb.d-nb.de/.

The paper in this book meets the guidelines for permanence and durability
of the Committee on Production Guidelines for Book Longevity
of the Council of Library Resources.

© 2018 Peter Lang Publishing, Inc., New York
29 Broadway, 18th floor, New York, NY 10006
www.peterlang.com

Printed in the United States of America

This book is dedicated to Dr. Mildred Pratt, my mother, who took time to write and share her journey so that she could become the shoulders for others to stand upon. Like Langston Hughes' *The Negro Mother*, she "has come back today to tell you a story of the long dark way that [she] had to climb, that [she] had to know in order that the race might live and grow." Like *The Negro Mother*, she encourages us to "make of her past a road to the light."

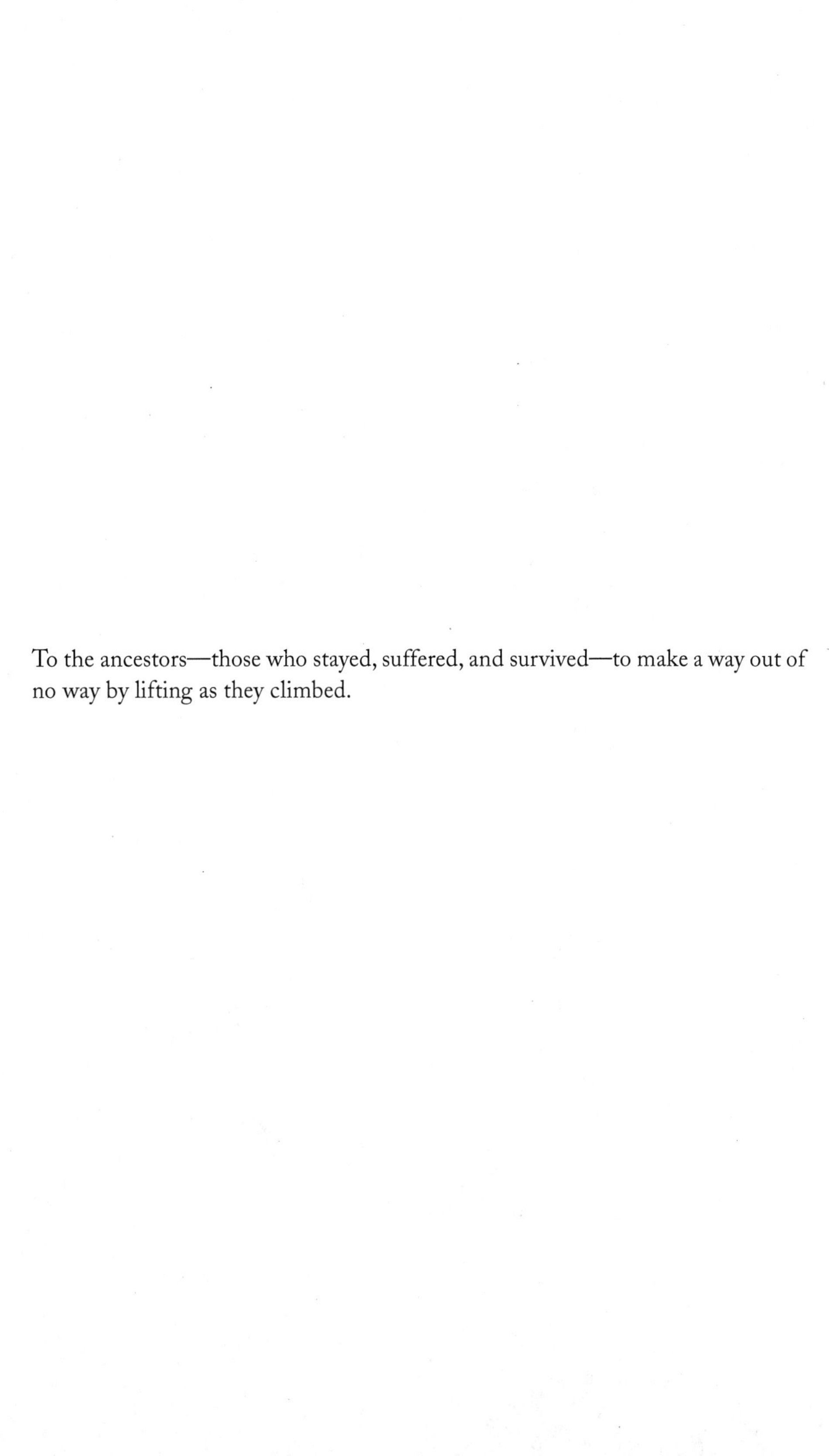

To the ancestors—those who stayed, suffered, and survived—to make a way out of no way by lifting as they climbed.

Contents

Illustrations

Foreword

Note: James D. Anderson is the Dean and Edward William and Jane Marr Gutsgell Professor of Education at the University of Illinois at Urbana–Champaign. His scholarship focuses broadly on the history of U.S. education, with specializations in the history of African-American education in the South, the history of higher education desegregation, the history of public school desegregation, and the history of African-American school achievement in the twentieth century.

At first glance, Dr. Mildred Sirls Pratt's story is one of the genesis, rise, and remarkable triumph of an extraordinary individual overcoming herculean odds. To be sure, noteworthy achievement is a central part of her story. Yet, the more we read about the things that tormented her, of the inner strengths she mustered to break down countless race, gender, and class barriers, and of her intellect and determination to carve out a better life for herself and her family, we realize that her experiences are reflective of the larger world made and remade by generations of ordinary Black men and women. However, her remarkable feats—despite successive setbacks—as she navigated a career as a tenure track professor without a blueprint is a story of legend. Learning of Mildred Sirls Pratt's experiences connects us with the life and culture of the generations of African-Americans who lived from the end of slavery through the postmodern Civil Rights movement. Her childhood experiences in the Jim Crow South connects us to the subterranean culture of African-Americans in various ways, from games and songs, to the language, food, clothing, medical remedies, religion, education, and labor of tenant farmers and sharecroppers. Her professional experiences as a graduate student, social worker, and professor in northern states reflect the persistent forms of racism inflicted on African-Americans irrespective of education, income, and class. Finally, her accomplishments reveal how individual Black women succeeded in spite of race and gender discrimination.

Her life as a sharecropper in East Texas represents a common experience for Blacks in southern states. At the turn of the twentieth century, approximately half of all Texas farmers were tenants and the highest proportion were African-American—69 percent compared to 47 percent for Whites (Harper & Odom, 2010). In Texas, as in other southern states, a hierarchy of tenant farmers developed, according to what resources tenant farmers could bring to the negotiation. At the top were share and cash tenants who could furnish their own mules, plows, seed, feed, and related necessities. At the bottom were sharecroppers who could only supply their labor. The Sirls family, like most African-American tenant farmers, was at the bottom. The Sirls were part of the East Texas cotton economy where approximately three-quarters of the state's cotton acreage lay prior to the end of World War II.

Mildred Sirls Pratt's memoir informs us of the African-American traditions and also of the economic and political conditions under which Black tenant farmers lived and worked in the pre-*Brown v. Board of Education* era. In short, her life channels us into the stream of African-American life and culture as it was being created in the farm tenancy world of the twentieth century. Sharecropping, above all else, meant poverty, hunger, and political exploitation. Still, African-American cultural forms emerged in the midst of a plantation-like society that systematically repressed and starved sharecroppers.

Every Sunday, her family walked miles to church where she learned to "line out" the music as the congregation followed. This practice was especially crucial in a community where there were few or no songbooks and people in general could not read. They sang such gospel songs as "Down by the Riverside" (also known as "Ain't Gonna Study War No More"). For recreation, they jumped rope and played croquet and other games like "Little Sally Walker." These games were played by generations of African-American children across the southern states and moved north and west with the Great Migrations. Such games, folktales, religious rituals, poems, and songs formed the foundation of African-American ethical values and shaped their views of a just and humane society. In his anti-Vietnam war speeches, Martin Luther King would draw upon words from "Down by the Riverside," calling for all people of goodwill to come to a massive act of conscience and say in the words of the old Negro spiritual, "we ain't goin' to study war no more." Such songs and rituals connected African-Americans collectively and individually.

More importantly, Mildred Sirls found within her culture the values and beliefs that propelled her to transform a childhood of poverty and exploitation into a remarkable career as a social worker and professor. Critical to her transformation was the long-standing tradition that poor African-American families placed on the value of education. In Mildred's words, "frostbitten feet were the norm. In spite of the situation we did not miss a day in school unless we were ill." Before going to bed at night she and her siblings would gather in their mother's room and listen to the reading from the Bible and a book of poems. The poems she learned to recite ("House by the Side of the Road" by Sam Walter Foss; "Invictus" by William Ernest Henley; and "The Creation" by James Weldon Johnson) were learned by African-American schoolchildren across the South. There is hardly a member of her generation that could get through school without learning to recite and interpret such poems and verses that remained the gold standard in southern Black education, at least until the end of racially segregated schooling in the post-Civil Rights era.

Mildred Sirls found that the value of education emphasized at home was also deeply affirmed in school. She recalls the great fortune of having excellent teachers who believed in children learning, asserting that "the Black teachers were relentless to teach." One teacher, Ira Henry, took great interest in Mildred and encouraged her to excel at the highest level. Mildred Sirls graduated Valedictorian of her high school in 1946, and with Ms. Henry's guidance she was admitted to Jarvis Christian College in Hawkins, Texas, a historically Black college. In the post-World War II era, historically Black colleges and universities enrolled more than 90 percent of Black college students, making her college experience reflective of the emerging postwar Black middle class (Harper, 2007). She excelled at Jarvis Christian and followed her undergraduate experience with work and graduate study. Following her graduation from Jarvis Christian College, she went on to earn three advanced degrees: a Master's degree in religion from Butler University, a Masters of Social Work degree from Indiana University, and a PhD in Social Work from the University of Pittsburgh.

Mildred Sirls' experiences in the north showed that intransigent racism and persistent discrimination were not peculiar to the South. Each milestone along the way taught profound lessons about the difference between Jim Crow segregation in the South and the day-to-day racism and discrimination that characterized close encounters with Whites in northern communities. As a child, she lived in segregated and insulated "Black enclaves" where the Whites she saw were usually the ones her mother worked for as a maid. Graduate school and professional life brought her into close encounters with different and more subtle forms of racism and discrimination in northern and Midwestern states—Indiana, Missouri, Michigan, and Pennsylvania.

Ultimately she was admitted to the doctoral program in Social Work at the University of Pittsburgh where she was the only Black student in the advanced degree program. While in Pittsburgh she would meet her future husband Theodore Pratt, a nuclear physicist graduate student at Carnegie Institute of Technology (now Carnegie Mellon University). They were married in 1964 and following the birth of their two children, Awadagin and Menah, issues of race discrimination took on a new and more ominous meaning.

Routine forms of discrimination became serious problems for the family. Racism was particularly painful when inflicted on their defenseless children in school and out of school. Mildred Pratt learned quickly that having three advanced degrees and a professional occupation did not shield her from the kinds of racism faced by ordinary Black men and women. Following the completion of her PhD, she and her husband took faculty positions at Illinois State University. While taking a walk in her residential community in Normal, Illinois, a White neighbor offered Dr. Pratt a job as a cook and a maid, reminding her that Black bodies were always presumed to be an available pool of cheap, uneducated, menial labor. Inside the academy was no less painful. Mildred Pratt describes her worst experience as the discrimination she faced when trying to get promoted.

Hence, it is not surprising that Dr. Mildred Sirls Pratt focused a significant part of her professional career on creating and sustaining the Bloomington-Normal Black History Project, which gathered the life stories of almost 100 elderly African-Americans. So much about her life had taught her the crucial lesson of knowing from whence you came and of transmitting from generation to generation African-American forms of resistance and the ways in which they affirmed their humanity through culture, music, and religion.

Her life is an amazing journey from sharecropping to the academy and the ways in which she traveled the stony road makes her life an all and sundry reflection of the African-American experience. Her self-respect, intellect, and self-determination led her to accomplish great things in life. She was an excellent scholar and teacher, traveled the world (Brazil, England, Czechoslovakia, Hungary, Sierra Leone, Jamaica, Bahamas, France, Poland, and Italy), met Presidents Clinton and Obama, watched her son give a piano recital in the White House, and saw her daughter become an Associate Chancellor at the University of Illinois at Urbana–Champaign. Her memoir is an insightful window into what it means to be Black in America, individually and collectively.

References

Harper, B. (2007). African American access to higher education: The evolving role of historically black colleges and universities. *American Academic, 3*, 109–128.

Harper, Jr., C., & Odom, E. D. (2010, June 12). Farm Tenancy. *Handbook of Texas Online.* Retrieved from http://www.tshaonline.org/handbook/online/articles/aefmu

Acknowledgments

This book would not have been possible but for the interest and commitment of Professor Rochelle Brock, editor of Black Studies and Critical Thinking Series with Peter Lang, to support the scholarship of African-Americans. Thank you, Rochelle, for your unwavering commitment and belief in me.

This book is the culmination of a five-year journey that began when my mother died on August 6, 2012. Writing her story enabled us to stay connected as I daily touched her handwritten notes and sought to feel and decipher her joy, pain, sorry, loss, passion, and wisdom. She walked alongside me as I wrote her story. Others accompanied us as well. The ancestors seemed to have orchestrated the universe in such a way as to ensure that this project would move toward fruition. At crucial moments, unexpected angels were sent my way to provide encouragement and assistance.

Shortly after my mother's death, Patty Sirls, my uncle's wife, sent my grandmother's quilt (book cover photo) and a crocheted bedspread to me in the spring of 2013. Just having the material possessions of my own ancestors near provided an ongoing reminder of our shared struggle. A few months later, during the summer of 2013, our family stopped at the Lawrence County, Alabama Archives on the way to the Thirkill Reunion (my mother's grandfather's family). Not only were the employees helpful, but Ms. Lisa Lentz, another visitor to the Archives who was researching her own family history, was a fabulous gift. She graciously took time away from her own research to look through documents and educate me on how to do genealogy and how to piece together little lines of data to understand a life. Being on the ancestral land of my great-grandparents in Alabama reminded me of the connection between my mother's story and their stories. Coming full circle, in November 2013, I visited the gravesite of my mother's grandfather, George Thirkill in Phoenix, Arizona. Patty and I placed flowers on his headstone.

In 2016, the writing and work had ground to a halt for this manuscript. Other book projects garnered my attention: *Journeys of Social Justice: Women of Color Presidents in the Academy* (Peter Lang, 2017) and *Reflections about Race, Gender, and Culture in Cuba* (Peter Lang, 2017). My friend, Alfreda Burnett, courageously suggested I contact Olivia Butler, an amazing scholar, historian, and writer, for a jump-start on the manuscript. Metaphorically, Olivia was the jump cable that I needed to restart the work. She provided invaluable suggestions and ideas that significantly strengthened the manuscript. I am very grateful to both Alfreda and Olivia.

I am thankful for family friends, including Darlene Miller, Marc Miller, Pam Muirhead, and Patsy Bowles, who were my mother's best friends. They were an invaluable source of inspiration and encouragement. My mother's colleague and friend, Professor Stephanie Shaw, worked with her at Illinois State University. She graciously offered to write the introduction. She believed in this work from the beginning. I am grateful for her. Professor Darlene Clark Hine, who also knew my mother, was so supportive of this project. Thank you, Stephanie and Darlene.

Professor Jim Anderson, who wrote the foreword, and Professor Chris Span, who took time to read the work and provided encouragement, are wonderful colleagues from the University of Illinois at Urbana–Champaign. I will always be grateful for Jim's role as a mentor, advocate, and sponsor. Laura Podeschi served as the initial editor by reading and editing every page, sentence, and word. My friends, PJ Fernandez and Mercedes Ramirez Fernandez, sustained me during difficult days of grief and I will always remain deeply grateful for the presence of their friendship.

Most importantly, I must acknowledge my family. No project of this magnitude can be accomplished alone. My children, Emmanuel and Raebekkah, helped immensely in transcribing documents and scanning photos. They also selflessly recognized the magnitude of the work and granted me the grace and time to write. My husband, Obadiah, was extremely supportive and kind. He lovingly encouraged me at each step of this journey. He also cared for my mother in our home in her last few months as if she was his mother. Thank you, Obadiah, for that gift of grace. My aunt, Bernice Miller—the only surviving sibling of eight—has been so gracious with her time to talk with me about her memories and recollections of her life and my mother's life. My brother, Awadagin, remains a source of inspiration, as well as my father, Theodore Pratt, who, despite a life of racism, ultimately triumphed. I also want to acknowledge my ancestors—my grandmothers, Eula and Elizabeth, my great grandparents, George and Rosa, and the generations of enslaved Africans and African Americans—who sacrificed in countless ways for future generations.

Finally, I want to thank Mama for taking time to write her own memoir and for entrusting me to bring it to completion. This is such a beautiful gift to me and to all those who are seeking to make a difference, regardless of their race, class, or gender. Thank you, Mama.

Part I Sunrise

The sound of silence breaking is harsh, resonant, soft, battering, small, chaotic, furious, terrified, triumphant.—Janet Miller[1]

The very act of writing, especially for people who do not occupy positions of status and privilege in the general society, is a bold and courageous enterprise.—Jacqueline Royster[2]

CHAPTER ONE

Introduction

In this introduction, Stephanie Shaw, Professor, Department of History, Ohio State University, a long-time colleague and friend of Mildred Pratt's, contextualizes the historical significance of the work and highlights issues of race, migration, gender, class, segregation, and discrimination in America. Her discussion of the historical context is followed by a discussion of the personal context by the biographer, Menah Pratt-Clarke (Mildred's daughter). An overview of each chapter is also provided.

Historical Context

For anyone who has decided or is in the process of deciding whether to read *A Black Woman's Journey*, it is a volume that holds a wonderfully complex story. It is simultaneously biography and autobiography, history and memory. It is an individual's story that includes both corroboration and contradiction from family members, and the story of a family's journey from economic stability to poverty and back to comfort, even privilege. The family here is sometimes significantly dysfunctional, but it mostly manages, sometimes with help, to function brilliantly. And ultimately this family, despite its regular economic deprivation, always remains strong and formidable.

Blending both personal and scholarly narratives, this book traces Jim and Jane Crow's paths from the Deep South to the Southwest, to the Mid-South, the Mid-west, the Far West, and the North—from the mid-nineteenth to the late-twentieth century. Part of that portrait is framed by the perspective of a child, though undoubtedly filtered through the lens of an adult. It becomes a portrait framed by the perspective of an adult, filtered through the eyes of a scholar.

This volume takes us from poverty to poetry, literally and figuratively. It is not a story of movement from the metaphorical and now clichéd "outhouse to White House" but, literally, to the White House—three times(!), and from once not even having an outhouse. *A Black Woman's Journey* is, indeed, a complex story. But, then, the story of a life, almost any life, is a complex one, especially if it is an honest account.

But *A Black Woman's Journey* is more than an individual biography and more than a multigenerational (beginning in slavery) family history. Beyond the brutally honest (and, remarkably, almost dispassionate) family history, scholars with interests in Deep South sharecropping and segregation, the various migrations of Black people beginning after the Civil War, the Civil Rights Movement, the women's movement, men's, women's, and children's labor history and sociology, the study of church and religion, the history of education, philanthropy, social networks (symbolic interaction), and more, will all gain from reading this book about the life of Dr. Mildred Inez Sirls Pratt.

And, perhaps of interest to academics in any field interested in translating their academic work into real-life, real-time relevance, Mildred's life story provides a model of an academic who knew how to, and did, connect her academic work to community people and created a local history project that was driven by the community people themselves. It is importantly also the story of an academic of very modest means who managed, throughout her life, to help look after others, whether family members or not.[3]

There are, ultimately, few fields of scholarly inquiry or general interests that are not at least touched upon in these pages. And so, sociologists, anthropologists, historians, critical theorists, political economists, philosophers, social justice, labor, and equal rights advocates, humanists, humanitarians, faith-based activists, philanthropists, and others, will find much of use in this volume. Here is, ultimately, an important commentary on race and rights, class and status, gender, and Jim and Jane Crow.

Mildred began her story with a list of "Important Dates in My Life." The list begins with the 1619 introduction of Africans, including slaves, to the United States (then, British colonies). In one way, it is interesting that Mildred would see this event as an important date in *her* life, even though she was born some 300 years later. As you will see, Mildred never viewed her life in isolation—whether one considers time or space. But there are events in this book that connect her to the beginning of the African slave trade, literally.

Whether Mildred knew it or not, African cultural traditions appeared throughout her life story. The naming patterns among her family members replicate those among slaves detailed by Herbert Gutman (1975, pp. 185–229) and Cheryll Ann Cody (1987) and characterized as uniquely African. Later, when Mildred's family home in Texas was destroyed, the only surviving artifact was a kitchen platter. Following an African tradition of grave decoration, years later Mildred's mother placed that dish on her daughter Ruby's grave after she died at the age of 6 (see Jamieson, 1995; Thompson, 1983; and Vlach, 1977, for African and African American traditions of grave decorations). Folk traditions ("superstitions" and homeopathic remedies) sometimes became fused with (probably) Euro-American and/or Native American ones, but there are at least remnants of African traditions there, too.

One of the most significant threads in this volume revolves around the experiences of a sharecropping family. The sharecropping stories in this book often resemble other first-person and scholarly accounts. As one might imagine, for example, there was significant deprivation, exploitation, and the occasional sneaking away in the middle of the night (or, the day) with the potential for facing more of the same in the next place. But, perhaps uncharacteristically, compared to many other accounts, most of the employers of the Sirlses provided decent living accommodations and paid the family according to the contract. These employers sometimes even exceeded the agreement by providing clothes for the children and extra food for the family.

But Mildred's account also presents an important opportunity for asking more questions and conducting a different kind of investigation. Many of their employers were Black, and often they were relatives. While other Black croppers undoubtedly worked under these kinds of arrangements, it is a story rarely (if ever) studied. The experience of the Sirlses suggests the great potential inherent in a scholarly examination of intra-racial sharecropping arrangements. Mildred's family always fared better in these intra-racial situations; the family often received their housing for free. While this was sometimes the way that better-off family members helped to take care of less well-off relatives, it is clear that this was not always a familial arrangement.[4]

Some of these employers benefited from the Depression Era Texas oil boom. Oil discoveries in Texas began in the late nineteenth century, but the 1930s discoveries dramatically and unexpectedly affected standards of living for Black landowners during The Great Depression. Mildred speculates that some of the people they worked for were "rich" because they sold their mineral rights to Whites. If they, in fact, sold these rights, they were not nearly as rich as they would have been had they kept them. There have been numerous (still sketchy and incomplete) studies of the Black loss of land in the South, a phenomenon that the Sirlses also mysteriously suffered. The study of the loss of Black family wealth as a consequence of losing control of the minerals in the land that they still owned lags much farther behind. This would, even generations later, have a crippling effect on families still in the possession of land, but land of little value without the mineral rights (which were often not bought, but stolen).[5]

Mildred's family was not always poor, nor was the experience of her immediate family replicated throughout the extended family. Mildred's family had owned land in Texas almost since their arrival there, and some of them were quite prosperous. Mildred believed that some family members received land as a consequence of the "40 acres and a mule" proposal. But the actual plan (General Sherman's Field Order # 15) was almost immediately reversed, and many former slaves immediately lost the possibility of owning the land they had always and were still working. Still, it is the case that some public lands were sold to former slaves.[6]

It is, however, clearest in this narrative that the Thirkill side of the family was part Native American: grandmother, Rosa Thirkill was half Indian and half White. Given that her roots were in Alabama, which was formerly primarily "Indian Lands" before becoming a state, it is not surprising. And even if they had been the slaves of Indians, rather than descendants of them, they would have been entitled to land.[7]

Mildred's mother and siblings descended into deep poverty only after her father irresponsibly destroyed the family home by setting it ablaze to conceal evidence of his earlier theft of cotton. After the fire, Mildred's father immediately relocated them and set them up as sharecroppers on someone else's land. And in this case, and in all others, as soon as he moved them, he disappeared, leaving his wife and children to do the work and to support themselves.

Although Mildred credits her brother George for contributing to their well-being, Mildred deserves much credit for the family's survival. She cleaned houses, prepared meals, tended children, worked in fields and in farms, while still a child. Her sisters remember her as always having been serious, even as the rest of them played. And her income (until she was preparing to go to college) was never her own; it was a much needed part of the family economy.[8] But Mildred's mother (Eula Thirkill Sirls) was especially responsible for how well this family seems to have functioned, despite its poverty.

Mrs. Sirls attended school only to the sixth grade (there were no higher grades available locally for Black children, and her father would not let her, an only child and a girl, leave home for school), but she clearly valued education and worked with her children when they could and when they could not attend school themselves. She also expected the older children to teach the younger ones. Among all their lessons, they all read, recited, and memorized poems. This activity was undoubtedly educational. It was equally a utilitarian form of entertainment for people who were poor (though activities like these might have been more typical in better-off families). But it was also a subtle and disguised lesson in discipline. This kind of activity focused one's thinking and efforts, vivified successes, and enhanced the potential for future success.

Ironically, the list of important dates in Mildred's life also includes the passage of the Thirteenth Amendment. That amendment obviously codified the end of slavery. But for many slave families, emancipation began family traditions of migration. While most former slaves left farms and plantations looking for other family members, wage work, adventure, and/or sometimes simply the proof of their freedom, Mildred's family elders left Alabama for Texas in search of property. Some of them (or their children) moved on to Oklahoma, Missouri, and other places.

Members of the next generation, Mildred's (Depression/World War II-era) generation, followed them, or went farther north or west or, in the case of the brothers, joined the military. In every case, one can see both the familiar step migration in which one moves, literally, step by step, from one place to another and then another until reaching an ultimate destination that becomes the permanent family home. And one can see, even more clearly, chain migrations in which one family member gets established in a new location, and then others join him or her (usually in dribs and drabs) until everyone (who wants to) is resettled in the same general area.[9]

There was usually both a "push" and a "pull" factor operating in most migration narratives and in the experience of Mildred's family. People were not simply pushed from a place by negative conditions, but were simultaneously pulled or drawn to another place for various positive reasons.[10] Mildred's own early moves were undoubtedly economically motivated, but they were also connected to her quest for education. Her example was different from the moves of migrating adults seeking destinations that would support the education of their children (one of the chief reasons migrants reported for leaving the South during the 1910s).[11] Still, Mildred's experience was practically the mirror image of hundreds of thousands of other migrants.

When she went to Missouri in 1946 to work during the summer before going to Jarvis Christian College, she joined the family of her uncle Booker T. Sirls, who had earlier migrated from Texas to Oklahoma and then to Kansas City. When Mildred's mother and younger siblings were unable to make it without her help, they also relocated to Kansas City. Friends from home who had friends and family members there also assisted them in living arrangements and finding jobs. Years later, after completing undergraduate and graduate degrees, Mildred moved to California (where other family members had gone earlier), and her mother later joined her. Eventually, Mildred's sister joined them, along with her children. In every instance, "friends of friends" networks went to work again.[12]

Mildred's work and college experiences, as a maid, paralleled the struggles faced by many Black "strivers" who wanted more than they had but possessed few family means of assistance. Traditionally, male college students had more lucrative options than women. Some of the men went north during the summers to work in segregated White resorts. While performing menial service work, they earned comparatively decent in wages, also counting their tips. The most fortunate of them spent their summers working as Pullman porters.[13] Women, however, had few options beyond domestic work. Even Black, college educated, female school teachers (particularly single women) sometimes spent their summers doing domestic work in private homes in the North because of the inadequate and unequal salaries paid to school teachers in the South.[14]

Mildred studied religion at Jarvis and at Butler. But before beginning a master's degree program in social work, she (with other Disciples of Christ missionaries) traveled to Jamaica to help rebuild a church after a very destructive hurricane. The experience seems to have launched her transition from almost passive acceptance of the way things were to active resistance. On the June 1951 Greyhound bus ride from Indiana to Florida, where all the volunteers were to meet to continue their journey by plane, Mildred befriended two of the White volunteers (graduate students from Indiana University), and they and two others decided not to ride Jim Crow. After shaming the others (including the two remaining Black missionaries) for their unchristian actions, the majority of the volunteers agreed that they would not continue the journey Jim Crowed, and the organizers had to scramble to find a bus that would carry an integrated clientele.

To be sure, this was a decade after CORE (The Congress of Racial Equality) began trying to force the integration of interstate transportation, but it was, importantly, a full decade *before* the famous, and history changing, Freedom Rides. Moreover, it was a decade before integrated interstate transportation had a federal mandate in the form of the 1961 Interstate Commerce Commission decision (which the Freedom Riders were testing) making it illegal to segregate such conveyances and their facilities. Integrated, *intra*state transportation, however, particularly in the South, remained illegal even after 1961, making Mildred and her colleagues something of a vanguard.[15]

Clearly, by the time Mildred returned and enrolled in her second master's degree program at Indiana University, she was a changed person. Upon the completion of the Indiana University degree in social work (Masters of Arts in 1955), she moved to Los Angeles and later to Detroit. Moving into her professional career created many opportunities for Mildred to come face-to-face with racial discrimination and to take a stand. Eventually, Mildred decided to pursue the PhD at the University of Pittsburgh.

Mildred's decision to go to Pitt was fateful in other, even more important, ways. While there, she met and married Theodore Pratt (a PhD student and later graduate in physics), gave birth to two children (Awadagin and Menah), and gained much more experience as an activist. After Mildred completed her dissertation, she, Ted (who was teaching at Hampton University at the time), and the children moved to Bloomington/Normal, Illinois, where she and Ted had been offered Assistant Professorships.

Mildred taught at Illinois State University for almost 30 years and had a successful career: former students and colleagues sang her praises, and still do, many years after their encounters with her. And while Mildred sometimes struggled in her own department, she also revived a moribund local history project, pioneered by interested Black citizens of Bloomington and Normal, and with her efforts, it thrived for many years. Mildred recognized the importance of this project to these local septua-, octo-, and nonagenarians.

Mildred made real the aspirations of these Black community residents who were interested in preserving more than their personal family histories but the significance of their experiences to the history and development of Bloomington and Normal—a story that they knew did not need, but did deserve, public recognition. With the subsequent creation of a permanent archive, their stories will no longer be silenced, but can and will continue to inform and guide other public programs, policy makers, and scholarly studies.[16]

In the Bloomington-Normal Black History Project, one can see some of the evidence of the essence of Mildred's life. In this project, one can see her educational philosophy; her deep appreciation for all of humanity; her understanding of all people's value; her willingness to sacrifice; her determination to succeed; her never having lived a separate, individualized, life; her love (and real understanding) of life; her boundless unconditional love; and her joy. As a young girl at the age of six standing up for her pride and dignity after a White man called her "boy," Mildred could not have imagined then that she would spend her adult life standing up for and supporting the dignity and humanity of all people.

Although her early life had enough heartbreak and disappointment to have crippled many human souls, Mildred just refused to define herself by these events, and she went on, still in the possession of a whole, healthy soul. She always just pushed on. She knew there was important work left to be done, and she was committed to doing all that she could. The world was made better by Dr. Mildred Pratt having been a part of it. Others will be left better for having read this story of her life.

Personal Context

In this section, Menah Pratt-Clarke provides the personal context and background for Mildred's autobiography.

My mother was Dr. Mildred Inez Sirls Pratt. "Mama," as I affectionately called her, wrote her own story—her autobiography. For decades my mother had been quietly filling up journals and notebooks by hand, and providing copious details about her life. To be sure, I had witnessed her writing. I saw her writing all the time—sitting on her bedroom floor, sitting on the living room couch, and sitting at the kitchen table. Even while visiting my father's family in Freetown, Sierra Leone, West Africa, in 1989, she was writing. She wrote almost daily the entire three weeks we were there, either early in the morning or late in the evening.

I recognized my mother as a scholar, but had no idea how challenging and difficult her life and career journey was as a Black woman. Somehow my mother recognized the intrinsic value of her personal narrative. She knew her story was important and had to be documented and shared. The content of her writings varied. Sometimes, her writings were reflections and memories about her childhood. At other times, her writing chronicled her daily experiences; but still at other times she chronicled epic moments, including her three visits to the White House to watch her son Awadagin, a classical pianist, perform for two U.S. Presidents. Ultimately, she wrote about how she, as a young Black girl who was sharecropping and picking cotton in the 1930s, became a full professor in the academy in the 1980s when Black women represented less than one percent (0.7 percent) of all full professors (Benjamin, 1997; Holmes, 1999, pp. 18–19).

Mama's death in 2012 prevented her from seeing the completion of her work. Toward the end of her life, she asked me—rather, she told me—to see that this project was completed. She left me, however, an almost complete autobiography of her life journey in her own words. As her biographer, I see my role as merely serving as the instrument responsible for conveying her experience to the world. Her own words inform the context. My task was to organize, arrange, and create coherence from the puzzle pieces of photographs, memories, reminiscences, diaries, and journals she left behind. Like Ida B. Wells' daughter, Alfreda Duster, who edited her mother's autobiography, this autobiography reflects "the dependence of the deceased mother on the living daughter for the revelation and publication of her autobiography" (Braxton, 1989, p. 106). In essence, as the daughter and biographer of Dr. Mildred Pratt, I sought to assemble and piece together a quilt from fragments of an incredibly rich life left behind.

The fragments that were left behind included not only her own writings, but also letters, notes, poems, and pictures that she asked her siblings—George, Clyde, Bernice, and Mozelle—to share. She asked each of them to send her their "recollections of childhood, names of places lived, names of schools attended, names of children, dates of military service."[17] She asked them to "write anything else you wish to write about yourself, most important influences in your life."[18] She asked for "interesting stories you remember when you were growing up, particularly stories told by older people."[19] She asked specifically for them to share information about their mother, Eula, and their grandparents, Rosa and George Thirkill. And the siblings responded. George, the eldest, sent a long manuscript. Mozelle, also, sent a long document, and included her poetry. Bernice sent little notes in envelopes, corresponding to each of the requests. Even Clyde, with whom Mildred had a difficult relationship, responded. Thus, the voices, stories, reflections, recollections, and memories of Mildred's siblings are part of the fragments of Mildred's life. This work, largely autobiographical, also includes biographical writing.

My mother entrusted me with telling these stories. She knew me not only as her daughter, but also as a scholar. She knew she was the impetus for me obtaining five degrees, because I wanted to have one more than her. She encouraged my scholarly pursuit of an undergraduate degree in English (with minors in Philosophy and African-American Studies) at the University of Iowa by completely financing my first year. Her financial support was matched by almost weekly letters of encouragement. After finishing the undergraduate program, I pursued a master's degree in Literary Studies at Iowa to more deeply study the work of William Faulkner and issues of race and class in the South. I, then, moved to Nashville, Tennessee, where I received a master's and doctorate degree in Sociology, as well as a law degree.

When I began my career at the University of Illinois in Urbana–Champaign as the Assistant Provost and Associate Director of the Office of Equal Opportunity and Access in 2006, Mama was still living in Bloomington-Normal. She even delivered a guest lecture for one of my classes at the College of Law. While I was working on my first book, *Critical Race Feminism and Education: A Social Justice Model* (Pratt-Clarke, 2010), Mama and I had numerous conversations about the academy, racism, sexism, and discrimination.

As Mildred's daughter, I accompanied her on many parts of her journey. I saw, heard, or experienced much of what she wrote. Like Joanne Braxton (1989, pp. 3–4), I, too, learned family history, genealogy, and folk medicine formulas from my mother. At various times in our combined life journey, she shared with me almost all of the stories that she wrote. Although she wrote about much, there is also much about which she did not write. What she did not share, however, reveals much about her character as a mother, a grandmother, a sister, a wife, and a friend.

From my earliest memories as a young child, I remember Mama getting up early every morning around 5:00 a.m. and making breakfast. Because my brother, Awadagin, and I played tennis from 6:00 to 7:00 a.m., almost every day before school with our father, my mother packed our breakfast—usually sausage or bacon sandwiches and hot apple sauce that she had canned from trees in our backyard. Awadagin and I ate them in the car on our way to school. Mama also made our lunches and dinner—every day. We rarely, if ever, ate out. Thus, she cooked almost every meal in our house.

Mama picked us up from school and took us twice a week to our piano and violin lessons. She did the laundry every weekend and hung the clothes out to dry on the clothesline. During the summer, she hand-peeled and cored apples, peaches, and plums from our backyard, and then preserved them by canning them. She made jam preserves as well. She planted a vegetable garden almost every year, as well as a flower garden. She was particularly fond of the "four-o'clock flowers," and she loved seeing the tulips bloom in the spring.

My parents owned apartment buildings—a total of 17 units, with a combination of two-bedroom townhouses, rental units in houses, and two-bedroom apartments. My mom was a maintenance worker for those apartments: she cleaned them, painted them, shoveled snow, and mowed the yards. When she could, she accompanied my father to court to deal with legal issues, since he served as a pro-se attorney for cases involving anything—landlord-tenant issues to bank lending practices to zoning matters.

Despite the numerous jobs she performed within our family, mama was a mama. Mama traveled with my brother, my father, and me as we pursued tennis careers as children. When my brother began his second year of college at University of Illinois at Urbana–Champaign, he was living at home in Normal. My mother drove him to his classes nearly every morning before returning to Normal to teach and work at Illinois State University as a professor. When Awadagin's music career took off, after he won the Naumburg International Piano Competition, she attended as many recitals and concerts as she possibly could. She often drove alone to Pennsylvania to his summer music festival.

Mama enjoyed being a grandmother and spending a great deal of time with her grandchildren, Alexander, Emmanuel, and Raebekkah. She loved her younger sisters—Bernice and Mozelle—and took special responsibility for them. My mom loved meeting people, being in community, and having fun. She often had dinner parties for special occasions—hand-cooking meals for up to thirty people in her small apartment. These meals of salmon, lamb shanks, oxtail, apple strudel, asparagus, knackwurst, rice, brussel sprouts, macaroni and cheese, and potatoes were legendary in Bloomington-Normal. It was always a grand feast with her friends. Mama was really funny and fun to be around, and she laughed a great deal. She fully enjoyed life and lived each day to its fullest potential.

Mama was a serious scholar, but also a quiet community activist with a deep commitment to lifting as she climbed through the academy. In particular, she sought to lift elderly African-Americans upon whose shoulders she knew she had metaphorically climbed to become a full professor. The Bloomington-Normal Black History Project in so many ways epitomizes her life and her legacy. It demonstrates her unwavering belief in the concept of empowerment. The Project—a seminal achievement in her journey—involved capturing the lives through oral histories and physical artifacts of almost 100 elderly African-Americans in Bloomington-Normal, Illinois, as part of a collaborative partnership with the university and the community. Though never explicitly calling herself a "Black feminist," she was a Black feminist in the traditions of Anna Julia Cooper who advocated for the education and empowerment of Black women; Hallie Quinn Brown, cofounder of the National Association of Colored Women; Nannie Burroughs, a Black woman educator; and Mary McLeod Bethune, founder of Bethune-Cookman University (Giles, 2006; Evans, Lamikanra, Jones, & Evans, 2004). Mildred was both an activist and educator.

One of Mildred's favorite poems was Langston Hughes' (1922) "Mother to Son." Her childhood reflects that, indeed, life for her "ain't been no crystal stair." Yet, like the mother in Hughes' poem, Mildred continued to climb and did not let her childhood events define her, undermine her, or deter her. Rather, they fueled her determination to leave the sharecropping lifestyle of East Texas, to "make a way out of no way," to survive, and to thrive. Mama chose to write about "making a way out of no way" (Reagon, 1982, p. 86). She frequently used this phrase in her writing and when speaking about her life. She recognized, as Frances Harper (Harper & Foster, 1990) did, that she needed to see herself as a "living force, animated and strengthened by self-reliance and self-respect," rather "than a stagnant mass, degraded, and self-condemned" (p. 221). As Bernice Reagon (1982, p. 82) reflected, "The roles that Black women have played in making a black space in the United States of America in which Black life can grow have been nationalistic, cultural, and also revolutionary." Mama felt a responsibility to share how she "made it" with the hopes that it could help others "make it."

Her life story is a rich multidisciplinary experience, covering literature, history, women's studies, political science, sociology, religion, and social work. Her journey provides a significant contribution to the Black women's literary tradition of education, activism, and community engagement. Her story is also a significant contribution to American history. Her life narrative spans a period of almost 100 years from the early 1900s through the early 2000s. Since her writing covers the entire twentieth century, this autobiography, then, is a story not only of Mildred's life, but also—and more importantly—of America's history.

Overview

This section provides an overview of the book and a short summary of each chapter.

A Black Woman's Journey is largely presented chronologically and in three parts. Each chapter is designed to highlight key themes and lessons about race, class, and gender in America. In addition, recognizing the importance of photographs in autobiographical writing, and the importance of creating visibility for the invisible—particularly Black women—images that represent and signify Mildred's life are included. True to Mildred's nature, she sought to include voices, experiences, and perspectives of her family. She asked her sibling to share their memories and recollections. These narratives are included and interwoven to help paint a comprehensive picture.

Part I (Sunrise) consists of Chapters 2 through 6. Chapter 2 (The Critical Black Feminist Autobiography) situates the work within the context of Black feminism, Critical Race Feminism, and Black women's autobiographical writings. It also includes the introduction that Mildred wrote for her own autobiography. Chapter 3 (Starting after Slavery) shares Mildred's family history on both her mother's and father's sides as slaves and descendants of slaves. It traces the family's journey from rural Alabama to rural East Texas. It also describes Mildred's first encounters with White people. Key lessons about race, class, and gender based on the experiences of newly freed slaves are discussed. The chapter concludes with photos of the Sirls and Thirkill family. Chapter 4 (Surviving the Great Depression) chronicles the Sirls' family's experiences and their daily life during the Great Depression and the 1930s. It explores the fortitude and resilience of Mildred's mother, Eula, as she cared for eight children without her husband, who was often absent and in jail. Chapter 5 (Segregated and Sharecropping) examines the Sirls' sharecropping experiences in the 1940s. It describes life in the Black community, including farming, taking care of animals, and dealing with health issues. It ends with a summary of the values and culture of African-Americans that helped them to survive. Part I ends with Chapter 6 (Black Girlhood). This chapter explores Mildred's traumatic experiences of Black girlhood, including sexual abuse, colorism, poverty, and sexism. The family's migration to Kansas City is discussed. The chapter ends with key lessons and photographs of the Sirls family, including Mildred's siblings.

Part II (Sunshine) consists of Chapters 7 through 10 and describes the sunshine of Mildred's life and her years of educational and academic achievement as a student and as a professor. Chapter 7 (A New Beginning) describes her college experiences at Jarvis Christian College, Butler University, and Indiana University in the 1950s, as well as a mission trip she took to Jamaica. It also discusses experiences of discrimination and segregation in Los Angeles, St. Louis, and Detroit in the 1950s and 1960s. It ends with key lessons about segregation in the United States during the 1950s. Chapter 8 (Pittsburgh and the PhD) explores Mildred's time in Pittsburgh as she pursued her doctorate in social work at the University of Pittsburgh and started a family. It examines her activism after the assassination of Martin Luther King, Jr., and her first efforts to connect social work to community engagement. It ends with key lessons and photos from Mildred's years in Pittsburgh. Chapter 9 (Normal University Racism) discusses the faculty journeys of Mildred and her husband, Ted, at Illinois State University in Normal, Illinois. The challenges of raising Black children in America during the 1970s and the 1980s are explored. The chapter ends with a discussion of key lessons about being a Black woman, mother, and wife, in the academy. Chapter 10 (Black History Project) is an in-depth look at the Bloomington-Normal Black History Project and Mildred's role as founder and co-director in capturing and preserving the oral narratives of elderly African-Americans. It explores the history of the project, the stories from the project, and the project's social impact. It concludes with key lessons about empowerment, the importance of narrative, the power of integration, and the crucial role of Black women scholar-activists in the academy.

Part III (Sunset) includes Chapters 11 and 12. It examines Mildred's later years in the twenty-first century. In Chapter 11 (A Legacy), Mildred's social justice views are shared through a speech at a celebration of the life of Martin Luther King, Jr. She also discusses her retirement from Illinois State University as a full professor of social work. Mildred's legacy to the academic community, as well as the Bloomington-Normal community, is shared through notes from faculty colleagues and former students on the occasion of her retirement. Chapter 12 (Travel, Trials, and Triumph) chronicles Mildred's recollections of meeting President Clinton and President Obama, as the guest of her son, Awadagin Pratt, who performed piano concerts at the White House. It also explores Mildred's role in creating a new legacy—the Pratt Music Foundation—in her husband's honor after his death, to ensure that children with talent and need are able to receive music lessons. Finally, the chapter details how Mildred prepared for the end of life, including recording a concert of spirituals and poetry for her own funeral. This final act encapsulates the power and spirit of a Black woman who feared nothing—not even death—and faced every challenge with a bold determination and conviction to overcome and to be an example for others of how to also overcome.

Notes

1. (Miller, 2005, p. 68).
2. (Royster, 2000, p. 104).
3. I am alluding here to the emergency fund (the Mildred Pratt Assistance Fund) that Mildred set up at Illinois State University in tribute to the secretary who made a small loan to her at a moment of dire need while a student at the University of Indiana. The Fund made gifts of up to $100 to students in emergency situations. Mildred also cofounded the more substantial Pratt Music Foundation at Illinois Wesleyan University to provide instruments and pay for music lessons for local children.
4. There is an extensive scholarly literature on southern sharecropping. Most of it concerns the general development of the regional economy. But the standard work on Black workers is Daniels (1971); also see Tolnay (1999).
5. On the Texas oil booms, see Hinton (2013). Again, very little has been written on black-owned mineral rights, but for one example, see Lewis (1979). Studies of Black land loss are much more extensive, but are still most reliable, state by state or county by county. Examples of the broader studies include Browne (1973), Mitchell (2006), and U.S. Commission on Civil Rights (1982). Government estimates indicate that black farmers lost, through various means, some of them nefarious, at least nine million acres of land between 1910 and 1969. And the loss continues. Since the late 1990s, there has been an Annual National Black Land Loss Summit that focuses on these issues and produces a report.
6. General Sherman's Field Order #15 would appropriate nearly half a million acres of confiscated land along the coasts of South Carolina, Georgia, and Florida and make that land available to former slaves in 40 acre parcels. President Johnson quickly reversed the policy. And as Mildred suspects, during the brief period of black possession of significant portions of land, it was indeed the Freedmen's Bureau overseeing the distribution process. See Oubre (1972) and Rose (1976).
7. Histories of American Indians that incorporate the experiences of black Americans are becoming more numerous. See, for example, Miles (2008), Reese (2013), Wicket (2000), and Yarbrough (2007).
8. Although there has been much research on the role of children and the family economy, much, if not most, focuses in the United States on the era of industrialization and on farm labor generally. One article that focuses on black children in the South around the time discussed here is Walters and Briggs (1993).
9. One of the first major studies of the post-emancipation migration is Painter (1977). On the Great Migration, see Marks (1989). A study that briefly surveys the historic migrations is Berlin (2010). And one should consider the prizewinning book by Wilkerson (2010).
10. Although not focused on the Great Migration, Reiff, Dahlin, and Smith (1983) provide an excellent discussion of the push–pull phenomenon. Most studies that focus on the Great Migration take the push–pull phenomenon up, and sometimes in great detail; see, for example, Grossman (1999).
11. For clear, first person statements that reveal education for children (and other reasons) as major incentives for migration, see Scott (1919a, July) and Scott (1919b, October) for

letters of Black southerners written to *The Chicago Defender* between 1916 and 1919 and collected and published in *The Journal of Negro History*.

12. Although the sources above in notes 9–11 reveal these patterns, also see Grossman (1999) for an excellent study that reveals all these patterns, and others, in detail, focusing specifically on the movement of Mississippians to Chicago.

13. Most people probably know that W. E. B. Du Bois worked during one summer at a Midwestern resort before he started teaching in the rural Tennessee schools during the summer. A. Phillip Randolph, who would later organize the Brotherhood of Sleeping Car Porters and Maids and organize the first planned march on Washington (in 1941) in support of the creation of a permanent Fair Employment Practices Commission, worked as a porter during summers while a student at the University of New Mexico. Their examples of summer employment are not exception, except that their jobs provided better pay and often better conditions than most.

14. An example of southern female schoolteachers going north to work as domestics and in factories during the summers is provided in Fields with Fields (1983).

15. Interestingly, events like these in Mildred's life do not appear in her list of "Important Dates." For an insider's account of CORE's (Congress of Racial Equality) philosophy and activities see Farmer (1965); also see Meier and Rudwich (1973). CORE's early activities are also discussed in most major studies of the civil rights movement.

16. For a brilliant study of all the ways history is made—when events take place, are remembered, are written down, become archival sources, and are retrieved by others—all of which the life and activities of the Bloomington-Normal Black History Project demonstrates, see Trouillot (1995).

17. (M. Pratt, personal communication, n.d.).

18. (M. Pratt, personal communication, n.d.).

19. (M. Pratt, personal communication, n.d.).

References

Benjamin, L. (1997). *Black women in the academy: Promises and perils.* Gainesville, FL: University Press of Florida.

Berlin, I. (2010). *The making of African America: The four great migrations.* New York, NY: Viking.

Braxton, J. M. (1989). *Black women writing autobiography: A tradition within a tradition.* Philadelphia, PA: Temple University Press.

Browne, R. S. (1973). *Only six million acres: The decline of Black owned land in the Rural South.* New York, NY: Black Economic Research Center.

Cody, C. A. (1987, June). There was no "Absalom" on the Ball Plantation: Slave-naming practices in the South Carolina Low Country, 1720–1865. *American Historical Review, 92*(3), 563–596.

Daniels, P. D. (1971). *The shadow of slavery: Peonage in the South, 1901–1969.* Urbana, IL: University of Illinois Press.

Evans, A. L., Lamikanra, A. E., Jones, O. S. L., & Evans, V. (2004). Hallie Quinn Brown (1845–or 1850–1949): Educator, author, lecturer, founder, and reformer. *Education, 124*(4), 727–733.

Farmer, J. (1965). *Freedom—when?* New York, NY: Random House.

Fields, M. G. with Fields, K. (1983). *Lemon swamp and other places: A Carolina memoir.* New York, NY: Free Press.

Giles, M. S. (2006). Dr. Anna Julia Cooper, 1858–1964: Teacher, scholar, and timeless womanist. *Journal of Negro Education, 75*(4), 621–634.

Grossman, J. (1999). *Land of hope: Chicago, Black Southerners, and the Great Migration.* Chicago, IL: University of Chicago Press.

Gutman, H. G. (1975). *The Black family in slavery and freedom, 1750–1925.* New York, NY: Vintage Books.

Harper, F. E. W., & Foster, F. S. (1990). *A brighter coming day: A Frances Ellen Watkins Harper reader.* New York, NY: Feminist Press at the City University of New York.

Hinton, D. D. (2013). *Oil in Texas: The Gusher Age, 1895–1945.* Austin, TX: University of Texas Press.

Holmes, S. L. (1999). *Black women academicians speak out: Race, class, and gender in narratives of higher education.* Retrospective theses and dissertations. Paper 12459.

Hughes, L. (1922). Mother to son. *Crisis Magazine, 25*(2), 87.

Jamieson, R. W. (1995). Material culture and social death: African American burial practices. *Historical Archeology, 29*, 38–58.

Lewis, J. A. (1979). Ownership and control of natural resources by minorities and small farmers in the South. In L. McGee & R. Boone (Eds.), *The black rural landowner—endangered species: Social, political, and economic implications* (pp. 135–154). Westport, CT: Greenwood Press.

Marks, C. (1989). *Farewell—we're good and gone: The Great Black Migration.* Bloomington, IN: Indiana University Press.

Meier, A., & Rudwich, E. M. (1973). *CORE: A study in the Civil Rights Movement, 1942–68.* New York, NY: Oxford.

Miles, T. (2008). *Ties that bind: The story of an Afro-Cherokee family in slavery and freedom.* Berkeley, CA: University of California Press.

Miller, J. L. (2005). *Sounds of silence breaking: Women, autobiography, curriculum.* New York, NY: Peter Lang Publishing.

Mitchell, T. W. (2006, April). Destabilizing the normalizing of rural Black land loss: A critical role for legal empiricism. *Wisconsin Law Review, 2005*(2), 557–615.

Oubre, C. F. (1972). *Forty acres and a mule: The Freedmen's Bureau and Black land ownership.* Baton Rouge, LA: Louisiana State University Press.

Painter, N. I. (1977). *The Exodusters: Black migration to Kansas after Reconstruction.* New York, NY: Alfred A. Knopf.

Pratt-Clarke, M. (2010). *Critical race, feminism, and education: A social justice model.* New York, NY: Palgrave Macmillan.

Reagon, B. J. (1982). My Black mothers and sisters, or, on beginning a cultural autobiography. *Feminist Studies, 8*(1), 81–96.

Reese, L. W. (2013). *Trail Sisters: Freedwomen in Indian Territory, 1850–1890.* Lubbock, TX: Texas Tech University Press.

Reiff, J. L., Dahlin, M. R., & Smith, D. S. (1983, Summer). Rural push and urban pull: Work and family experiences of older Black women in southern cities, 1880–1900. *Journal of Social History, 16*(4), 39–48.

Rose, W. L. (1976). *Rehearsal for reconstruction: The port royal experiment.* New York, NY: Oxford University Press.

Royster, J. J. (2000). Traces of a stream: Literacy and social change among African American women. Pittsburgh, PA: University of Pittsburgh Press.

Scott, E. J. (1919a, July). Letters of Negro migrants of 1916–1918. *Journal of Negro History, 4*(3), 290–340.

Scott, E. J. (1919b, October). More letters of Negro migrants, 1916–1918. *Journal of Negro History, 4*(4), 412–465.

Thompson, R. F. (1983). *Flash of the spirit: African and Afro-American art and philosophy.* New York, NY: Random House.

Tolnay, S. (1999). *The bottom rung: African American family life on Southern farms.* Urbana, IL: University of Illinois Press.

Trouillot, M. (1995). *Silencing the past: Power and the power of production of history.* Boston, MA: Beacon Press.

U.S. Commission on Civil Rights. (1982). *The decline of Black farms in America: A report of the U.S. Commission on Civil Rights.* Washington, DC: Government Printing Office.

Vlach, J. M. (1977). Graveyards and Afro-American art. *Southern Exposure, 5*(2–3), 161–165.

Walters, P. B., & Briggs, C. M. (1993, April). The family economy, child labor and schooling: Evidence for the Early Twentieth Century South. *American Sociological Review, 58*(2), 163–181.

Wicket, M. R. (2000). *Contested territory: Whites, Native Americans and African Americans in Oklahoma, 1865–1907.* Baton Rouge, LA: Louisiana Southern University.

Wilkerson, I. (2010). *The warmth of other suns: The epic story of America's great migrations.* New York, NY: Vintage Books.

Yarbrough, F. A. (2007). *Race and the Cherokee Nation.* Philadelphia, PA: University of Pennsylvania Press.

CHAPTER TWO

The Critical Black Feminist Autobiography

Our young African-American children must grow up knowing who they are, where they came from, who they came from—who suffered, died, was humiliated so that they can be where they are. They must know on whose back they were carried. …We, our children, and their children must be the storyteller—we must assure that the story is told like it was and is. Mildred Pratt[1]

This chapter situates Mildred's auto-biography[2] in the context of literature about Black women's autobiographical writing and it demonstrates the connections between Black women's autobiographical writing and Critical Black Feminism. It ends with Mildred's introduction to her autobiography.

Black Women's Autobiography

White men's lives have often dominated the biographies and autobiographies that provide a window into the past. White men who worked in public or official capacity were often able to document their experiences. As such, their story was seen as the official, and only, legitimate, perspective and account of history:

The rise of professional history in the late nineteenth and early twentieth centuries brought with it a reverence for written sources as the most authoritative, transparent

> windows into the past. The serious historical biographer came to believe that he or she could only write about people who left extensive documentation behind; more often than not, the subjects were white men who worked in a public or official capacity. For most of the twentieth century, such methodological preferences caused African American women to suffer the worst kind of biographical neglect. (Des Jardins, 2006, p. 15)

As a result, Black women's history was once "neglected, obscured, distorted, or relegated to the back pages of our collective consciousness" (Hine, 1992, p. 125).

Much work has been done to create visibility for the lives and life histories of African-American women and the distinct and powerful tradition of writing about their lives and their activism through autobiographies and biographies (auto-biographies). The tradition includes Black women like Maya Angelou, Toni Cade Bambara, Daisy Bates, Elaine Brown, Lorene Cary, Shirley Chisholm, Septima Clark, Angela Davis, Charlayne Hunter Gault, bell hooks, Flo Kennedy, Harriet Jacobs, June Jordan, Audre Lorde, Anne Moody, Pauli Murray, Barbara Omolade, Faith Ringgold, Assata Shakur, Barbara Smith, Alice Walker, Gloria Wade-Gayles, and many others (Braxton, 1989; Foner, 1984; Guy-Sheftall, 1999; Murray, 1989; Perkins, 2000).

Black women have felt a responsibility and obligation to ensure that the history of the United States is representative of their lives and experiences. This responsibility includes not only recovering and excavating the stories, voices, lives, and experiences of those who have been ignored, but also challenging the historical dominance of White and male historians. It extends to questioning the content and construction of history, and the legitimacy and accuracy of historical presentations (Des Jardins, 2006; Lanza, 1994; Wilkerson, 1990; Zinsser, 2009). Even within the African-American community, while the important role of African-American male historians such as Carter Woodson, W. E. B. Du Bois, and Arthur Schomburg is often given prominence, the contributions of Black women, particularly Black women librarians and archivists who played a critical role as custodians of African-American culture, is often ignored (Des Jardins, 2006, pp. 15–18). These women identified, collected, organized, indexed, and served as experts and scholars on Black history. The role of Black women as historians, librarians, archivists, biographers, and autobiographers is consistent with the recognition that Black women are the "major cultural carriers and passers-on of the traditions of our people" (Reagon, 1982, p. 82). This is exemplified by West African storytelling tradition where women have served as the "oral archives of their culture" through stories and songs passed down from mothers to daughters (Stover, 2003, p. 151).

Joanne Braxton (1989, pp. 3–4) notes that from her female elders she learned about family history, genealogy, and folk medicine formulas. She heard prayers, ghost stories, preacher tales, lullabies, and nursery rhymes. She also learned about the difficulty of being a Black mother and raising children. The role of Black women has often been about ensuring the survival of Black people, particularly of Black women, in the midst of the "tri-partite crossfire of masculine prejudice, White illogical hate, and Black lack of power" (Angelou, 1969, p. 231). As Nellie McKay (1995, p. 93) asserts, Black women's autobiographical writing is an act of witnessing against racism, sexism, and classism and reclaiming the identity of Black women.

Because of their invisibility, silence, and marginalization, Black women have constructed their history with a focus on establishing "their humanity and self-worth in the eyes of a dominant White American society that grant[s] them neither" (Stover, 2003, p. 133). As Jacqueline Royster (2000, p. 104) notes, "the very act of writing, especially for people who do not occupy positions of status and privilege in the general society, is a bold and courageous enterprise." Royster (2000, p. 104) further notes that Black women's writing often addresses social, political, and economic power and involves interrogating issues of peace, justice, and equity. Thus, autobiographical and biographical writing by Black women is often a radical and rebellious act that illuminates the personal and private spheres, as well as the professional, public, and political spheres, which are often hidden from view (Neumann & Peterson, 1997, p. 7). Black women are increasingly shining light on experiences in arenas and spaces that were previously silenced. The world of higher education and the academy is one such sphere.

The literature about the experiences of Black women and women of color in the academy is growing (Battle & Doswell, 2004; Berry & Mizelle, 2006; Gutiér-rez y Muys, Niemann, Gonzalez, & Harris, 2012; Li & Beckett, 2005). Such works contain personal narratives and often reflect an autoethnographical style in which the narrative is contextualized within a larger framework involving experiences of racism, sexism, classism, and homophobia in the academy.[3] These works are powerful documentaries and testimonies about empowerment and survival, oppression and resistance, isolation and marginalization, and success through struggle. The works illustrate that White men and Black women often have completely divergent paths and experiences in the academy. Whiteness and maleness often becomes a passport for a smooth and comfortable ride into tenure (Johnson-Bailey & Cervero, 2008, p. 314). Without this passport, Black women have found themselves struggling for legitimacy, validation, self-recovery, and liberation.

bell hooks (1989, p. 29) challenges women of color to transform the academy to "a place where the oppressed gather to talk our way out of bondage, to write our way into freedom, publishing articles and books that do more than inform, that testify, bearing witness to the primacy of struggle...." The academy, then, can be a sphere and a space of resistance, revolution, and transformation for Black women and a place where counter-hegemonic discourses and strategies can emerge. Critical Black feminism, then, provides a lens and framework from which to understand Black women's experiences in the academy.

Critical Black Feminism

Critical Black Feminism is a conceptual framework that is a synthesis of Black feminism and Critical Race Feminism. These concepts inform the critical themes associated with Black women's writings. Patricia Hill Collins (2009) articulated the conceptual framework of Black feminist thought. Building on Collins' work, Juanita Johnson-Bailey and Ronald Cervero (2008, p. 314) defined Black feminist thought as

> a body of knowledge which asserts that the daily living of Black women in a society that is racist and sexist has produced a collective consciousness that resists being defined as 'less than,' resists being stereotyped as undesirable, and seeks to define and empower its members by interpreting existence as a triumph.

As April Few (2007, p. 455) notes, Black feminists have four areas of focus. Black feminists (a) acknowledge Black women's historical struggle against multiple oppressions; (b) examine how Black women and their families negotiate the intersections of race, ethnicity, gender, sexual orientation, and class; (c) eradicate malignant images of Black womanhood; and (d) incorporate an activist perspective into their research through the cocreation of knowledge with informants, consciousness raising, and empowerment within the context of Black women's lives.

Black feminist thought also recognizes the role of power domains—hegemonic, disciplinary, structural, and interpersonal—on the lived experiences of Black women (Collins, 2009, pp. 291–309). Understanding these domains becomes a source of knowledge and empowerment for engaging in the revolutionary work of social justice. For example, although the hegemonic domain often reflects the dominant ideologies of White supremacy, capitalism, segregation, and Black inferiority, the domain provides a framework for developing counter-ideologies, such as Black pride, Black nationalism, Black feminism, and community empowerment. Similarly, the Black community recognized that the structural domain of macro and micro social structures, systems, and institutions, such as the political system, the economic system, and the education system, could serve as sites of oppression, but also as places of restoration, regeneration, affirmation, and empowerment. They often transformed segregated spaces designed to disempower into spaces of power and knowledge.

Likewise, it was equally essential for African-Americans to understand the disciplinary domain of Jim Crow, social codes, rules of conduct, and the laws in order to survive and to be able to help their children understand how to survive within those constraints and parameters, but also when and how to challenge those constraints. Those constraints were often challenged through the interpersonal domain and the confusing, inconsistent, paradoxical, and complex relationships between Blacks and Whites. Understanding how to restructure and reconstruct power domains designed to perpetuate oppression and inequality into forms of resistance and activism connects the work of Black feminism to Critical Race Feminism.

Critical Race Feminism builds upon Black feminism and recognizes the vital necessity of Black women using their voices to tell their stories and validate their experiences; the inseparability of their intertwined identities, particularly those of race, class, gender, and sexuality; the permanence of racism, sexism, classism, and homophobia; the relentless nature of White privilege, White female entitlement, and White male oppression; and the importance of social justice and equality (Wing, 1997). Black feminism and Critical Race Feminism share a commitment to the important role and power of individual experiences, narrative, and voice as part of a revisionist history project to retell what has been told and also to tell what has never been told (Pratt-Clarke, 2010, p. 102). This telling may include a variety of sources and methodologies, such as interviews, surveys, autoethnographies, poetry, diaries, creative art, and photography (Bell-Scott, 1994).

Black feminism and Critical Black Feminism seek to empower both the storyteller and the storytelling. They validate the unique ways of knowing of Black women; recognize the impact of intersectional and intertwined identities of race, class, and gender; appreciate the role of family and community within an individual journey; and underscore a commitment to activism. They focus on the personal and interpersonal; the political and community; and survival and empowerment (Gutiérrez, Oh, & Gillmore, 2000). This focus is reflected by the recurring themes in Black women's narratives: Black community cohesiveness and empowerment; family and community rituals; the Black church and revivals; quilting and sewing; gardening and canning; and most importantly, survival. Critical Race Feminism informs our understanding of the ways in which Black women have survived (Braxton, 1989; Guy-Sheftall, 1999; Perkins, 2000).

For Black women, surviving—especially during Jim Crow—meant working within and outside the home, while caring for families and children. It also meant navigating complex gender dynamics, including physical and sexual abuse by both Black and White men, as well as degrading ideas about self-worth and beauty based on skin color (see Andrews, 1990; Chafe, Gavins, & Korstad, 2001; Estes-Hicks, 1993; Griffin, 2011; Liberato, Fennell, & Jeffries, 2008; Taulbert, 1989;

Valk & Brown, 2010, for an extensive discussion of the Jim Crow experience). In the midst of property losses, socioeconomic struggles, violence, and discrimination, Black women survived by their determined commitment to maintaining their dignity and self-respect through courageous acts of subversion and resistance. Activism, social justice, and fighting for space, place, and equality, defined the journeys of Black women activists. This auto-biography of Dr. Mildred Pratt not only bears witness to struggle, but also to success and the importance of voice and advocating for one's self and others.

Autobiographer's Introduction

Mildred wrote an introduction to her autobiography. Mildred introduced herself in her autobiography by asking the essential question about her life: "How did I get here from where I came from?"

My 80 years living in several different states—Texas, Indiana, Missouri, California, Pennsylvania, and Illinois—and practicing and teaching social work automatically directs me to be analytical and to search for factors that motivate people to demonstrate certain behaviors. How, for example, does a person born to a poor Black sharecropping family of eight children who never left the rural areas in Texas and the Blackest girl in the family go on to become a full professor and earn four degrees?

I think I was able to accomplish as much as I did because of a variety of factors. I was carefully taught by my mother to accept the state of my life and not to overtly complain. In my own way, I somehow decided that I would live a better life. I decided very early that I wanted a life very different from my life in East Texas. There was something about my character that drove me to make something of myself. I recall when growing up that I sort of marched to my own drum. This has guided me throughout my life. As with most people, my life was shaped by family, environment, and my particular qualities.

This book charts my life from my birth through good days to almost unbearable situations. There were several factors with which I had to cope as I grew up. My life from birth through adulthood was, in fact, "making a way out of no way." My mother often used these words when supporting us became very difficult. I believe my life was painful for several reasons. A list of obstacles included my skin color (Black), my height (short—sometimes I was called "Shorty"), my position in the family (middle), an irresponsible father, growing up in a sharecropping family in the South in a period of discrimination and segregation, and instability since we were constantly moving. As I reflect on them now, I have learned to use them to help me as I trod on upon this earth.

I was born and grew up in an era in rural Texas when Black people were not viewed as human beings entitled to all the rights and privileges as the White people in the state. My life during that period, 1928 to the late 1960s, was characterized by legal segregation. This book presents my life as I experienced and coped with segregation, discrimination, and my skin color.

I have protested the treatment of African-Americans and females since I was a child. I could go on and on with examples of my protest on behalf of African-Americans and the shaft that many Black women get. Many of us paved the way for so many who now reap the benefits of our protest. Many Black females protested to open the doors for the current generation. We must remember, as Colin Powell (2003) said, that we rode on the backs of those who went before us, and we have a responsibility to be the backs for those who come after us.

While not all people might require mentors to help them navigate their lives, my life experience demonstrates that I needed them. Most people can recall having special teachers who played important and critical roles in their development. While formal counselors can make a difference, it is usually an informal, unanticipated encounter with a special teacher or other person at some point in a person's life that has a major impact. I hope this information about my life helps motivate those in positions to help young people navigate their lives to do so. Sometimes this might be considered intrusive; however, it depends upon how it is done. I tried to give back when I was in position to do so.

This book is dedicated to the following:

All my relatives: those who survived slavery and those who succumbed to the brutal system and never got to experience freedom.

Charlotte Surls, the slave who bore many children and started the birth of the host of Surls (Sirls) who were to come later—those who were "professional" slave breeders and sharecroppers.

My grandfather, George W. Thirkill, who packed up his family of three after slavery and moved to Texas, where he bought land with his wife, Rosie, whose father was her slave master.

My beloved husband, T.A.E.C. Pratt, a PhD physicist from Sierra Leone who, though brilliant, was stopped dead in his tracks from becoming a major contributor to physics research by 1960s racism.

Ms. Ira Henry, a great teacher who saw my talents and counseled me as to how I could go to Jarvis Christian College without tuition money—an experience that I never thought would be a part of my life.

My mother, Eula Sirls, even though I still feel the sting from her calling me her "little Black girl" at a time when being dark-skinned was not cool. This book is also dedicated to her because I know all too well how much she suffered just to keep her children alive and to "make a way out of no way."

My brother, George, who helped us survive when my father was not around and shared his remembrances of our family's history with me.

My children, Awadagin and Menah, their families, and my three grandchildren, Emmanuel, Raebekkah, and Alexander, who have and continue to bring me much joy and make my senior years worth living. You have been the "wind beneath my wings." I certainly could not have navigated the computer age without you. Be well. Love and protect each other.

My two sisters, Bernice and Mozelle, who have made considerable contributions to this book. They have given me family history documents and materials that they themselves have written; my sister Mozelle made her poetry available to me.

My very close friends, who know who they are, have looked after me, protected me, made me laugh, and invited me out with them to basically "couple events." My dear friends in Bloomington-Normal have been so generous in their friendship to me and my family since my husband's death. I know that without your friendship, particularly the Pratt Music Foundation members, I would have found it impossible to have navigated my life.

Those people who put stumbling blocks in my path and all those who lived to discourage me, because I turned your opposition into my determination. Those many actions made me more determined to "keep on keeping on." While there have been people in my journey in life who have not been supportive to me and indeed were negative forces, as I review my life, I turned those negatives into positives. Those negatives made me determined to make it.

These are important dates in my life:

1619—First slaves brought to the United States
1865—13th amendment to abolish slavery, Bureau of Refugees, Freedmen and Abandoned Lands, 40 acres and a mule promised
October 15, 1928—Date of birth during the Great Depression
1929—Great Depression
1935—Social Security Act
1943—Fair Employment Practices Act
May 24, 1946—Graduated from Shiloh High School (lived in Camp Switch, Longview, Texas). Moved to Kansas City, Missouri, to work and save money for college (lived with Uncle Booker T. Sirls)
1946–1952—Lived in Kansas City during summers and attended Jarvis Christian College in Hawkins, Texas
May 30, 1951—Graduated from Jarvis Christian College in Hawkins, Texas, with a Bachelor's degree in Religion

1952–1953—Moved to Indianapolis, Indiana, while studying at Butler University School of Religion for a Master's degree in Religion (lived with Cleo Blackburn and family)

August 1, 1952—Graduated from Butler University School of Religion, Master of Arts, Indianapolis, Indiana

1953—Lived with the Blackburns for about a year and worked at Flanner House during the year. Enrolled in Indiana University School of Social Services to take a few courses part-time

1954—Brown v. Board of Education argued by Thurgood Marshall to end school segregation

June 13, 1955—Graduated from Indiana University School of Social Services, Master of Arts

1955—Emmett Till was lynched. Heard his mother, Mamie Till, speak in Los Angeles after the death of her son

1964—Civil Rights Act banning discrimination in public accommodations was passed. Experienced discrimination in hotel accommodations, restaurant service, and housing in Pittsburgh

April 14, 1968—Death of Dr. Martin Luther King.

April 18, 1969—Graduated from University of Pittsburgh, Graduate School of Social Work, in Pittsburgh, Pennsylvania

1969–1993—Academic career at Illinois State University, Normal, Illinois, from Assistant Professor to Emeritus Professor in the Department of Sociology, Anthropology, and Social Work

August 21, 1974—Promoted to Associate Professor

August 16, 1979—Promoted to Full Professor

July 31, 1993—Retired from Illinois State as Professor Emerita

Notes

1. (M. Pratt, personal communication, n.d.).

2. Auto-biography is hyphenated to reflect that this work is simultaneously the autobiography and biography of Mildred Sirls Pratt. The work contains both autobiographical and biographical writings.

3. For more on Black women in the academy, see Agathangelou and Ling, 2002; Aguirre, 2000; Benjamin, 1997; Brown-Glaude, 2010; Burke, Cropper, and Harrison, 2000; Calafell, 2012; Chalis, 1994; Chambers, 2011; Davis, 1994; Dowdy, 2008; Evans & Grant, 2008; Few, Piercy, and Stremmel, 2007; Garner, 2002; Generett and Cozart, 2012; Gregory, 1995, 2001; Hartman, 1994a, 1994b; Holmes, 1999; Jackson and Johnson, 2011; James and Farmer, 1993; Jean-Marie, Williams, and Sherman, 2009; Johnson-Bailey and Cervero, 2008; Johnson-Bailey and Lee, 2005; Mabokela and Green, 2001; Mitchem, 2003; Rodriguez and Boahene, 2012; Souto-Manning and Ray, 2007; Thomas and Hollenshead, 2001; Turner, 2000; Vakalahi, Ofahengaue, and Peebles-Wilkins, 2010; White, 2007; Williams, 1991; Yenika-Agbaw and Hidalgo-de-Jesús, 2011.

References

Agathangelou, A. M., & Ling, L. (2002, December). An unten(ur)able position: The politics of teaching for women of color in the U.S. *International Feminist Journal of Politics, 4*(3), 368–398.

Aguirre, Jr., A. (2000). Women and minority faculty in the academic workplace: Recruitment, retention, and academic culture. *ASHE-ERIC Higher Education Report, 27*(6), 1–127.

Andrews, R. (1990). *The last radio baby: A memoir.* Atlanta, GA: Peachtree Publishers.

Angelou, M. (1969). *I know why the caged bird sings.* New York, NY: Random House.

Battle, C. Y., & Doswell, C. M. (2004). *Building bridges for women of color in higher education: A practical guide for success.* Dallas, TX: University Press of America.

Bell-Scott, P. (1994). *Life notes: Personal writings by contemporary Black women.* New York, NY: Norton.

Benjamin, L. (1997). *Black women in the academy: Promises and perils.* Gainesville, FL: University Press of Florida.

Berry, T. R., & Mizelle, N. (Eds.). (2006). *From oppression to grace: Women of color and their dilemmas in the academy.* Sterling, VA: Stylus Publishing.

Braxton, J. M. (1989). *Black women writing autobiography: A tradition within a tradition.* Philadelphia, PA: Temple University Press.

Brown-Glaude, W. R. (2010). But some of us are brave: Black women faculty transforming the academy. *Signs: Journal of Women in Culture and Society, 35*(4), 801–809.

Burke, B., Cropper, A., & Harrison, P. (2000, December). Real or imagined: Black women's experiences in the academy. *Community, Work & Family, 3*(3), 297–310.

Calafell, B. M. (2012, April). Monstrous femininity: Constructions of women of color in the academy. *Journal of Communication Inquiry, 36*(2), 111–130.

Chafe, W. H., Gavins, R., & Korstad, R. (2001). *Remembering Jim Crow: African Americans tell about life in the segregated South.* New York, NY: The New Press.

Chalis, J. (1994). "All I'm askin' is a little respect": Black women in the academy. *Black Scholar, 24*(1), 2–6.

Chambers, C. R. (2011). Candid reflections on the departure of Black women faculty from academe in the United States. *Negro Educational Review, 62/63*(1–4), 233–260.

Collins, P. H. (2009). *Black feminist thought: Knowledge, consciousness, and the politics of empowerment* (2nd ed.). New York, NY: Routledge.

Davis, A. (1994). Black women and the academy. *Callaloo: A Journal of African American and African Arts and Letters, 17*(2), 422–431.

Des Jardins, J. (2006, January). Black librarians and the search for women's biography during the new Negro history movement. *OAH Magazine of History, 20*(1), 15–18.

Dowdy, J. K. (2008, December). Fire and ice: The wisdom of Black women in the academy. *New Horizons in Adult Education and Human Resource Development, 22*(1), 24–43.

Estes-Hicks, O. (1993). The way we were: Precious memories of the Black Segregated South. *African American Review, 27*(1), 9–18.

Evans, E., & Grant, C. (Eds.). (2008). *Mama, Phd: Women write about motherhood and academic life*. New Brunswick, NY: Rutgers University Press.

Few, A. L. (2007). Integrating Black consciousness and critical race feminism into family studies research. *Journal of Family Issues, 28*(4), 452–473.

Few, A. L., Piercy, F. P., & Stremmel, A. (2007). Balancing the passion for activism with the demands of tenure: One professional's story from three perspectives. *NWSA [National Women's Studies Association] Journal, 19*(3), 47–66.

Foner, P. S. (1984). *Three who dared: Prudence Crandall, Margaret Douglass, Myrtilla Miner: Champions of antebellum Black education* (Contributions in Women's Studies No. 47). Westport, CT: Greenwood Press.

Garner, R. (2002). *Contesting the terrain of the ivory tower: A study examining the spiritual leadership of African-American women in the academy*. Miami, FL: Miami University, Department of Educational Leadership.

Generett, G. G., & Cozart, S. (2012, January). The spirit bears witness: Reflections of two Black women's journey in the academy. *Negro Educational Review, 62/63*(1–4), 141–165.

Gregory, S. T. (1995). *Black women in the academy: The secrets to success and achievement*. Lanthan, MD: University Press of America.

Gregory, S. T. (2001, June). Black faculty women in the academy: History, status, and future. *Journal of Negro Education, 70*(3), 124–138.

Griffin, J. H. (2011). *Black like me*. San Antonio, TX: Wings Press.

Gutiérrez, L., Oh, H. J., & Gillmore, M. R. (2000, April). Toward an understanding of (em)power(ment) for HIV/AIDS prevention with adolescent women. *Sex Roles, 42*(7–8), 581–611.

Gutiérrez y Muhs, G., Niemann, Y., Gonzalez, C., & Harris, A. (Eds.). (2012). *Presumed incompetent: The intersections of race and class for women in academia*. Boulder, CO: Utah State University Press.

Guy-Sheftall, B. (1999). Preface. In K. Springer (Ed.), *Still lifting, still climbing: Contemporary African American women's activism* (pp. xix–xxiii). New York, NY: New York University Press.

Hartman, S. (1994a). Black Women in the academy, 1894–1994: Selected papers from a conference at the Massachusetts Institute of Technology, January 13–15, 1994. *Callaloo: A Journal of African American and African Arts and Letters, 17*(2), 407–439.

Hartman, S. (1994b). The territory between us: A report on "Black Women in the Academy: Defending Our Name: 1894–1994." *Callaloo: A Journal of African American and African Arts and Letters, 17*(2), 439–449.

Hine, D. C. (1992). International trends in women's history and feminism—Black women's history, White women's history: The juncture of race and class. *Journal of Women's History, 4*(2), 125–133.

Holmes, S. L. (1999). *Black women academicians speak out: Race, class, and gender in narratives of higher education*. Retrospective theses and dissertations. Paper 12459.

hooks, b. (1989). *Talking back: Thinking feminist, thinking Black*. Boston, MA: South End Press.

Jackson, S., & Johnson, III, R. G. (Eds.). (2011). *The Black professoriat: Negotiating a habitable space in the academy* [Black Studies and Critical Thinking Series, 6]. New York, NY: Peter Lang.

James, J., & Farmer, R. (1993). *Spirit, space, and survival: African American women in (White) academe.* New York, NY: Routledge.

Jean-Marie, G., Williams, V. A., & Sherman, S. L. (2009, November). Black women's leadership experiences: Examining the intersectionality of race and gender. *Advances in Developing Human Resources, 1*(5), 562–581.

Johnson-Bailey, J., & Cervero, R. (2008, June). Different worlds and divergent paths: Academic careers defined by race and gender. *Harvard Educational Review, 78*(2), 311–332.

Johnson-Bailey, J., & Lee, M. (2005, January). Women of color in the academy: Where's our authority in the classroom? *Feminist Teacher, 15*(2), 111–122.

Lanza, C. D. (1994). "Always on the brink of disappearing": Women, ethnicity, class, and autobiography. *Frontiers: A Journal of Women Studies, 15*(2), 51–68.

Li, G., & Beckett, G. H. (2005). *"Strangers" of the academy: Asian women scholars in higher education.* Sterling, VA: Stylus Publishing.

Liberato, A., Fennell, D., & Jeffries, W. (2008, September). I still remember America: Senior African Americans talk about segregation. *Journal of African American Studies, 12*(3), 229–242.

Mabokela, R., & Green, A. L. (Eds.). (2001). *Sisters of the academy: Emergent Black women scholars in higher education.* Sterling, VA: Stylus Publishing.

McKay, N. Y. (1995). The narrative self: Race, politics and culture in Black American women's autobiography. In D. C. Stanton & A. J. Stewart (Eds.), *Feminisms in the academy* (pp. 74–100). Ann Arbor, MI: University of Michigan Press.

Mitchem, S. Y. (2003, March). No longer nailed to the floor. *Cross Currents, 53*(1), 64–74.

Murray, P. (1989). *Pauli Murray: The autobiography of a Black activist, feminist, lawyer, priest, and poet.* Knoxville, TN: University of Tennessee Press.

Neumann, A., & Peterson, P. L. (1997). *Learning from our lives: Women, research, and autobiography in education.* New York, NY: Teachers College Press.

Perkins, M. V. (2000). *Autobiography as activism: Three Black women of the sixties.* Jackson, MS: University Press of Mississippi.

Powell, C. (2003). My American journey. On principles and values. *On the Issues.* Retrieved from www.ontheissues.org/Archive/American_Journey_Principles_+Values.htm

Pratt-Clarke, M. (2010). *Critical race, feminism, and education: A social justice model.* New York, NY: Palgrave Macmillan.

Reagon, B. J. (1982). My Black mothers and sisters, or, on beginning a cultural autobiography. *Feminist Studies, 8*(1), 81–96.

Rodriguez, D., & Boahene, A. (2012, October). The politics of rage: Empowering women of color in the academy. *Cultural Studies/Critical Methodologies, 12*(5), 450–458.

Royster, J. J. (2000). Traces of a stream: Literacy and social change among African American women. Pittsburgh, PA: University of Pittsburgh Press.

Souto-Manning, M., & Ray, N. (2007, October 1). Beyond survival in the ivory tower: Black and Brown women's living narratives. *Equity and Excellence in Education, 40*(4), 280–290.

Stover, J. M. (2003, November 1). Nineteenth-century African American women's autobiography as social discourse: The example of Harriet Ann Jacobs. *College English, 66*(2), 133–154.

Taulbert, C. L. (1989). *Once upon a time when we were colored.* Tulsa, OK: Council Oak Books.

Thomas, G. D., & Hollenshead, C. (2001). Resisting from the margins: The coping strategies of Black women and other women of color faculty members at a research university. *Journal of Negro Education, 70*(3), 166–175.

Turner, C. (2000). *Faculty of color in academe: Bittersweet success.* Boston, MA: Allyn and Bacon.

Vakalahi, H., Ofahengaue, F., & Peebles-Wilkins, W. (2010). *Women of color on the rise: Leadership and administration in social work education and the academy.* New York, NY: Columbia University Press.

Valk, A., & Brown, L. (2010). *Living with Jim Crow: African American women and memories of the Segregated South.* New York, NY: Palgrave Macmillan.

White, D. G. (2007). "Matter out of place": Ar'n't I a woman? Black female scholars and the academy. *Journal of African American History, 92*(1), 5–12.

Wilkerson, M. B. (1990, Spring). Excavating our history: The importance of biographies of women of color. *Black American Literature Forum, 24*(1), 73–84.

Williams, P. J. (1991). *The alchemy of race and rights.* Cambridge, MA: Harvard University Press.

Wing, A. (1997). *Critical race feminism: A reader.* New York, NY: New York University Press.

Yenika-Agbaw, V., & Hidalgo-de-Jesús, A. (2011). *Race, women of color, and the state university system: Critical reflections.* Lanham, MD: United Press of America.

Zinsser, J. P. (2009). Feminist biography: A contradiction in terms? *Eighteenth Century: Theory and Interpretation, 50*(1), 43–50.

CHAPTER THREE

Starting After Slavery

Mildred and her siblings, George, Bernice, and Mozelle, share their knowledge of the family history. The ancestry and lineage of the Thirkills (on the maternal side) and the Sirls (on the paternal side) are discussed. The siblings' recollections include the stories of survival from their ancestors and elders. Their stories often involved experiences in multiple states: Alabama, Kentucky, Texas, Oklahoma, and Kansas. Their memories reveal the challenges of recently freed slaves and their descendants as they sought to live independently, build community, and raise children.

The Thirkill Family

Mildred begins by sharing her recollections about her mother's side of the family, the Thirkills[1]:

I was born into a family whose ancestors moved from Alabama and Georgia shortly after the Emancipation Proclamation and the establishment of the Freedmen's Bureau. The earliest relative that I know about was Charlotte Surls, born in slavery in 1806. Charlotte died in 1880. My mother, Eula X. Thirkill,[2] was born in Landersville, Alabama, on January 14, 1898, as the only child of George W. Thirkill (born in Landersville, Alabama, in 1870) and Rosa[3] Hubbard (born in Landersville, Alabama, in 1863).

My mother was three years of age when they traveled by train with many other Blacks to rural East Texas. It seems that a large number of former slave families left Alabama at the same time in wagons, resettled in Texas, and began to farm. Most got their initial start with land gained through the Freedmen's Bureau and from land acquired from the Indian Bureau. It seems that somehow my mother's parents, as well as some of my father's relatives at the time, acquired land through their Indian heritage and the special act of Congress.

It is well known that there were many former slaves who owned land in those days. My mother remembers that they were a well-to-do family who lived in a lovely house, which included an organ. As I understand the history, her mother, Rosa Thirkill, was a fair-skinned person who was born to a slave mother and her White master. My mother's mother died of some disease when my mother was about in her 20s. It seems that my mother was left on her own after her mother died.

Shortly after her mother died, my mother got swept off her feet and married my father, R.P.[4] Sirls, in January 1922. Her father, who was now a well-to-do farmer with an organ in his living room, was so distraught about his only child marrying what he considered to be below her status that, legend has it, he left for Arizona and was never seen by my mother again. My oldest brother, Lowell, found his grave in Phoenix, Arizona.[5]

My mother never spoke to me about her parents. In the days when I was growing up, it was not a done thing for children to ask such questions of parents. My best description of my mother is that she was a light-skinned lady who wore her hair in braids on each side. I recall that she always wore old lady clothes that she made. I do not recall that she was very talkative with me. She talked very little.

Mildred's brother, George, remembers more about his mother and her parents. He wrote his recollections at Mildred's request in April 1992 and sent them to her[6]:

The author of this draft is George Lowell Sirls, the eldest of the children born to R.P. and Eula. Much of the information results from my memory and information provided to me by my mother and my grandmother, Etherline. The information contained in this writing involves primarily the Sirls family that was headed by Jesse and Etherline Sirls. Children born to that union were R.P., Annie B., Booker T., Sam, Clara, Frank, Eugene, and Griff. Those to whom this writing most pertains is the family resulting from the union between R.P. Sirls and Eula Thirlkile.[7] R.P. and Eula were married sometime during January 1922. After I was born came Jesse Clyde (Clyde), born December 23, 1923; Irmagene, born April 1, 1925; Erie Geneva (Era), born August 17, 1926; Mildred Inez, born October 15, 1928; Bernice Etherline, born June 18, 1931; Mozelle Oleta, born November 3, 1935; and Ruby Pauline, born May 12, 1938. Irmagene and Ruby predeceased both our parents.[8]

After my mother and father married, they lived with her father, George, in Panola County, Texas, near Long Branch. Long Branch was a township near Carthage, Texas. I was born in November 1922 in that house. While discussing the Thirlkile house, I shall pause to give a little bit of information about my mother and her immediate and extended family.

George and Rosa Thirlkile were parents of my mother, Eula. At the age of three, my mother, along with her parents, migrated from the state of Alabama by train. There were several families and some of my grandfather's cousins, including the Stevens family.[9] My mother was the only child. Rosa was a midwife during most of the time she lived in Texas. She died around 1918. She left my mother and grandfather living in a house on a 25-acre farm that my grandfather owned. They were farmers of a rich spot of land, which gave them a better than average lifestyle. The midwife activities of my grandmother helped to make a fairly privileged life for my mother.

Rosa was born of a Black housekeeper and her employer, who was White. Rosa had nearly predominantly White features, except her complexion was olive. Pictures of Rosa provoked me to question my mother as to why Rosa looked different from the rest of us with her waist-length braids and thin nose. Mom did not really want to talk about it when I was young, but later conceded that grandmother was half Anglo.

Some disagreements occurred between my father and my grandfather, resulting in Grandpa leaving his home and moving to Arizona. My dad managed to borrow money with mom's consent against Grandpa's home in which they then lived. Early one winter morning after the cotton had been harvested, our house burned to the ground. My dad had a Model T truck that he used to transport workers from the city of Henderson back and forth to the fields. It had to be moved during the burning of the house. While all the kids were out in the road watching the house burn and my mother was screaming, my dad made one more trip in the house and came out with a frightened baby, Mildred. My dad burned his ears while in there rescuing her. With that fire went all of the furniture and most of the memorable artifacts that my mother had inherited from her parents.

Mildred's sister, Mozelle, also remembers her mother talking about her childhood. She describes a photograph of her mother as a child with her parents[10]:

Mama had had her picture taken with her parents around the time they moved to East Texas from Alabama, Mama being about three years old. She is standing on an unseen barrel behind her parents, who are seated side by side. Grandma is a little pudgy with fine features and an abundance of hair. Grandpa is slim, looking sternly into the camera. Mama is cute and has both little hands on her parents' shoulders, looking curiously into the camera. Rosa looks like a grand dame (see Figure 3.1: Photograph of George, Rosa, and Eula Thirkill, circa 1901).

Mama told us that when she was a small girl, her Mama, Rosa, would try to give her castor oil. Mama would take off running. Rosa would call to her, "If you don't get back here, I'm going to kill you!" Mama said, "Are you going to kill me?" Rosa would smile and say, "No!" Mama had no sisters and brothers. So I suppose she got her share of being spoiled. Her parents were well-to-do. Mama had an organ, but she did not play it. Her father, George, farmed. Mama got a sixth-grade education and could not get further in school because her parents would not let her go away from home to school in order to get higher grades (see Figure 3.2: Photograph of Eula Thirkill, circa 1914, at age 16). Rosa got chronically ill sometime during Mama's teens, and Mama had to attend to her. Rosa did not recover from this illness and died shortly before Mama got married at age 23 or 24.

My grandfather, George, did not like Papa, and he left and went to Arizona after Mama got married. That left the farm to Papa and Mama. Papa quickly destroyed the house in the attempt to disguise his cotton-thieving activities in the fire. My sister, Mildred, almost got caught in the fire. Papa saved her. She was the baby at this time. After the house burned down Mama lost contact with Grandpa because his address was lost or burned. It was not until much later that Lowell discovered Grandpa had lived in Arizona and died there in 1945. We might have been able to see him if we'd known where he was.

Mildred's sister, Bernice, shares similar memories[11]:

Mozelle and I set at Mama's feet, and she talked about her life as a little girl. She would tell the story over and over again about the family. She was the only child, and they owned their property and owned land and animals. She had an organ that her father bought from Sears. He had to be rich—"high on the hog," they called it.

Mama and her family came on a train from Alabama. She said she would never forget the porter who was so nice. She remembers there were cattle in the boxcar behind her. They were at the tail end of the train because they were Black. She remembers the smell and sounds and the conductor shouting, "Fresh bacon and red-eyed eggs!" Her father and his three to four cousins could not buy property in Alabama. Grandpa borrowed money to buy his house in Texas. The bank is still there where he borrowed the money. It was the first bank in Henderson, Texas.

Mama never talked much about her mother, Rosa. Mama's papa was a very bright man. He was very intelligent. Mama told me she would ask her father about everything. She would say, "I would ask Papa." At school, the teachers insisted that her name started with a "U." She asked her father, and he let her know that it started with an "E." She said he told her how to spell her name. He would bring her lunch and pick her up on his horse and buggy. She remembers saying, "Yon come Papa." Mama was also very bright, very smart. Mama stopped going to school at sixth grade because there was no high school in those days.

Mama's mama was a housewife, not a midwife. I know my brother George said she was a midwife, but she wasn't. She was seven years older than her husband. She was born in 1863. The master's family told her that they didn't want her because she looked White. They put her out. She never learned anything. She had no schooling. She was half Indian and half White. She had big, fat braids as thick as the wrist on my arm. My grandfather found her sitting by the side of the road. She had sisters and brothers she never knew. She was born a slave and illegitimately by the slave master. That was bad in those days, so my mother didn't talk much about her. She was ashamed. In those days, they thought it was their fault—that slavery was their fault. Mama's mama got real sick, maybe from diabetes. Her legs swelled up so big and leaked so much that there were stains on the floor after her mother died. Mama had to constantly rub her legs.

Mama told me that Papa picked and stole cotton from the White man at night and stored it at the house. When he learned that the White people found out, he set the house and everything on fire. He burned the organ, and the only thing mama was able to save was a platter that she put on my sister Ruby's gravesite. After Papa burned the house down, we were vagabonds until he left and went to California. We never had a house after that. Mama's daddy left after she got married. He sent one letter, but it was destroyed in the fire. She grieved so much for her father. She never knew where he was, and we moved so much. Even if he tried to find us, he wouldn't have been able to find us.

The Sirls Family

Mildred shares about the Sirls family[12] on her father's side[13]:

My father, R.P. Sirls, was born in Texas in August 16, 1901, to Jesse and Etherline Sirls. Jesse Sirls, my father's father, had 16 brothers and sisters and was the son of a man named Abram Surles, who lived on a plantation near Mount Enterprise. My grandmother, Etherline, was born in 1899, about 40 years after the Emancipation Proclamation. Freed slaves who could prove that they had Indian blood (as many had) were entitled to free land in Oklahoma. My grandmother, Etherline Taylor, and her husband, Jesse Sirls, left for Oklahoma to claim their land, as did many freed slaves. I know that my father moved with his family initially to Oklahoma with support of the Freedmen's Bureau and land acquired from their Indian ancestry. My father, RP Sirls, had two sisters, Clara (born 1908) and Anna B. (born 1903), and five brothers, Griff (born 1914), Sam (born 1906), Frank (born 1911), Eugene (born 1912), and Booker T. (born 1904).

My grandparents put their children and their few belongings in the wagon and left for Oklahoma. Unfortunately, they were only there for a few days with their eight children when Grandpa Jesse was struck by lightning and died immediately.[14] My grandmother, Etherline, moved back to Texas, where her father [Sam Taylor] now lived, and settled to raise her children, all of whom followed her to Texas except a son and daughter who remained to carve out productive lives for themselves. The two older children, Uncle Booker T. and Aunt Annie B., decided to remain in Oklahoma. Aunt Annie B. got a certificate in hairdressing, married, and had a rather good life. Uncle Booker T. later moved to Kansas City. Of my father's siblings, Uncle Booker and Uncle Sam were the best of the litter among the boys. Uncle Sam was a great cook and earned his living in the better restaurants in Henderson, Texas. He was a fair family man, but word is that all of the Sirls men were skirt-chasers.

Uncle Booker T. Sirls was a smart, industrious person who did not finish high school. He was a handsome, ambitious ladies' man who "married up" to Aunt Jessie, who was from a fairly well-off family. He dressed well, had a great figure, and carried himself like an executive, as was the practice when relatives were north and made it big. They moved to Kansas City, Missouri, where he eventually bought a nice middle-class home, earning his living as an expert janitor of office buildings. He made his home available to close relatives, nieces, and nephews who needed a place to stay until they got on their feet. My two oldest sisters, Irmagene and Era, and I benefited from his largesse. My sister Era lived with Uncle Booker until she got a job as an elevator operator in an office building and rented a room for herself. My sister Irmagene only stayed for a little while and went back to Texas.

The next sibling in line, I went up for several summers and lived with Uncle Booker and Aunt Jessie and worked to make money to support my college education at Jarvis Christian College. Uncle Booker and Aunt Jessie let us know that we were the poor relatives from Texas and treated us like the poor relatives. They had no children. Uncle Booker was protective of his wife. She had nice clothes, a well-furnished house, and worked as a volunteer for the Girl Scouts.

Grandpa Sam Taylor [Mildred's great-grandfather and her father RP's grand-father] owned a large house on 200 acres of land that he farmed, as I recall.[15] I understand that my great-grandpa, Sam Taylor, acquired the land through a federal law that provided that freed slaves were to be given "40 acres and a mule." When the Civil War ended, the newly established Freedmen's Bureau was to administer the law and assure that each freed slave did indeed get 40 acres and a mule. Some freed slaves did get their land and a mule. By most accounts, it was a poorly administered program. Grandpa Sam Taylor got more than 40 acres and a mule. He also was fortunate to have oil on his land and got money from that.

In those days he would have been characterized as a wealthy man. We called him Grandpa Sam, but he was really Great-Grandpa Sam. I didn't realize he was my great-grandpa until I was in my 40s.

Papa took us to the farm in an old, beat-up car, and Grandpa Sam showed us all the land he had. He hired people to do his farming. I was in my teens. I recall going to his house several times in wagons, and he was very kind to us. We went there on Sundays. It was a big, happy house. He was rich. He had a big dining room with a long table, and there would be a big dinner in his house. We liked the large tables of food prepared when we visited. There were always many relatives there. His house had a fireplace, and there was always a kettle on the fireplace. He also had a vault in his house for all his money and valuables. Many years after his death, we, along with Uncle Booker T. Sirls, tried to get ownership of the land, which my father should have inherited from Grandma Etherline, but we only got several legal papers.

Grandpa Sam Taylor had three daughters by one wife (Ann McAlister)—my Grandma Etherline, Aunt Amy, and Aunt Mandy. The oldest, Grandma Etherline, had a very hard life (see Figure 3.3: Photograph of Etherline Sirls, circa 1938). When she left Oklahoma, she moved to Texas and managed as best as she could with her children. I do not know how she managed. My first memory of my Grandmother Etherline is that she would come to visit us when I was perhaps 12 or 13 years of age. I do not recall if she arrived in a car or was walking. What stands out in my mind is that she behaved strangely. She would stay for a few days and would then wander off without telling us where she was going. The police would often find her sitting or lying down on the side of the road. The police would sometimes put her in jail because she did not know where she lived. She was jailed several times, but she was mentally ill and people did not understand. She would not stay at any place very long. At one point, mama was nursing Ruby [Mildred's sister] and she told Papa she couldn't take care of his mother and Ruby. Papa took her to live with his brother, Uncle Sam. But Uncle Sam killed his wife by beating her to death. Eventually, Grandma wandered away and was put in jail. There was no place for mentally ill people in those days, especially if you were Black. She just died in jail. Etherline Taylor's cause of death is listed as falling during epileptic seizure in jail.

When I was grown and married and a professor of Social Work at Illinois State University, our family decided to have a Sirls reunion in rural Mount Enterprise, Texas. We visited the courthouse to try and get information about my grandmother. The record that we found indicated that she had been put in jail for wandering, with no indication about her mental illness. In the days when I grew up, we did not know the term "mental illness" and would simply label people who demonstrated the kind of behavior as my grandmother as beggars and put them in jail. Adults would usually say that they just acted strange or "She or he is tetched (touched meaning crazy) in the head." It is very important to know the health problems of relatives. It is not always possible to get this information. It is perhaps even more difficult to get this information in Black families because adults (at least within our family) rarely discussed these matters around children. I learned in various ways that several of my relatives suffered from mental illness.

We would go visit the "mean lady," Aunt Mandy. We would go to her house and she was not nice to us, and I think it was because she had this nice, big house and we didn't have anything. But I just remember her not being nice to us. We would visit her often, and she would laugh at our tattered clothes. Aunt Mandy married a school principal and lived a very good life. As I recall, some of my relatives owned land, owned their homes, owned cars, were teachers, and lived a middle-class life. Several owned oil wells. They were always available to help us.

George shares more detail about the lineage of the Sirls family[16]:

I would like to begin dealing with the Sirls lineage and my understanding of how my great-grandfather became a Sirls. The information I am about to impart was provided by Grandmother Etherline, the wife of Jesse, my grandfather. Jesse was killed by lightning near Okmulgee, Oklahoma, around 1918. Shortly after his death, grandmother moved most of her family back to Texas. She had eight children, of whom my dad, R.P., was the oldest. However, the two next oldest, Annie B. and Booker T., remained in Oklahoma. Jesse is reported to have had 16 brothers and sisters whose father (I never knew his name) was a slave to a man named Sirls living on a plantation in the vicinity of Anadarkus Community in East Texas near Mount Enterprise. The ages of these 17 children varied up to as much as 24 years. Jesse was the third youngest. He married Grandmother Etherline Taylor before she was 16 years old. My dad was born when she was 16.

Other information about the Sirls has come from interviews I have conducted with some White members of the Sirls family. The most reliable information reveals that their relative (and the owner of my great-grandfather) moved from Eastern Kentucky to East Texas, bringing with him my great-grandfather as his house slave. The owner set up a plantation headquarters comprised of a community store and a cotton gin. The older White Sirls revealed a long-held and often repeated story common among them, stating that my great-grandfather and his fellow slaves were "not branded" as was common. Instead, the Sirls slaves wore headbands identifying themselves as property of their master. It is said that my great-grandfather always suffered headaches as a result of the headband being too tight. His master trusted him enough to remove the headband, and the headaches ceased immediately. I have spoken with seven or eight members of that Sirls group and have learned that other than my grandfather's owner, none of the White Sirls were wealthy enough to own slaves. The most reliable speculation is that the name "Sirls" has a French origin and that a Sirls migrated from Arcadia, Canada.

The only explanation available to me that would explain why none of the 17 Sirls children remained on the plantation, which I am told was left to them by their master, is that they were so glad to be free that they just plainly left. They may have also left due to their inability to appreciate property ownership. I do not know where Great-grandfather Sirls died or when. I am aware that at least three of his sons were Baptist ministers. Great-grandfather acquired the Sirls name from his slave master, as was the case with most freed slaves.

Uncle Lawyer Sirls was the husband of Mandy Biggers Sirls. He apparently lived a very good life economically. Others of the Sirls descending from the slave branched out into other parts of Texas, but at least one named Sam settled in Oklahoma. Sam was reported to have had a large number of children by his Indian [Native American] wife. I cannot attest to the tribe to which she belonged. My dad introduced me to one of those Sirls in Los Angeles. He was apparently of mixed blood and was spelling his name "Searles."

The following will deal with Grandmother Etherline's family and her known relatives. She was the oldest daughter of my great-grandfather, Sam Taylor, and my great-grandmother, Ann McAlister Taylor. Great-grandmother Ann died when her three daughters were young children. The names of those daughters were Etherline, Mandy, and Amy. After Great-grandmother Ann's death, Great-grandpa Sam Taylor married a woman named Laura. Laura had three daughters of her own, only one of which I have ever known. Her name was Lucinda Montgomery. Her husband was named Offie Montgomery, and her only son was named Finis.

I visited the site where Grandmother Etherline was born, which was near a house where we lived in a community called Union Spring. My dad attended grade school and also church at Union Spring. After Great-grandpapa Sam married Laura, he purchased a farm about seven miles from Mount Enterprise and about two miles from where Great-grandmother Ann died. It was on this farm that the six girls (my great-grandpapa's three and Laura's three) grew up. The house was a rambling farmhouse with a long hallway separating two sections. I am told that when I was a baby, Great-grandpapa's dad held me in that house. It is reported that he was 120 years old at that time. In later years, between the ages of 12 and 14, Clyde and I spent many hours with Great-grandpapa Sam at his farm talking and eating fruit from his orchard. I remember Great-grandpapa Sam's mule named Maggie.[17] His farm was always neat, and he had a girlfriend named Becky (at this time, Laura had passed on).

About then, his daughter Mandy married Joe Starling. Joe Starling taught my father and later taught me in the eighth and ninth grades at Union Spring. The youngest sister of Grandmother was named Amy. Amy married James McCany. James was a farmer living real close to the township of Mount Enterprise. Aunt Amy maintained the neatest house I have ever seen. Her behavior always seemed correct. She looked out for her dad, Great-grandpapa Sam Taylor. She loved to cook for Clyde and me when we would visit her, which was often. She had two boys, the oldest James Grady and the youngest nicknamed "Gold-Child."

Great-grandmother Ann only had one full-blooded sister but had several half-brothers and half-sisters. Some of the McAlisters had White fathers. Some of her half-sisters were also half White; however, Ann was not. One of Ann's nephews, John Lee Riding, is reported to have dated my mother. Mom kept in contact with him. He was a preacher at the time and he visited us often. John Lee had a sister who appeared to be White and did not associate with the rest of us. Another half-brother whose last name was Cadell sired a large number of children, all of whom were very fair-skinned, some passing for White. The Cadells and McAlisters never got along with one another—due to jealousy, I assume. One of Great-grandmother Ann's nephews, John McAlister, killed (shot) one of the Cadell men in an open field for allegedly molesting his sister. He was never punished for this crime. John was also known as one of the meanest men in East Texas. He was so mean that we all thought he was crazy and were afraid of him and his brother, Neal, and his sister, Mandy Stein. They were good-looking people with beautiful, wavy hair. Great-grandpapa Taylor never fooled with them and stayed well away.

Great-grandpapa Sam Taylor was represented as having one brother whose name was Henry Taylor. Henry Taylor had a farm within 1,000 yards of the Union Spring school and church. We lived in a house on Henry Taylor's farm for nearly three years. Henry Taylor was reported to be living in Nacogdoches, Texas. I never knowingly met Henry Taylor. I am told he was a good man and quite prosperous. I was later told by other relatives that Henry Taylor was Great-grandpapa Sam Taylor's bastard son.

Early Years

George shares his recollections of the family's early years as very young children in Texas. In particular, he remembers the kindness of the Black community in its care for each other[18]:

I remember when we were living in a house owned by Mr. Luke Water, the father of two of my mother's good friends, Sammie and Mimmie. Both of these women taught me during my elementary school days. This house was located in the Antioch School District for Black children, about seven miles from the school itself. However, I had not begun school at this time. This was a time of economic prosperity. My dad had bought a Buick automobile that I recall was generally parked by two big oak trees. I recall on one occasion my mom tried to drive the car while Dad was gone and ran it into one of the trees. To my knowledge, she never tried to drive again. Also, while living in Mr. Water's house, my sister Irmagene was born and was named by one of the two sons of Luke Waters, whose name was Harrison. I recall vaguely that Sammie more than Mimmie seemed always to be at our house. Their father, Luke, was one of the more prosperous farmers in the area among both Black and White.

To my knowledge, the next house we lived in was on a farm leased by Clyde Green. Clyde Green was a White farmer whose wife was named Lois. Despite this period of rigorous segregation in the state of Texas, the Green family was very kind to us, and they considered my mother their personal friend. This house was also located in the Antioch School District. In this house I recall learning to read fairly well, to recite the timetables, and to spell commonly used words accurately. In January 1929, my father took Clyde and me to Antioch School for the first time. I was seven years old and Clyde had just turned six, the minimum age required for that district's primary school. The first teacher for Clyde and me was Miss Nova Lewis, a friend of my mother's. When school was out in late May, I was promoted to third grade due to my mother's efforts before I entered school. Antioch School at that time was three rooms. Its senior class was seventh grade. The principal of that school was Mrs. Dora Ballinger.

We were later taken to Aunt Mandy, who lived in the city of Henderson. Aunt Mandy was the wife of one of my dad's uncles, a Baptist minister who had passed. Her house was very, very large. Clyde and I finished the semester at Henderson Elementary School. However, when school ended, we would go with my dad out to the country place to work on the farm near the house that had burned earlier. I recall counting days of the week leading up to Saturday, when we would go home. I recall also once when we became lost in a wooded area while looking for my dad, who had failed to return for us as promised.

A brother of Aunt Mandy Sirls ran a profitable grocery store about six doors from Aunt Mandy's house. His name was Bud Biggers, who was also a friend of my mom and dad but later fell out of favor with my dad. Bud Bigger's wife was named Jackie. She wore fine clothes and drove expensive cars. I recall my dad buying a five-pound wood ax from Bud Biggers. The typical weight of an ax was three pounds. Even at the tender age of seven, after we moved for the second time to Luke Water's place, I thought my dad was unfair to my mother for buying such a heavy ax, which she had to use in his absence.

Also in the vicinity of Mandy Sirls' home was the Walter Simmons family, who had a very pretty daughter named Pauline. Too bad she was too old for me then. Walter's wife was Aunt Mandy's sister. Living nearby was Felix Jenkins and his parents, whose name I do not recall. They, too, were well-to-do by contemporary standards. The Jenkins family established the Jenkins Funeral Home. This particular funeral home handled Grandmother Etherline's burial.

From Aunt Mandy's home, we moved again to Luke Water's home, which was about eight miles from Henderson. It was at this location that real hard times for our family began. The year is believed to be 1930. Clyde and I enrolled at Antioch School for the second time. The school was located seven miles from where we lived. We walked to and from school every day regardless of weather conditions. There were people along the route to school who played a great part in easing the pressure on us resulting from the long walk and bad weather.

The first family that we knew along the route belonged to Fred and Clara Durkee. They had two children, Freddie and Ruby. Clara and my mother were friends from childhood. Fred belonged to a family whose physical characteristics were unmistakably White, even though there was Black blood in the family. Clara was also Caucasian-appearing and was very pretty. Down the road from Fred Durkee lived Fred's dad and mother. His mother was named Ann, and the father's name escapes me. Ann and her husband lived in a three-story, big white house at an intersection in this rural area. Mrs. Ann Durkee would insist that Clyde and I come in and warm our hands at their fireplace each cold morning we went to school. She would wrap our hands in cloth using warm water to avoid the near-frozen fingers from aching.

At this same intersection, no matter the weather condition, we were often met by two older girls and a boy named Braxton Pryor, who accompanied us to school. The girls' names were Nadine Durkee, the granddaughter of Mrs. Ann Durkee, and Beatrice Skyan. Nadine's mother was also a long-standing friend of my mother. Nadine was the oldest of several children, including twins who went to school with Era and Irmagene. She also had a sister named Erma Fae and a brother, Curtis, with whom I graduated from high school. Beatrice Sykan was the adopted daughter of an immigrant from some African country. One of the reasons that Braxton, Nadine, and Beatrice Sykan walked with Clyde and me to school was that we were afraid of a little area around a creek crossing. We thought the area was haunted because it was extremely woody.

Further down the road from Mrs. Ann Durkee and her husband lived John and Willie Hall. Willie Hall was the oldest daughter of Mrs. Ann Durkee and the sister of Fred. The Hall family's children were Anna Lois, Clifton, Lorraine, and Ruth. This family also looked White, with the exception of Clifton. John Hall knew my mother's mom and dad. I graduated from Antioch High School with Ruth. She and I also first linked up in classes in the fifth grade. Clifton married

Annabelle Cadell, who was a cousin of my dad on his mother's side. It must be noted that the Hall family was extremely kind to all of us in times of need.

The majority of the people known by us lived in the Antioch area—some of whom touched our lives very significantly. I recall families like Frank Lewis's, with three boys and two daughters named Carnell and Arnell, and Buster Montgomery's, whose wife was the daughter of Luke Waters. The Montgomery family had two daughters, Irene and another (name forgotten), and some six or seven boys. Another family in the area was the Greenwoods, who had a son named Nelson and daughters named Clara C., Eloise, and another one whose name escapes me. The principal of the school, which grew from a seven-grade school to a high school level, was A. W. O'Neal. His wife was named Irmagene. Mrs. O'Neal taught me, Clyde, Irmagene, and Era in the early grades.

Among other families of significance were the Burnetts, who had several kids who went to school with us, and Cornelious and Essie Trimble, who had two children, Roscoe and Hattie Lou (Shang). Essie was also a longtime friend of my mother's. There was the family of Clyde and Lois Green, a White family who had a daughter who let me play with her wagon before I got one. I recall also the Lewis's, Nava's parents. I recall two of their sons, the youngest named Ray. Ray was my playmate, although he was older than I. Another of my classmates was Ivey Young, who had a brother named Dewalt Young. Through this writing I wish to acknowledge the many other fine families who lived in the Antioch community whose lives touched our family. It is reasonable to understand that we knew more people than most because we lived at five locations in the Antioch School District over a period of about 17 years.

White People

Mildred shares her memories of one of her earliest experiences with White people[19]:

In all of the places where we lived, we were in an area where our neighbors were Black. The Whites, in most instances, lived long distances from us. I do remember that in one place, Clyde Green's farm, they were our closest neighbors. My mother worked for the family as a maid. My mother and Mrs. Green had an interesting relationship, not unlike that which existed between maid and mistress in the South. I recall that while she was required to enter the back door, she and the lady had a very friendly relationship.[20] The lady discussed her personal and marital problems. Indeed, as I recall, Mrs. Green would confide in my mother, sharing with her difficulties coping with her alcoholic husband. The relationship between them was very much like that existing between sisters.

Mrs. Green did all of the cooking, and when Mother came home, she brought some of the food for us. We looked forward to the food, and the cornbread was the best I've ever eaten. I also remember my mother saying that Mrs. Green was very nice and respectful to her. The relationship between Blacks and Whites in the South was peculiar. Formally, it was racism; informally, it was friendship. The Green's daughter played with my sister Bernice as best friends. I do not remember if Bernice ever went into the Green's house.

Bernice remembers playing with Mrs. Green's daughter, June, and not being able to go inside her house[21]:

I played with June Green. She invited me into her house once. I remember her mother said, "You can't bring your playmates in the house." But I knew she meant, "You can't bring your Black playmate in the house." Even then, I knew. I got the message. But she came to my house. Her brother was Justin, and he would call her to play with me.

Mildred shares one of her early encounters with a White man while living at the Greens' house, reflecting the uneasy relationship between Whites and Blacks[22]:

I have few recollections of experiences with Whites. I rarely saw White people because few lived near us. In most instances, we lived in rural areas not near other houses and had very little direct association with Whites. We lived in houses provided by the people for whom we were sharecroppers. The times when we saw or had contact with Whites were when we worked for them as maids, went to the grocery stores, or saw them when we worked in the fields. As Blacks, we had our own infrastructure. The schools were all of course segregated, and we never had contact with Whites in the school system. With respect to economics, we raised our own food, had some Black grocery stores, and also had an effective system of borrowing from relatives and neighbors.[23] My life was protected from the worst physically brutal aspects of the segregated South because we lived in the rural South in "Black enclaves," where the only Whites that we saw were usually the ones for whom my mother worked as a maid.

When I was about six or seven years of age, I came face-to-face with a White person. We were living in the Green's house when I had walked about a mile to get our mail. I met the postman, and he said, "Hi, boy."[24] It was clear that I was not a boy because I wore braids and a dress, because in those days girls did not wear pants. I remember being very insulted and just instinctively said, "I am not a boy; I am a girl." I recall feeling no fear or anger, just a feeling of being insulted. The postman's only response was to simply smile and go about his business.

I was proud of myself. I could hardly wait to walk the two miles home to tell Mama what I had told the White postman. When I arrived home, I gleefully told my mother what I had done. She immediately said angrily, "Don't you ever speak to a White person in that way."

I remember saying to my mother, "I won't, Mama." I did not understand why, but I never spoke to a White person again until later in my life when I was on my own. I later learned why my mother retorted as she did and handled the situation the way she did. I could have been beaten or worse.[25] Her life in the South had taught her the danger of doing so. When I look back on this event and the setting in which it took place [segregation], I realize that he could have killed me. While I took my mother's advice, deep down in my gut I knew that I was right to defend my dignity.

This is my first experience with any confrontation dealing with a White person. As I reflect on this encounter and why I did not feel afraid to express myself, I think it was because I had no previous experience of hostility from a White person. All of my contacts had basically been with Blacks. While our family experienced tremendous poverty and hardship, I never made the connection that racism in all of its forms was the primary cause for our suffering. My father doubtless felt it directly, because he always referred to Whites as "old peckerwoods," "crackers," and "rednecks."[26] It was clear that he blamed Whites for our suffering. I got the impression that my father had had some very humiliating experiences with Whites. He literally hated White people. Shortly before my father's death, I was to learn that he had once been involved with the Garvey Movement.[27]

As I was growing up in Texas, I do not remember anyone except my father speak about White people as our oppressors. It seems that Blacks just accepted our status and made the best of it. We existed in two different worlds and accepted it. I do not recall that my mother taught us about segregation, etc. I never recall having been called a "Nigger" until I went to the North.

Key Lessons

1. *The legacy of slavery significantly impacted African-Americans as they attempted to survive in the immediate generations after Emancipation. Many families moved across multiple states as they sought to find and create community and provide stability for their families. The challenges of building a new life required strength and perseverance. Rural East Texas became the home for Mildred's parents as they migrated there from Alabama and Kentucky.*

2. *The legacy of slavery also is reflected in the inconsistent spelling of names. The challenges of identity for African-Americans is reflected by the multiple spellings of names (Surls and Sirls; Threkild and Thirkill; RP and R.P.; Eula X and Eula). The difficulty of identifying actual names reflects the reality of slavery in which slaves were stripped of their original names.*

3. *The legacy of slavery is evidenced by the reality of land ownership. There were complicated relationships between African-Americans, Native Americans, and Whites involving entitlements to land ownership. Some former slaves did in fact own land and were wealthy, as reflected by Mildred's great-grandfather, Sam Taylor, who owned almost 100 acres of land. Some obtained land through their Native American lineage, as was the case for Mildred's great-grandfather, Jesse Sirls in Oklahoma. Some bought land, like Mildred's grandfather, George Thirkill, who bought a 25-acre farm in Texas. In many cases, the wealth and land ownership did not pass through generations and was eventually lost, often through theft and deceit of Whites, or the inability of Blacks to manage the expenses, costs, and taxes associated with land ownership.*

4. *The legacy of slavery also impacted issues of education. Many former slaves' descendants received very little education. Mildred's mother, Eula, only had a sixth-grade education. As George's narrative reflects, African-Americans who were able to get an education had to walk many miles and rely on the support of the Black community along the way to school.*

5. *Jim Crow and other social norms dictated the relationship between Blacks and Whites—what could be said, what could be done, and what was acceptable in daily life. Bernice knew she could not go inside the White family's home (the Green's house) to play with her playmate, June. Mildred's mom, Eula, had to enter the back door to clean the Green's house, yet their relationship in Mildred's eyes was that of sisters, in many ways. As Eula's response to Mildred reflects, Mildred was not supposed to speak to the White postman, even though he called her a boy. Transgressing protocols could be deadly. Nonetheless, Mildred's indignation at such an insult at a young age and her decision to "stand up for herself" foreshadow her future activism and advocacy for herself and others.*

Photos

It is rare to have photos and pictures of African-Americans, particularly those portrayed positively that reflect beauty, dignity, and grace. The photos below reflect important images of Mildred's journey. Photo 3.1 is the photo of her grandparents—George and Rosa Thirkill—and their daughter, Eula, at age three, taken in 1901. Photo 3.2 is a photo of Mildred's mother, Eula, at age 16, taken in 1914. Photo 3.3 is a photo of Mildred's grandmother, Etherline. Despite her difficult journey, losing her husband, and raising six children alone, the photo—taken around 1938—is an important reminder of the presence, role, and strength of Black women.

Figure 3.1: George, Rosa, and Eula Thirkill, circa 1901
Source: M. Pratt.

Figure 3.2: Eula Thirkill, age 16, circa 1914
Source: M. Pratt.

Figure 3.3: Etherline Sirls, circa 1938
Source: M. Pratt.

Notes

1. A visit to Lawrence County Historical Society in Alabama in June 2013 provided some additional information about Mildred's grandparents. The Threlkelds file of the Lawrence County archives references a Captain Threlkeld, noting that "prior to the war, the Threlkelds had slaves who were forced to hold window panes in the house during the storms. After the war was over, the Threlkelds lost their slaves and their fortunes. Today, some Threlkeld Blacks get their name from the old Bankhead family." The marriage registry shows a George Threlkild married Rosa Hubbard in 1892. Likewise, the records reference a Dave Hubbard plantation in the same Bankhead area (Threlkeld's File, Lawrence County Archives). There are multiple spellings of Thirkill, including Thirlkill, Threlkeld, Threlkild, Thirkle, and Thirlkile. George Sirls, Mildred's brother, always spelled the name, "Thirlkile." The cemetery records list him as George Thirkle, though his name on the tombstone is spelled George Thirkile.

2. No birth record is available, but Eula is listed as three years old on the 1900 census. Bernice Miller confirms her mother's birth name was Eula X. Thirkill (B. Miller, personal communication, June 7, 2013).

3. Rosa Hubbard's first name is spelled in multiple ways, including Rosie and Rose. The marriage license in Lawrence County refers to her as Rosa, as does the 1900 United States Federal Census.

4. RP Sirls is spelled as both "RP" and "R.P." The correct version is believed to be RP, without any periods.

5. I [Menah Pratt-Clarke] visited the tombstone in November 2013. It reads: "Beloved Father, George Thirlkile, 1875–1945."

6. (G. Sirls, personal communication, April 1992). Permission received from Pat Sirls, May 27, 2017.

7. According to Bernice, RP had a child out of wedlock: "I remember that Papa had a daughter before he married Mama. That was shameful in those days. My brother Lowell knew because he was in school with her. He told me her name but I forgot. When Mama found out, she took Lowell out of school and said, 'Don't share her name'" (B. Miller, personal communication, June 7, 2013).

8. The following is Mildred's mother's (Eula X. Thirkill's) genealogy: George Thirkill (1870–1945) married Rosa (Rose; Rosie) Hubbard (1863–1918) in 1892. They had one child, Eula X. Thirkill (1898–1975). Eula Thirkill married RP Sirls in 1922. They had eight children: George Lowell (1922–2002), Jesse Clyde (1923–1995), Irmagene (1925–1973), Erie Geneva (Era; 1926–1998), Mildred Inez (1928–2012), Bernice Etherline (1931–present), Mozelle Oleta (1935–2011), and Ruby Pauline (1938–1944). George and Jesse were often called by their middle names: Lowell and Clyde.

9. Mildred's brother Clyde shares his recollections: "Mama was born on January 13th, 1898 to George and Rose Thirkill. They moved to Texas sometime in the early 1900s. She had some people there. I don't know if they came together or not, but they were Loches Thirkill and his wife and Cousin Kate" (C. Sirls, personal communication, March 28, 1992).

10. (M. Perry, personal communication, n.d.).

11. (B. Miller, personal communication, June 7–9, 2013).

12. The following is Mildred's father's (RP Sirls') genealogy: Charlotte Surls (1806–1880) had two children, Abraham and Stephen Surles. Abraham Surles (1827–1898) married Amanda Surls (1832–1914). Abraham had 16 children, including Jesse Sirls. Jesse Sirls (Mildred's grandfather) married Etherline Taylor, and they had eight children, including RP Sirls (Mildred's father; 1901–1983). RP's siblings were Annie B., Booker T., Sam, Clara, Frank, Eugene, and Griff. Etherline Taylor's parents (Mildred's great-grandparents) were Sam Taylor and Ann (Mandy) McAlister (McAllister) Taylor. Etherline had two siblings, Amy and Mandy.

13. (M. Pratt, personal communication, n.d.).

14. Bernice remembers this incident: "Papa's father was struck by lightning. They used male children to support farming, and the boys were out on the farm. Papa said his father came out of the house and said, 'Goodness, boys, you have done a fine job.' He said this was the only time he said a kind word. Then it started to rain and thunder. He went to a tree for protection, lightning struck the tree, and he was killed by the lightning. Papa's mama came back to Henderson to her father [Sam Taylor], who had outlived two wives. He had a big farm and a big barn, and we would go there on Sundays" (B. Miller, personal communication, July 21, 2013).

15. A letter from the law firm of Caves, Waldrop, and Shaw dated October 15, 1941, suggests that Sam Taylor owned between 90 and 101 acres that he purchased between 1889 and 1902, which was referred to as the "home place." Sam Taylor died in 1939. It appears that by 1941, his heirs only owned 18 acres. By 1982, a final judgment by the District Court of Rusk County, Texas, found that the heirs did not have "any right, title, or interest in the lands" (M. Pratt, personal communication, n.d.).

16. (G. Sirls, personal communication, April 1992).

17. Clyde shares his recollections about Maggie, the mule: "Now, Grandma's father was Sam Taylor. Lowell and myself youst [used to] spend a lot of time with Grand Pa. I remember he had and [an] old mule name [named] Maggie. That old mule had more sence [sense] than a lot of us. You could plowing [plow] in the field, and at 12 o'clock he would stop and would not move until you take him a luce [loose], take him and fed him" (C. Sirls, personal communication, March 28, 1992).

18. (G. Sirls, personal communication, April 1992).

19. (M. Pratt, personal communication, n.d.).

20. As part of Jim Crow, Blacks were often required to enter White homes through the back door (Beeth & Wintz, 1992, pp. 98, 176; Chafe, Gavins, & Korstad, 2001, pp. 212, 268).

21. (B. Miller, personal communications, February 8, 2013. April 7, 2013, and June 8, 2013). For another example of Black children playing with White children as friends, see Valk and Brown (2010, p. 48).

22. (M. Pratt, personal communication, n.d.).

23. Borrowing was often necessary in the Jim Crow South (Valk & Brown, 2010, pp. 89–90).

24. Blacks were often called, "boy" (Beeth & Wintz, 1992, p. 98, 176; Chafe et al., 2001, p. 268).

25. "Talking back" to a White man was an act of defiance and a challenge to Jim Crow. Physical abuse, including lynching, was often the punishment for violating Jim Crow norms (Chafe et al., 2001, pp. 268–269).

26. These were common phrases used to describe Whites (Taulbert, 1989, p. 87, 103, 106; Valk & Brown, 2010, p. 11).
27. For more on the Garvey movement, see "African-Americans: The Garvey Movement."

References

African-Americans: The Garvey Movement and the Harlem Renaissance. In *Encyclopaedia Britannica's Guide to Black History*. Retrieved from http://www.britannica.com/blackhistory/article-285192

Beeth, H., & Wintz, C. D. (Eds.). (1992). *Black Dixie: Afro-Texan history and culture in Houston.* College Station, TX: Texas A&M University Press.

Chafe, W. H., Gavins, R., & Korstad, R. (Eds.). (2001). *Remembering Jim Crow: African Americans tell about life in the segregated South.* New York, NY: The New Press.

Taulbert, C. L. (1989). *Once upon a time when we were colored.* Tulsa, OK: Council Oak Books.

Threlkeld's File. (n.d.). Lawrence County Historical Society.

Valk, A., & Brown, L. (2010). *Living with Jim Crow: African American women and memories of the segregated South.* New York, NY: Palgrave Macmillan, 2010.

CHAPTER FOUR

Surviving the Great Depression

The Great Depression, occurring only a few generations after Emancipation, presented significant challenges to the formerly enslaved African-Americans. The experience for African-Americans was largely defined by basic survival, household chores, school, and church. In this chapter, Mildred and her sisters, Mozelle and Bernice, share their recollections of their childhood lifestyle. These are stories of persistence and resilience, as well as family and community. This chapter explores life in the 1930s, including the challenges associated with the Great Depression, segregation, and poverty.

Daily Life

Mildred begins by describing her recollection of her early childhood and daily life[1]:

I was, according to my mother, born in 1928. I have no birth certificate to prove it because I was not born in a hospital and we knew nothing about hospitals and birth certificates in the eastern rural area of Texas where I was born. I lived in dire poverty in the throes of legal racial segregation through the Great Depression and World War II—living in a separate and unequal social and economic society from my birth until I graduated from high school. My life was shaped by the economics of sharecropping and segregated schools through grade school, high school, and college in various areas of East Texas. My mother gave birth to eight children. I had two brothers, Clyde (1923–1995) and George (1922–2002), and two sisters, Irmagene (1926–1973) and Era (1927–1998), who were older than me. Three more were to follow me: Bernice (born 1931), Mozelle (1935–2011), and Ruby (1938–1944), who died at age 6.

Since my birth in 1928 until I completed high school, my family lived in a sharecropping structure. During my life in Texas, I think I lived in at least seven or eight sharecropping systems. The properties were owned by Black relatives, Black landowners, and White landowners. Sharecropping was a system that followed slavery. It can be defined as a social and economic system that provided housing, some food or free products from the farm (which may include vegetables, fruit, milk, butter, meat, etc.), and a little money in exchange for working on farms.

Sharecropping was primarily practiced in the South. It was basically the only system of livelihood for newly freed slaves. African-Americans, who had served as slaves on farms, sometimes remained on the farm after being emancipated and worked as sharecroppers. Most sharecroppers were Black. The work involved farming and tending the livestock. To be exact, we plowed the land, planted the seeds, and harvested the products. It was usually cotton and corn.

The basic treatment of African-Americans in the system varied a great deal, as there were no basic standards that those who operated the system were obliged to follow. My family was fortunate that the seven or eight different systems we experienced were fairly acceptable, except one. From the time I was born until I left for college, if there had not been a sharecropping system, I do not know how we could have survived.

My mother had nothing that she could share with us after the house burned and she became a poor sharecropping lady. She found herself moving from one sharecropping system to another. My father would negotiate the arrangements and manage the system by which we moved from one tenant system to another. He found wealthy people who needed help with their farm work. We lived in various parts of East Texas in rural areas of Henderson, Longview, and Mt. Enterprise.[2]

For most of my life, my family was tenant farmers who moved frequently.[3] We had little stability in our family as I was growing up. I never knew when we would be moving from one rural area to another until a couple of days before the move took place. As a child, I never knew why we moved so frequently and never asked. It was not proper to ask parents a lot of questions. We barely stayed at any place very long. It was not possible to develop friendships with other children, and we were always changing schools. Life as a sharecropper, as I experienced it, meant almost always being on the move. I have difficulty even remembering all of the places we moved because my father (who rarely was home) failed to carry out all of his responsibilities.

My father rarely worked in the fields. We rarely saw him. He was more like a stranger who came home whenever he wished. I was to learn in my 40s or 50s from my mother that he was away "wrestling cows" and "herding cattle," whatever that meant. He was a sweet-talking dude until his death. The females he called, "Baby." While my father was not physically cruel to my mother, he dated other women. He was a womanizer, even courting one of my elementary school teachers. I have the impression that he came from a slave breeder where men were treated as studs because, as I recall, all of his male siblings I knew were womanizers—many openly so.

While my father was home infrequently, he was always kind in his own way to my mother. I do not recall that he ever hit or spoke mean to her. I was to later learn that my mother's father, who disliked my father, informed him that he must never lay a hand on her. He always called her "Baby," and she seemed happy whenever he was around. She would groom him. They would sit in the yard and she would pluck his eyebrows and shave him. That was something that most people did.

He somehow managed to have eight children. One of the things that I never understood was how I could suddenly find a newborn baby in the house. Interestingly enough, I never knew the answer until I was in high school. My older sisters told me that my mother went to an old lady in the neighborhood who delivered the baby. We never talked about those things with adults.

I recall always being excited when my father came home. When he came home it was like Santa Claus had visited our house. We always looked forward to his return because he always brought guilt gifts—some special food like mac and cheese, canned salmon, sardines, cheese, crackers, and cheap candy. My father was rarely home, but my mother stuck with him until he decided to go to California, as many Blacks did after the war [World War II]. Since my father was away most of our growing-up years, our mother performed the functions of both parents to the extent that she could. For discipline, if we were arguing with each other, fighting, etc., Mom would make each of us get a switch (a limb from tree) and whip each other. She was a smart lady, because we could not really hit each other hard with the switches. It solved the problem. My mother tried to solve problems without whipping.

Bernice shares some memories and reflections from her early years in the 1930s[4]:

In the year of 1931 in June, I [was born and] came to live with Eula and RP Sirls. At that time they already had two boys and three girls. My middle name is Etherline. I learned it came from my great-grandfather's first wife. He gave this name to his oldest daughter who was my grandmother. I did not like the name. My sisters and brothers would make fun of me because of the name. There was also my red hair and the freckles on my face.

Just before I started to school, my sister Mozelle [was born and] came to live with us. I did not like that one bit. Mama gave her more time than she gave to me. I didn't like Mozelle; she was pretty and Mama spent too much time nursing her. I named her, "The Food." She was always hungry. So I had to do something to get my part of the attention. I was always vying for attention to be number one. So I became an informant. They called me, "Red-Head, Tattle-Tailing Bernice." I did not think those other people (my sisters) liked me, and if they could catch me they would hit me and laugh at my middle name, red hair, and freckles.

I did not care. In the summer I got at least two switchings a day. I only got myself in trouble: starting a fire in the fireplace, using real eggs to make mud pies, and drinking my older sisters' fingernail polish because it smelled good. After drinking the nail polish, I gave up eating everything that smelled good; it is not always good. I remember starting fights in the bed just to get out of sharing the bed. I'd start hollering and Mama would say, "Get in here young'un." As I grew older, I always stayed close to Mama. I followed Mama wherever she went. She loved her garden. Once, I didn't think she recognized how fast the plants were growing, so I pulled them up to show her. That was the last time I got to go in the garden.

The only time I felt sad was when I would see it on my mother's face. Other than that life was OK, even when there was not enough food. I didn't know we were poor.[5] Mama dressed us well. But we had malnutrition. I just knew my stomach was hurting; I didn't know I was hungry. It is amazing what God does. He didn't let me know I was poor. But Papa didn't feed us. He spent most of the time in jail. He was a very smart man but did not know how to use it because the White man just put stops on everything: "Stop this, stop that, stop there, and stop here."

As I grew up among all five of my sisters, life was not easy, but I did not suffer because I thought that was the way life was. I did not know any other way. Mozelle and I had fun! Mildred didn't think it was funny. She washed many things out of her mind because it was a terrible life, but I didn't see it that way. Somehow we were able to weed out fun. But it wasn't fun for Mildred because she knew what was green and what was purple. She knew more than Mozelle and me, and she couldn't tolerate it. Mildred did not laugh that much. She knew why she was hungry. Life was serious for her, and she knew a lot about what was happening and she wasn't happy about it. Mildred would have to do all the work because Mozelle and I did not want to do work.

I was a happy child as long as I was near Mama. I did not do any work; I was too young. I would bring in stove wood and water. What I did best was play house in the summer. I would go out in the yard after breakfast and make a diagram with a stick to mark out the bedroom, kitchen, etc. I also had children—12 children and some friends made out of sticks; they all had names. I would play with them and then get busy with my mud pies.

Mildred was very intelligent. She was always reading a book. I was not good at school. Mama helped me and had Era help me, too. Once when we were supposed to be doing homework, I started wiggling my nose. I thought everybody could do it, but Era couldn't. She started laughing and we were both laughing. My mom shouted at us to stop laughing and finish the work. Era just did it for me. I didn't learn anything.

I once changed an F to an A on a test and gave the paper to Mama and went out to play. Mama just put the paper in her pocket. Later, I saw Mama go to the teacher when the teacher was walking home and have a long talk with her. When Mama found out from the teacher that I got an F, she got a switch from the persimmon tree and I got in double the trouble: for the F and for lying. Those persimmon tree branches would bend but not break. I was a terrible little one!

I wonder what life would have been like if I had not come to live with them. I was an outsider in that family. I clung to Mama to keep from being killed for tattling on everyone. I tattle-tailed all the time. I was always getting someone a whooping. They did not like Bernice. Now that I have become a Christian I know why.

My mother to me then and now was a diamond trimmed in gold. She fed eight children, taught us right from wrong, and made us do well. I was baptized at Sabine Valley in a pond where folks went fishing, and there were lilies on the water.[6] I remember seeing the white lily. After the preacher put me under, I remember I walked into Mama's arms into one of her quilts. Papa was not there. He rarely went to church. When he did, it was just a lot of flirting.

My father was a dashingly handsome man whom everyone seemed to like. Papa was a ladies' man. He was going with everyone—the schoolteacher, the candlestick maker, the church ladies, everyone. I remember that one of our ancestors was used as a stud and had 50 sons. His only job for the master was to make children. It is on record in Texas about this African. Maybe that's where Papa got it from! I remember that Mozelle wrote with her left hand. Once a teacher hit her, and Mama went to talk to the teacher and told her not to hit Mozelle again. I later learned that Papa was going with this schoolteacher.

Papa was gone a lot. My Papa was a jailbird. He stole mostly cattle, chickens, cows, and pigs. The last time he went to jail in Huntsville, Texas. He said he was never again going to the penitentiary. I remember once Mama told me she heard "Bam, bam, bam" on the door and the police say something about Papa stealing a White man's cow. He would steal the cow and sell it to the butcher and give the money to his women. When the police arrested him, they told Mama, "Eula, we going to see that you don't get no welfare this time." Every time he'd come out of jail, they'd make another baby. When Papa would get out of jail every two years I was glad to see him. "Here come Papa, y'all," Irmagene would say.

When he got out of jail, I remember when he would come home. I would be so happy to receive his hug and kiss; he would rub my tender face with his. I would frown and turn up my nose, and he would laugh that loud laugh as only he could. I still loved him. I told Mozelle once, "Papa calls me, 'Baby.'" She said, "That's because he doesn't know our names." I learned that Papa's mama [Etherline] wanted him to go to school, but his father [Jesse] would not let him go to school and would have him work and pick cotton, putting Papa to work like he was a slave.

What I liked about Papa was that he didn't beat his wife. His other brothers beat their wives to death.[7] When I asked Mama why Papa didn't beat her, Mama said she told him the day they got married that if he beat her, he needed to kill her. I asked Mama what she was going to do, and she said that she was going to boil some hot grits and throw it on him. She said she told him, "Don't go to sleep if you beat me."

Growing up, I also remember only one Christmas. I got three English walnuts, an apple, an orange, and little candies, and that was the happiest time for me.[8] Everybody got something. I went outside and I screamed for Mama, "Here are Santa Claus' tracks, right here!" I also remember Papa coming in one Christmas night and saying to Mama, "This is the last Christmas when we will have nothing for us and the kids." I remember one Christmas when we had nothing, not even food to eat.

June 19th was always a holiday for Black people that was celebrated by making ice cream.[9] I was born on the 18th, and my mom had to stay in a dark room after giving birth.[10] She was mad because she couldn't go outside, but she still got her ice cream.

Mozelle has similar memories about growing up in poverty, but also important holidays[11]:

We were very poor. There were eight children in our family. The boys, Clyde and Lowell, were oldest; actually, their names were Jesse Clyde and George Lowell. The name Jesse came from Papa's grandfather, and the name George from Mama's father. The girls were Irmagene, Era, Mildred, Bernice, and Mozelle (myself), then the youngest, Ruby. Lowell was more conservative while Clyde tended to be carefree, getting into scrapes and getting out of them. Our oldest sister, Irmagene, was a beautiful girl. She helped Mama with the younger children. She was quiet as well as beautiful. The next sister, Era, also helped out with the younger children. She looked and acted like Clyde. She was of medium height and was a bit on the hefty side. She and Clyde teamed together against Lowell when playing baseball.

Our oldest brother, George Lowell (we called him Lowell), tells a horror story about the family being in a starving situation while Papa played around in town with fancy women. Mama was pregnant with me, the seventh child, second to the youngest, and was in need of nourishment, which she was not getting. After weeks of going without food and slowly starving, my big brother, Lowell, watched us. He loved his beautiful mama dearly and it hurt him to see her in this state. At the tender age of twelve, Lowell, in desperation, set out for town on foot, miles away. He asked around town until he discovered Papa in a house with what was called then "sporting women." Lowell persuaded him to come home and bring food. He saved our lives that day. Papa was more favorable to Clyde, our youngest brother, I think because he was named for Papa's father. Papa would sometimes take Clyde with him on his jaunts into town.

On the 19th of June each year, Papa made homemade ice cream, usually with peaches. We had a barbecue and other goodies like cakes and cookies and pies, celebrating the 19th of June. Droves of cars would pass the house on the 4th of July. I did not know what the 4th meant. I learned later that all the White people were going to celebrate the 4th of July, probably at a nearby lake to the west of us.

For birthdays, we always had birthday cake. Mama always gave each of her children something for their birthdays, even after we'd grown up; we'd get a card with a handkerchief or money in the card. And for Christmas, there was a Christmas tree and we always had fruit. At Christmastime we would get a tree from the woods and decorate it with store-bought and handmade decorations. I remember Mama taking down a red paper bell that folded and unfolded like an accordion. This sat atop the tree. Though our gifts were not fancy, everyone got something: fruit, apples, oranges, and nuts that we had gotten from the woods, along with those Papa (acting as Santa) had bought. We had special candy for Christmas, and ribbon-like candy that I liked to eat with the nuts. We had gathered hickory nuts, black walnuts, and pecans. Mama made Christmas dinner and almost always baked a black walnut cake. I always placed my dessert on the same plate with my dinner. I liked it this way because I had learned to do this from my older brother, as I almost worshipped him and did as much like him as I could. He did not eat green vegetables and neither did I, except for green beans.

When Lowell was a small boy, he was afraid of Santa Claus. He did not know Papa was Santa. Clyde and Lowell schemed to trap Santa one Christmas. In the dark, Lowell peeked into the living room and saw a red suit, got panicky, and ran out of the house down to a creek nearby and stayed out all night. I firmly believed in Santa Claus[12] and did until I was told differently by Mama and Bernice when I was about the age of 11. I was so disappointed. Sometimes snow occurred around Christmas, only enough to barely cover the grass, but we would gather some snow and make snow ice cream by adding sugar and milk. It was very good, but I always got a sore throat. I had bad tonsils.

Mildred and her sisters share their memories about daily life in sharecropping houses, including chores and hair-washing. Mildred begins[13]:

The houses usually had at least three bedrooms and large yards. Girls always slept in the same room and boys always slept in the same room. My parents had their own room. We never owned a house. In fact, I never lived in a house my family owned until I [got] married and we moved to 1405 West Hovey in Normal, Illinois. The persons for whom we were sharecroppers provided us a small amount of money. It was the children who did the work. While as children we had many chores to do around the house, we also worked outside performing chores related to tasks that sharecroppers were required to perform.

We washed our clothes by making a fire from logs outdoors and boiling the white clothes clean in a large cast-iron black pot. We took wood and poured kerosene on it. We would strike a match and then boil the white clothes, using a wooden paddle to stir the clothes around until they were clean. The colored clothes were placed in a tub of water and rubbed on a board. We used soap made from the fat of pigs, oil, and lye. We would then rinse the clothes in two tubs of water and hang them out on a clothesline with clothespins. We would iron all of the clothes with an iron heated on the heater that we used to keep the house warm. In the summer we would make a fire outside and heat the iron. All clothes were ironed with a smoothing iron. We usually starched all of our clothes. This was a laborious process, as my mother liked clean.[14]

Mom made aprons, washcloths, sheets, and pillows. We made our own quilts.[15] My mother cut the pattern from newspapers that we got from the White lady for whom she worked as a maid. She also used the Sears and Roebuck catalogs to make patterns. In the winters we would piece and sew the pieces for the quilts and put them on "horses" to quilt them. We bought the bed frame, and we made our own pillows and mattresses from flour sackcloths, cotton, and straw.

My mom bought our shoes and socks. She, of course, could not make our shoes and stockings. Incidentally, my brother Lowell was a fantastic buyer. We always liked the shoes that he bought for us. He would draw our feet on newspaper or pages from catalogs so he would purchase proper sizes. He would take those to town and purchase our shoes. Our shoes lasted as long as they could, but we regularly found ourselves wearing torn shoes. I recall one situation in which my shoes and those of most of my siblings were so old that the soles were quite worn. My mother would have us replace the soles with folded-up newspapers and cardboard to augment the torn soles to protect our feet from the cold and frostbite. Frostbitten feet were the norm. In spite of this situation, we did not miss a day in school unless we were ill.

My mother would wash and braid our hair once a week. I recall that every Saturday night was full bath and hair-washing time in the tub. My mother believed in being clean, and I can see her now saying, "Go bathe yourself." We bathed in a metal tub.[16] She would use an ordinary bar of soap. When we became teenagers, she would heat a straightening comb to straighten out the hair and use a hot curling iron to curl it. She would braid it while it was wet. The only memory I have is that of my sister Bernice screaming as loud as she could when her hair was being washed as she was taking a bath in a washtub on the open back porch of the house. She would yell so loud that the neighbors could hear and know that it must be Saturday and Bernice was taking a bath and having her hair washed and braided. Bernice knew how to fake being hurt but was unable to make the tears cooperate.

Bernice admits this[17]*:*

During hair-washing time, I would scream so loud the neighbors would come over and say, "Ms. Sirls, please don't wash her hair." I screamed like a siren. Era, who was like a mama, said, "Bernice, I'm not going to hurt you. Be still and don't cry." But when that P&G soap, which was like Clorox, started running toward my eye, I just screamed. I was a pickle and I knew it. I didn't shed any tears. I just screamed.

Mozelle also remembers hair-washing and clothes-washing time[18]*:*

Bernice furnished entertainment to the whole county when she had to get her hair washed. Irmagene would hold Bernice's head down over a galvanized tub and begin to scrub. Bernice would immediately begin to yell her head off. I believe the whole county could hear her. Bernice was of a reddish color and so was her hair. She had freckles, as did all of Mama's children, whether they were light colored or dark. Once a passing neighbor heard Bernice yelling and begged Mama to quit washing her head. I believe Bernice yelled and hollered just to keep from getting a head-washing.

When taking baths in the tub, I recalled how in Texas, Bernice got the idea of deceiving Mama by rattling the galvanized tub that we bathed in and pretending we were bathing. Bernice, Ruby, and I would participate in this deception. But it did not last for long, for soon Mama's nose and Ruby told her we were not bathing. Once, Ruby got out of the tub and for some reason decided to go into the living room where other members of the family were. She placed a towel in front of her and made her appearance. After saying what she had to say, she turned and went back, leaving her little behind exposed!

There were porches on each end of the house. The porch by the living room faced the large, empty space. This is where Mama washed clothes. Washing day was on Monday. Mama put a fire under the big iron washpot and boiled the clothes, rolling them with a stick while they boiled. There were two ring tubs. Bernice and I were placed at these. I always got my dress wet. Mama would tell me I was going to marry a drunkard. (Indeed, one of [my] husbands was a drunk). We hung the wash out on the fence to dry, Mama having starched everything—including sheets and pillowcases, although she used only a slight amount of starch for these. Everything else was starched stiff and ironed neat. I wanted to iron, but I was too short. Then I wanted to wash dishes. Mama finally placed a box under me and allowed me to wash dishes. I still got my dress wet.

Church and Religion

Church and religion were very important parts of the sharecropping lifestyle. Mildred describes the role of church and religion in her daily life[19]:

We had our own churches which served many functions for us. Outside of our family and extended family and neighbors, our social life was the church. Church was an important aspect of our lives. We walked miles every Sunday for Sunday school and church service. We went to a Baptist church, and baptism was in a waterhole. In the early years, someone lined out the music and the congregation followed. There were no songbooks, and most people could not read. Songs were about God, Jesus, and hard times. There is an interesting joke about lining out songs. My religion professor said one Sunday in jest that the person lining out said, "My eyes are blind, I cannot see, I did not bring my specs with me," and the congregation followed!

Every summer the Baptist Black churches always had what were called revivals. This included a full week ending on Sunday with a huge dinner. Sunday was church all day. Long tables were set up outside the church buildings. We ate outside on tables and everyone brought food. These tables were filled with many traditional African-American and Southern foods. Among the traditional foods were collard greens, cakes, pies, chicken n' dumplings, black-eyed peas, cornbread, biscuits, fried chicken, corn on the cob, and punch.

During the revivals, there was the "mourner's bench."[20] This bench was on the first row of benches nearest the pulpit. When the preacher completed his long sermon, he dramatically called all of the unsaved or sinners to come up to the first bench. I found myself going up each night to the bench. On the last night, I was the lone person on the bench, as all of the other people had felt the Spirit and committed themselves to the Lord, with the minister now looking at me as the lone sinner. While I did not feel the Spirit, I was not only conscious of the minister's glare, but also the apparent disgust of the parishioners. So, I reluctantly went up and shook the preacher's hand to the obvious relief of the parishioners and the preacher.

We had certain rituals and would say Bible verses before eating. I recall that as each of us children waited our turn, we were hoping that no one ahead of us would say, "Jesus wept." Each of us knew that one. One day I was listening to my sister, and I heard her say, "Get day, be done breakfast!" There was also a ritual at bedtime, which was to say prayers. "Lord, I lay me down to sleep. I pray the Lord my soul would keep. If I should die before I wake, I pray the Lord my soul to take."

I recall one day (at age 11 or 12) that I did not want to go to church. My mother approved with some reservations and said that I should have dinner ready when they returned from church. I had no apprehension about remaining at home alone and making dinner. While I cannot remember all of the items I prepared, I do remember vividly the cake that I baked. Cooking meant making a fire in the wood stove and sustaining it. When the family arrived, I was excited with the meal that I had prepared. As I recall, all went well until it was time for the dessert. The cake, as I recall, looked good, but when the family began to take the first bite, I observed frowns on their faces. My mom asked for the ingredients in the cake. They all heard "salt" instead of sugar, and that was the end of that cake!

Mozelle remembers this time, and shares similar memories about the role of church and religion in her life[21]:

Mildred, who took care of us when Mama was away doing housework for White families, cooked a cake one day. Only it turned out she'd used salt instead of sugar in error. I was especially disappointed, and I supposed Mama was too, for she as well as Papa had a sweet tooth.

At mealtime we all sat down together to eat, and regardless of how meager the meal, Mama would say the blessing: "Bless this food we are about to eat for the nourishment of our bodies for Christ's sake. Amen." Then each of us would recite a Bible verse. We all tried to recite a new verse except for the younger children, who mostly recited, "Jesus wept." Mildred would most often say, "He that hath an ear, let him hear." Era prayed, "Get day, be done breakfast!" At bedtime we would all get on our knees by the bed and say the Lord's Prayer.

Mama did not allow us to sing any church songs other than the ones sang at our church, Sabine Valley. I liked to hear the choir sing. Era sang in the choir as well as serving as an usher. I was so enamored with the singing and piano music that I would try to copy the singing and piano playing at home by sitting on a pillow, beating the rungs at the end of our iron bed, and singing the songs they'd sang at church. Someone would soon shut me up.

We went to Sunday school, to the regular preaching services, and then back at night for Baptist Training for Youth. One Sunday, Bernice got the idea that we would snatch the tray carrying the grape juice at the Lord's Supper and carry it outside and drink it all. I got the giggles and so did Bernice. Mama looked back at us and frowned, but we were too far away from her for her to scold us. There was a lady who lived near the church called Mrs. Fannie. Mrs. Fannie would always shout and get the Holy Ghost as soon as Reverend Spellman began preaching. She knocked the ushers about, one of whom was Era. It took all the ushers to subdue Mrs. Fannie. They would take her outside, whereupon she'd promptly walk home. When we got out of church hours later, Mrs. Fannie would be sitting on her porch in the shade, fanning. Smart lady!

At revival time, the minister would preach each night and sometimes we had preachers and singers from town. This would go on for a week, and at the end of the week all the members would bring covered dishes and serve in the church annex. This little building was filled with goodies: all kinds of chicken, vegetables, and desserts. I liked this part of the revival. After the feast that evening came the last sermon of the revival. I can recall gazing at the stained-glass windows in the back of the pulpit, which was all lit up by the setting sun. I would be filled with awe and it seemed Heaven itself was close by, shining in the windows. Gospel singers often came to the church, but after the singing when they passed the plate, they would "brook no nonsense" with brownies [pennies]. They wanted green [dollars], but few of us had what they wanted.

Not too often, the minister, Reverend Spellman, came to dinner. Everyone sat down to dinner but the younger children. I waited and got chicken feet, much to my regret. I had waited patiently for at least a drumstick. But I did like Reverend Spellman and his wife very much. They were nice people.

Struggling to Survive

Mildred and her siblings remember one of the most difficult sharecropping housing experiences involving the "Schmeling shack." Mildred begins[22]:

The earliest memories that I have of my life involve working. My guess is that I began work at age six. My earliest memory of sharecropping is when we were on a place called Sandy Hill, owned by our relatives. When we left that place, we moved to the worst living place I ever experienced. I recall the most frightening and poverty-stricken experiences in growing up as a child in Texas. It was life in a jungle—the most inhumane place that we ever lived.

My father had moved us into a house and property owned by a rich White man whose last name was Schmeling. He was very wealthy, and my older brother Lowell was to learn later that this man was related to the professional boxer from Germany, Max Schmeling.[23] My mother served as his maid. The man my mother worked for had a big house about a mile from us, and she had to walk there in very cold weather. We as children never got to see the house, but my mother told us that it was like a mansion. He lived alone and he was a very mean man. My mother would leave us eight children at home while she worked. We were there for one winter. It was a small house tucked deep in the woods with no houses near us. Life in this Schmeling hut was our worst. The unfinished, old house was located several miles from a road. There was no indoor toilet or indoor water.

I don't recall that my father ever lived in the house with us. There was my mother, two brothers, and five girls all under 14 years of age. The house had about three rooms. It was a very cold winter when we were there, and water dripped from the tin roof. The place had no cooking stove. We had one room where my mother slept that had a wood heater. We cooked with what little wood we had on the stove. The iron stove served two functions—cooking and warmth. Most of us eight children slept on the floor with badly torn blankets. We drew water from a well to drink and bathe. Occasionally, Mom would bring us a bit of food from the "master's" house.

The older siblings just spent the day in the forest looking for food and playing. One of the older girls would look after the younger children. We found a garbage dump and ate the food there. I'll never forget that there was one car dump. We scraped some tar from the car battery and chewed it for gum. I am surprised that it did not make us sick or even kill us. I think God must have saved us. I recall that we would eat red berries from trees and sometimes just weeds that we thought might be edible. In the evening when my mother would return from work, she had us bring her buckets of snow, which she mixed with sugar and vanilla to make ice cream. She made traps from clothespins, put them on the windowsills, and caught blackbirds. She defeathered them and fried them for us to eat. She would cook them and tell us to pretend that they were chickens. We also caught squirrels and rabbits to eat. She was an incredibly creative lady.

Since for the first time we were not able to attend school because there was no school near us for Black children, my mother set up her own school. With respect to learning when we were in the jungle, my mother and older brother Lowell were our informal teachers. While sitting around the fireplace, Lowell would teach us what he had learned when he had attended schools at the numerous sharecropper houses where we lived. For example, we learned our spelling and ABCs, and we had [the] Sirls Spelling contests. There was reciting times tables and naming the various states. Mississippi was spelled "M-i-crooked letter-i-crooked letter-i-hump back-i-hump back-i."[24]

When my two older brothers were learning geography and math, they taught us in the evenings around the potbelly heater. We also memorized poetry. My mother loved poetry and read it to us when we were children. My mother always read poetry even up until she died. My older brother Lowell had memorized several poems and taught them to us. The poems were from such poets as Langston Hughes and Paul Lawrence Dunbar. We all sat around the old iron stove, cooking, eating what food there was, and singing and reciting poetry. We would also piece quilts using the few rags we had.

For recreation and entertainment, we would play croquet, jump rope, and baseball. We played with rag dolls made by my mother. For toys, we made balls from newspaper strung, wrapped, and held together with flour paste and starch. We made paper balls for catch and played baseball with stuffed stockings.[25] Sometimes we listened to [President Franklin D.] Roosevelt on a small radio we were lucky to have.[26] Whenever he made major speeches they were broadcast on the radio. We would all gather around the heater and listen to his speeches. It was during the Great Depression, and we wanted to know what he would do to improve our lives. We played games like "Little Sally Walker, sitting in a saucer; rise Sally rise, wipe your weeping eyes; put your hands on your hips, let your backbone slip; shake it to the east, shake it to the west; shake it to the one you love the best."

I cannot recall just how long we were at this place. But I recall that it was in the winter; it snowed almost every day. We almost froze to death roaming around in the woods and in the snow and ice. We got out of the jungle when late one night my father drove up in an old truck (I do not know where it came from or where he had been). Through ice and snow, my father, out of breath, hastily got out of the truck and told us to quickly grab as much stuff as we could and run with him. Very frightened, we followed orders. We grabbed stuff and ran with him to a truck, where we quickly jumped in and were driven away to a place that he had found for us—another sharecropping farm.

Where my father had been I do not know. I doubt that my mother knew. In any event, we were moved to a safer place. We learned from Mama that Papa rushed to get us because this man Schmeling, for whom my mother worked and on whose property we lived, had plans to literally enslave us if we did not get out of that place. I only know that Papa saved us from death or slavery.

Mozelle shares a similar memory of this experience with Schmeling[27]:

I believe the next place we moved to was a cabin in the deep woods, with pine trees all around. I recall it being cold and rainy. Papa was not with us at this place. We were destitute as usual. What we ate I do not know. Papa had brothers and sisters and other relatives, and they were particularly friendly with Mama. Papa's younger brother, Uncle Griff, would often help us in hard times. Our Uncle Griff came to visit often, and I am sure he brought food, for I remember him bringing clothing. Among these was a blue-green coat he gave to me. This coat had a rooster on the pocket, and I was very fond of that coat. Uncle Griff was proud of his nieces and nephews. He was tall and handsome with bright, sparkling eyes.

We were on the property of a White man called Schmeling, who wanted to make slaves of us, but Papa came in time and moved us to another place, called Greenville. This was also in the country. I think this place was located in Gregg County. Here there was a school and a store nearby. I liked this house. I remember it being rainy and stormy, but I felt safe here. I would look out on the trees and green grass, for it was springtime.

Bernice also remembers this time at the Schmeling house[28]:

I remember Schmeling. Papa said he was a redneck cracker. He would walk through the yard. Lowell had a pig, and Schmeling said, "Get that pig out of the barn." Papa had dumped us there. The man wanted the girls to iron his clothes at his house, but Mama said no. She said he could bring his clothes to us. It was cold and snowing, and we weren't accustomed to that. We hardly had any food. My stomach hurt a lot, but I didn't know then that it was from being hungry. I remember Mama going to the garbage and getting potato peels and frying them. She had to kill blackbirds for us, too. One night, Papa came and put us in a truck—not his truck, but someone else's. He covered our heads and told us not to look up. The man was going to make slaves of us. We were always moving.

Key Lessons

Mozelle wrote a poem summarizing the siblings' childhood experiences as sharecroppers entitled "The Good"[29]:

The good old days or modern ways,
(A few would really go back);
But not many people would want to raise
Six kids in a two-room shack!
Babies were rocked in an old straight chair,
All clothes hung to dry outside
By hands that were cracked and bled, why care?
'Twas badge of a mother's pride.
Rainwater caught off the eaves of the house,
Clothes scrubbed on an old washboard;
Cracks in the floor (to let in a mouse),
No stop for the wind could afford.
Kids' clothes were all ironed, slipped under the bed,

Each child had a box of its own,
Three dresses for girls, overalls for each lad,
But mended and starched 'til they shone.
Water was carried uphill from the spring
For drinking and cooking and such.
On the opposite side to the outside "thing"
A path that was traveled as much.
The wood was brought in (ashes went out),
For heating and cooking stove, too;
The kitchen in summer, a steam bath, no doubt,
But cooking you *had* to do.
Cows had to be milked, pigs and chickens were fed,
Every morning and night;
You stirred up and straightened each old straw bed
And read by a kerosene light.
You ran to the garden, then jogged to the field,
Made hay when the sun shone *hot*;
Canned vegetables, fruit (saved all summer's yield),
Made lard in an old iron pot.
I guess it shows, some memories of mine,
Going back wouldn't "hack it" for me;
But if we could choose the best of each time,
What a better life it would be.
So much can be said for the days gone by,
Like pride in a work well done;
Belief in the aid of a God on high,
And that man and wife are one.
We'd show more concern for a neighbor in need,
Teach our kids more obedience, too,
By living more love in each word and each deed
Teaching honesty's value anew.

As Mozelle's poem reflects, despite the challenging circumstances of segregation and poverty, African-Americans persevered and survived. Surviving as a Black family in a racially segregated economically marginalized society steeped with hegemonic values of White superiority and Black inferiority required certain qualities. Strength, perseverance, determination, creativity, wisdom, pride, and respect were qualities that Black women needed to raise children, often in the absence of husbands. Mildred's mother, Eula, like many Black women, worked as a maid to provide for the family, but also worked within the home to cook, clean, and sustain a household. In addition, the community created and sustained by the Black Baptist church provided an important foundation for survival. The church also had a significant influence on Mildred as she chose to study religion when she eventually went to college.

Notes

1. (M. Pratt, personal communication, n.d.).
2. Bernice (Mildred's sister) shared with Mildred a list of important places in their lives: "Sandy Hill; Union Spring; Camp Switch (our address Route 4, Box 354); Longview Texas; Sabin Valley (we lived here when Ruby died); Greensville (the place we lived where the teacher made you repeat a grade); Nacogdoches; Henderson; Greggton (where we lived when Mozelle, Mom, and I caught the train from Texas for Missouri); Huntsville (where Papa was in jail); Center (where Ruby Pauline Sirls is put to rest); Lubbock (where most of Mom's people lived); Prairie View (where Lowell went to college for a semester before the war)" (B. Miller, personal communication, n.d.).
3. For a discussion of the transient nature of sharecropping, see Valk and Brown (2010, pp. 51, 208–211).
4. (B. Miller, personal communication, February 8, 2013; April 7, 2013; June 8, 2013; and June 13, 2013).
5. Because of segregation, many Black children did not know they were poor (Andrews, 1990, p. 52; Chafe, Gavins, & Korstad, 2001, p. 237; Valk & Brown, 2010, p. 47).
6. For another example of public baptisms, see Taulbert (1989, p. 105).
7. Spouse abuse was not uncommon (Andrews, 1990, pp. 65–66).
8. Fruit and nuts were common Christmas treats (Andrews, 1990, p. 52; Taulbert, 1989, p. 11).
9. For more on the significance of June 19th, see "History of Juneteenth" that describes Juneteenth as "the oldest known celebration commemorating the ending of slavery in the United States. Dating back to 1865, it was on June 19th that the Union soldiers, led by Major General Gordon Granger, landed at Galveston, Texas, with news that the war had ended and that the enslaved were now free." This was two years after January 1, 1863, at President Lincoln's "Emancipation Proclamation." See also Beeth and Wintz (1992, p. 98) for a description of Juneteenth and De-Ro-Loc ("colored" spelled backward) celebrations in Houston, Texas.
10. Staying in a dark room after giving birth seems to have been a common midwife practice (Taulbert, 1989, p. 50).
11. (M. Perry, personal communication, n.d.).
12. For related experience about Santa Claus, see Andrews (1990, pp. 108–109).
13. (M. Pratt, personal communication, n.d.).
14. For another description of washing clothes, see Valk and Brown (2010, p. 20).
15. Making quilts was an integral part of the Black South experience (Andrews, 1990, p. 77; Chafe et al., 2001, p. 209; Taulbert, 1989, pp. 48–49, 1992, p. 88).
16. See Chafe et al. (2001, p. 45) for a description of bathing.

17. (B. Miller, personal communication, June 13, 2013).
18. (M. Pratt, personal communication, n.d.).
19. (M. Pratt, personal communication, n.d.).
20. For more about the mourner's bench, see "Mourner's Bench." See also Taulbert (1989, p. 102) and (1992, p. 193).
21. (M. Perry, personal communication, n.d.).
22. (M. Pratt, personal communication, n.d.).
23. For information on Max Schmeling's family, see "People and Events: Max Schmeling"; "Oscar Schmeling"; and "Nick Schmeling Flies to Join."
24. Mildred notes that her husband, Theodore, from Sierra Leone, West Africa, said they learned to spell in a similar way. For example, mud was "m-u-one butt" (M. Pratt, personal communication, n.d.).
25. See Andrews (1990, pp. 104–105) for a discussion of recreation.
26. The radio was an important connection to the "outside" world during Jim Crow (Andrews, 1990, pp. 213–221; Chafe et al., 2001, pp. 92–93).
27. (M. Perry, personal communication, n.d.).
28. (B. Miller, personal communication, June 13, 2013).
29. (M. Perry, personal communication, n.d.).

References

Andrews, R. (1990). *The last radio baby: A memoir*. Atlanta, GA: Peachtree Publishers.

Beeth, H., & Wintz, C. D. (Eds.). (1992). *Black Dixie: Afro-Texan history and culture in Houston*. College Station, TX: Texas A&M University Press.

Chafe, W. H., Gavins, R., & Korstad, R. (Eds.). (2001). *Remembering Jim Crow: African Americans tell about life in the Segregated South*. New York, NY: The New Press.

"History of Juneteenth." *Juneteenth.com*. Retrieved September 1, 2013 from http://www.juneteenth.com/history.htm

"Nick Schmeling Flies to Join Cousin Max." *The Spokesman-Review*. Retrieved September 1, 2013 from http://news.google.com/newspapers?nid=1314&dat=19371217&id=1m5WAAAAIBAJ&sjid=zOMDAAAAIBAJ&pg=3684,549718

"Oscar Schmeling." *BoxRec*. Retrieved August 5, 2013 from http://boxrec.com/list_bouts.php?human_id=60129&cat=boxer

"People and Events: Max Schmeling." *PBS*. Retrieved September 1, 2013 from http://www.pbs.org/wgbh/amex/fight/peopleevents/p_schmeling.html

Taulbert, C. L. (1989). *Once upon a time when we were colored*. Tulsa, OK: Council Oak Books.

Taulbert, C. L. (1992). *The last train north*. New York, NY: Penguin Books.

Valk, A., & Brown, L. (2010). *Living with Jim Crow: African American women and memories of the Segregated South*. New York, NY: Palgrave Macmillan.

CHAPTER FIVE

Segregated and Sharecropping

Segregation, while clearly separate, and often unequal, facilitated the development of a close-knit community among African-Americans. African-Americans often served as sharecroppers for other African-Americans who owned land. Mildred's family served as sharecroppers for a wealthy Black man named Bob White in Longview, Texas. Mildred and her sisters remember their time in Longview: sharecropping, farming, picking cotton, harvesting corn, and raising cows and pigs. They also share fond recollections of family, friends, and community.

The Black White's Houses

Mildred and her siblings remember their experiences growing up in Bob White's houses. Mildred shares[1]:

After leaving the Schmeling's place, we were taken to a farm owned by an African-American man, or a "Negro," as we called him then. The long and short of it is that I was delighted when this page in my life changed. My father, who was gone most of the time as was his pattern, found us a place to stay. He was a bright man who could sweet talk one out of anything. This time my father had arranged with a well-to-do Black man whose last name was White for us to be sharecroppers. Mr. White owned a nice house and a grocery store in a Black section of Longview. He lived in the city of Longview and owned several properties in the surrounding areas.

My father promised that he, my two brothers, and [my] sisters would take good care of his farm. This was a sizable farm with cows, hogs, horses, and produce. It turned out that as soon as my father made the deal, he skipped [out] as usual. I think Papa was in jail. Back then, he used to steal people's horses and sell them. Papa was a horse thief. This left my mother and the children trying to manage the farm. Because we could not manage the farm properly, we were only there for a couple of years. I recall that our economic situation was so precarious that we found ourselves eating the food provided for the animals.[2]

The first of Mr. White's houses in which we lived was an unfinished mansion-like house. We all lived there and worked on his farm. It had about three rooms. This was the house that was being built for Mr. White. It had a fireplace. It was old and elegant but incomplete. Mr. White also owned at least two other farms. We lived for a short time in all three. We lived in this house for only a few months and [then] moved to another of Mr. White's houses.

As I remember, the houses were large enough for our family to have at least three bedrooms—one for my parents, one for my two brothers, and another for all of us girls. The five girls shared one bed. Sometimes some of us would sleep on pallets. With respect to sleeping, there was much fighting for space all night. I had no problem because I just decided to sleep on the floor.[3] My two brothers were lucky because just the two of them slept together.

There was no toilet, and we had to build our own outdoor toilet. We used Sears and Roebuck catalogs and old newspapers for toilet paper.[4] We found the toilet to be a great place to hide from doing work. The toilet was about a quarter block from our house and therefore a good place to hang out to avoid work—at least until Mom began to count and found absentees, and sent a sibling to find the "runaway." At night we had buckets that we used for the bathroom, which had to be emptied every morning.

We drew our water from wells, had iceboxes, and used wood stoves and heaters. For water, we would make our own well or use buckets to have water from springs. There was no electricity or gas. We heated the house with an iron heater, fed by wood. We used lamps with kerosene and cooked on a stove fueled with wood.

The second of Mr. White's houses in which we lived was perhaps the equivalent of one-and-a-half miles from the first of his homes in which we lived. There was an all-Black school less than half of a mile from us. The school that we attended was the Gregg County Industrial School.[5] I think it was constructed with funds from the series of alphabet programs that President Roosevelt had established just prior to the passage of the Social Security Act to deal with the Depression.[6]

In the Gregg County Training School, Ms. Star, my elementary school teacher (a mulatto), gave me an F for reciting poetry and required me to repeat the grade.

It was the first F I ever received in all my education. I had always done well in school—all A's. This time I had a light-skinned teacher who, for some reason, seemed not to like me from the beginning. I was livid, because I had always made A's in all of my courses. I had no recourse.[7]

I recall that the winters in the rural areas of East Texas could be incredibly cold. When I was in grade school we had to walk several miles to school in bitter cold, as we owned no car and no bus service was available. The girls wore thick, ugly, cotton stockings held up with garters that covered our legs past the knees, and we used an elastic band to keep them from falling down our legs. Incidentally, the stockings were so ugly that when the weather was less cold, my sisters and I would take them off when we were out of our mother's sight before we got to school.

There was a honky-tonk directly across the road from the second of Mr. White's houses in which we lived. The owners were Mr. and Mrs. Boarders. They had a big house set on several acres of land. We used to live across the road from them, and they had a little restaurant. They called each other "Nigger." We never knew why. How they came to call themselves this I don't know. I always wanted to ask why but never did.

At the honky-tonk on the premises, they played the music of the day, and on Saturdays and Sundays the place was jumping with loud music from the jukebox.[8] On Saturday nights the place was packed with people. We had no trouble hearing, as the music could be heard throughout the neighborhood. When my mother was not home, we all tried to dance to the music. This couple was always nice to us, and at any time we could borrow food from them.

Mozelle also remembers her experiences at Mr. White's houses[9]:

Our family made many moves in the eastern part of Texas where I was born. We moved to one house up the road that was not quite finished being built. There was a large garden. Papa was with us here. Once I was playing near the back door, which had no steps yet, and it was quite a distance to the ground. I got myself pushed out that door. I must have passed out, because I do not remember anything afterward. Bernice was the culprit. She says she did it because she was mad at Papa for having her get him a glass of water.[10] I played alone and made my own toys; I made dolls out of rags and sticks, and we had conversations. Bernice was given to sneaking up on me and poking fun, but I was very content with my little families.

Across the road from us lived a funny couple who affectionately called each other "Nigger." There were two or three buildings on their property. One was a place where Mrs. Boarders had Bernice and me dry fruit—peaches and apricots— for her on the roof. Another building was in the process of being built. In my few years, I had not had the experience of seeing a structure being built. So I asked my rascal of a brother, Clyde, "What are they making?" Clyde replied with a straight face, "Why, little sister, they're making a car."

I was satisfied with this answer and waited patiently to see a car. Instead, the building was completed and was called a "honky-tonk." I heard music coming from the honky-tonk. The jukebox played songs like "Someone's Been Digging My Potatoes," or "Someone's Been Stealing My Tomatoes." My older sisters liked the music and would go into a room, close the door, and dance. They called this dance "trucking."[11] This consisted of shaking a finger in the air and shuffling across the floor. I was not to come into the room at all, let alone tell Mama. I don't think I told, but maybe I did.[12]

We moved to another house that had a fireplace that warmed your front, leaving the back cold.[13] We used coal oil lamps to read. This did not harm our eyesight. Up the hill from our house lived a White family who had a girl named June. This girl was of the same age as my sister Bernice, and they played together. At this house I recall digging in the sugar barrel and eating the contents until I got caught at it. My older sisters and brothers were at school, and in my brothers' case, in the fields working. Papa believed in the boys doing his work. Papa did not like farm work, but Mama foiled his plan by keeping the boys in school as much as possible.

There was a family that lived across the road back in some woods. One of those children, called by the nickname, "Stick-horse," was given to paying visits and saying, "Ma said, 'Send some snuffer,'" meaning, Mama said, "Send some snuff," for our Mama dipped snuff named Tube Rose.[14]

At the first house we lived in a railroad was next to it and our peace was disturbed by the train roaring through. This house was the one in Camp Switch, or Kemp Switch. This place's name is not clear to my mind, for some people called it Kemp Switch. We called it Camp Switch.[15] I had not started to school yet, so I had long periods of time alone with Mama at home. To her chagrin, I had a habit of hanging onto her dress tail. I liked the texture of the dress seams at the hem of the dress and would finger it, scooting around on the floor and following her as she did her chores—cooking, etc. This would sometimes cause her to smile and sing, "If I could only touch the hem of His garment," part of a church hymn. Mama liked to sing, and she usually sang as she cooked or washed dishes or sewed. Mildred remembers her singing, "I'm gonna lay down my sword and shield down by the riverside"; "Oh, don't you want to go to that land?"; "What you gonna do when Death comes creeping in your room?"; "Rock of Ages"; and "Amazing Grace."

Before going to bed at night, we would gather in Mama's room where the pot-bellied wood stove was and get our lessons or listen as Mama read from the Bible or a book of poems from the older children's [school] books. We read by kerosene lamps or coal oil lamps. The older girls, Irmagene, Era, and Mildred, went to high school. One of their teachers was the principal, who had studied in a college in Boston and was very well educated. In their curriculum, they studied from the book *Prose and Poetry*. This was the book Mama read to the younger ones.[16]

Some days when Mama was not otherwise occupied, she would read love stories to Bernice and me from her *Love Story* magazine.[17] Bernice and I would get the giggles from this, too. When this happened, Mama would toss the book down on the porch and get into her duties in the house.

We had stayed in the other house long enough for me to learn to read before I started to school. I learned by listening to my older sister read and memorized a poem by reciting it aloud. I would stand by her and look at the book as she read. One day she left the book at home, and I picked it up and turned to the page that poem was on. I taught myself to read by repeating the words I'd heard her read, hence recognizing words in other books. From that day on I loved books, and then I would read everything from labels on food containers to schoolbooks. I never forgot this poem.

My favorite things were playing with my dolls, sitting by Mama as she sewed her quilts and our clothing, and reading. I could not do things like play ball or climb trees or ride bicycles as Bernice did. We were not allowed to do any of these things.

Bernice liked to explore and get into trouble; only she did not see it as trouble. She was not too interested in playing with me; I guess I was too young. She was four and a half years older, so her interests went in different directions. She did not associate with Mildred either because Mildred would have nothing to do with any of us. Mama made a poor referee between the kids and their disputes. Usually Era and Clyde won the disputes. Mildred usually just watched her sisters and brothers argue or ignored them, as she did when Bernice and I came along.

The boys, Clyde and Lowell, were the oldest, and they were not expected to do housework. These were the girls' duties. One day Mama was out working. Three of us, Mildred, Bernice, and I, were left at home. We were supposed to be cleaning. Bernice had said something funny to me, and we were in a corner giggling while Mildred cleaned. We could not stop giggling. It was one of those times when one of us would look at the other and begin giggling all over again. Well, Mildred must have had just had enough, for she pitched us out of the door into the yard and continued to clean!

Bernice was funny. She was always shrewd, even if she did have a strange way of standing and staring at the hot sun, a habit that gave Clyde great amusement. Clyde liked to tease Bernice just because he liked to see her reactions. We all went barefoot in the summer, and we'd often get cuts from the sand or glass. Bernice would yell to high heaven and place dirt on the cut. She would somehow heal. I sought more practical medical help from Mama, who would put alcohol on the cut and tie it with a clean rag.

I liked to listen to the rain on our tin roof. I felt so safe on Mama's feather mattress under an abundance of her safe quilts. Some of her quilts were gaily colored with pieces from her dressmaking; some were coarse, with the pieces coming from the boys' worn-out trousers. But we all felt safe and warm under these covers, even though the only heating stove was in Mama's room.

We were supposed to use the toilet before going to bed, but Bernice always had to use the toilet in the middle of the night. Mama did not allow chamber pots unless someone was sick. Bernice slept by Era, and she would whine until Mama awakened. Era would wallop Bernice with her left hand. Mama would say, "Era, take that child to the toilet." I slept at the foot of the bed among all those toes, though sometimes I would get to sleep by Irmagene, and I was happy with this.

One of my friends at Camp Switch was a girl named Geraldine, who once while we were playing with our dolls asked me to help her make doll clothes. Other friends were some kids who stayed in town going to school but came home to their grandmother's house in the summer, when we would play together. Bernice had as her playmate a girl named Jessie Mae. They adored playing together. As well as paper dolls, Irmagene bought puzzles for me, which I loved working.

Boxes were another fascination for me. I quickly grabbed up every empty box I came across. I used them to make many different toys. After losing my store-bought paper dolls to Irmagene's house-cleaning too often, I learned to make my own paper dolls and their furniture with the discarded paper and cardboard. I made the clothing from the paper in my Big Chief writing tablet, drawing the dolls and clothing, coloring them with my crayolas, and using glue to fix the paper onto the cardboard. I loved these boxes. One day I found a *Kotex* box and was using it for a dollhouse until my older sisters caught me and threw the box away. I was quite indignant and told Mama. Mama had no other comment but that I should not use that particular box.

When we soon moved from this first house in Camp Switch, I had started to school—first grade. I came home one school day to an empty house. I was six years old and terrified. I did not have the sense to inquire of the neighbors where my family had gone. I waited on the steps wondering what to do. After a long while and having succumbed to deep anxiety, I started walking back toward the school. After a few steps down the road who should appear out of the woods but Bernice. She had come to take me to our new home. This house was also owned by Mr. White, a nice Black man who lived in Longview, the nearest town. He did not charge us to live in the house.

A large garden was on the side of the house, and on this side of the house was the path that led to the road and the line of houses where our other neighbors lived. Past that was a stretch of woods, beyond which were the house where we'd stayed before, a store, Sabine Valley Church, and Sabine Valley School where Bernice and I attended.

There was a Black family who lived near us whose last name was Madiera. Their people were wealthy from oil, which was unusual down in Texas because the White people would buy the mineral rights from Black people. The Madeiras were friendly and were well-acquainted with Papa. Papa went grocery shopping one day and brought back sacks and sacks of groceries. I heard him when he said he'd spent all of $5.00. I felt rich. When someone would give us a nickel, we would go to the store and get candy. My favorite was a coconut bar colored pink, brown, and white.

It was in this house that I recall Papa getting watermelons from the garden, placing a watermelon in the tub of ice, getting it cooled, and then handing slices of it to each of his children. This watermelon was so good that I wanted to eat the rind. But at night I would invariably pee in the bed, and I would get a whipping in the morning. I did so hate the whippings that I started to eat only a spoonful of watermelon and kept this practice even into adulthood.

Cotton Pickin', Corn Shuckin', and Cow Milkin'

One of the requirements of being a sharecropper was to work the land. Mildred shares her early experiences working on the farm and in the fields[18]:

I remember that I began working in the field as a water girl, taking water to my older brothers and sisters and my parents. As I grew older, I chopped cotton, picked cotton, and thinned corn. All of the money earned went to my father. As I recall, we spent springs and summers working in the field, picking cotton, hoeing corn rows, and taking care of house duties. We picked cotton during "cotton-picking time."[19] If there were too many cotton plants close together, we took some away so the good ones would grow. Chopping cotton was done with a hoe. When the cotton got to a certain level, it was necessary to separate it with a hoe so that there were only two sprouts, rather than five or six. This was back-breaking work, which required tremendous work in the hot Texas sun. Regardless of how hot it was, we had to work in the fields.

What I abhorred the most was handpicking the cotton which was the primary crop. We had to carry a handmade bag, which we called a "tow sack," on our backs, hanging down from our shoulders, and drag it on the soil to harvest the cotton. To pick cotton, you take the rotten cotton off and throw it away. The good cotton is in a boll and you have to take the leaves off it. When it is ripe and white and in the boll, then you have to take the cotton out. It was difficult to do.

You had to get the cotton boll out with your fingers and put that in your big ole cotton sack. That was no fun. Your fingers would feel like a needle was sticking them. Once those sacks were filled we took them to the wagon, or someone picked them up in a wagon at the end of the rows and took them to the storage area or cotton gin to be weighed. The bags were approximately six to seven feet long. We worked from sun up to sun down.

As one can imagine, this was tedious work out in the Texas sun. My mother made the girls bonnets to help shield us from the hot sun. I hated those things and would pull them off. You did cotton all day long until it got too hot. The person who is the boss tells you when it is too hot. Otherwise, you stay out there. We could stop for lunch, which we generally carried to the field with us and ate under the shade of a tree.

There was also corn. With respect to the corn, we plowed it, hoed it, and harvested it when it was ripe. We would chop the weeds from the corn when they just started coming up with a hoe. The first thing you would do was hoe if you had one. If not, you used your hand. You had to shuck the corn and pull the white stuff off. We had to pull the corn from the stalk by hand once it was ready. Thus, as one can imagine, this was rather rough on the hands. You put the corn in the tow sack, made out of cornmeal, around your head.

After the corn was dry and you shucked it, you took it to the corn mill for them to make cornmeal. You'd stay out there as long as you could to maybe get some of the corn for yourself. The landowner would usually permit us to eat the corn. Dry corn was used for bread for cornmeal. As I was engaging in this horrible work, I was telling myself that I would not do this forever.

With the sweet potatoes, when they are little plants, you put them in the ground until they grow big. You pull those out of the ground with your hand. You put sweet potatoes in a bag where your dry food is, and you pull the white potatoes off the limbs. You keep that for the balance of winter to eat. It was horrible. If you were wealthy, you got gloves. If not, you just had to pick with your hands. The worst part was picking those things with your hands.

Mr. White asked us to move to his property at Camp Switch, a rural area. At this site, Mr. White specialized in cows and hogs. Our tasks involved looking after the cows and hogs. We fed the cows, put them out to pasture in the mornings, brought them into the pens in the evening, and milked them with our hands. For example, we sometimes milked cows, put the milk in buckets, and let them set overnight. In the morning, the "sweet milk," as we called it, would turn to clabber milk. We would churn the milk in the morning. We would put it in a bowl and beat it by hand up and down for about an hour until all the butter was freed from the milk and came to the top. We would then beat the butter, arrange it in squares, and put it in the icebox or refrigerator (if we had one). The milk was sold by the owner. We could keep some of the milk for ourselves. Sometimes we would just drink the clabber milk.

Other functions that our family performed as sharecroppers were killing and processing hogs. In the fall, hogs were killed, cleaned, cut up, and put in a smokehouse and sold. Cows were sometimes killed, processed, and sold. The fall was hog-killing time. We would kill the hogs, cut them up, cure (salt) the legs, and hang them in the smokehouse for winter. We would clean the hog intestines, which we called "chittlings."[20] We processed the heads into hog's head cheese. The feet were cleaned and boiled—sometimes pickled—to eat.

We also canned a great deal of vegetables, beans, black-eyed peas, jellies, corn, peanut butter, sauerkraut, and greens of all types—collards, mustard, cabbage, and turnip.[21] My mother rarely worked in the fields, but she would can [make preserves of] the fruit and vegetables. I recall that we almost always had plenty of food to eat except when we were in the Schmeling house. In most situations, we had adequate food from sharecropping and our own gardens. We ate well when we were share-croppers for the Whites. We were fortunate to have plenty food because we grew it. We had a large garden. Some of the food was sold and some we ate. We grew watermelon, which was sold, but we ate as much as we liked.

A typical meal for breakfast would be eggs from chickens we raised, bacon from hogs we raised, grits we made from corn, biscuits we made, gravy, cereal, milk we got from cows, butter from churning, and hoe cakes (meal on a pan put on coals). Lunch was leftovers. For dinner it would be chicken, chittlings, corn-bread, potatoes, greens, milk, pig's feet, pig ears, pig tails, crackling bread, clabber milk, poke salad, berries, butter, black-eyed peas, beans, potatoes, rice, cornbread, green beans, squash, and whatever was available. Sometimes my mom brought back cooked food from families she worked for. We used food stores to buy certain items that were rationed and got some things from the federal government pro-gram during the Great Depression.

Health and Medicine

Healthcare was difficult in segregated Texas. Families had to cope as best as they could and often relied on folk remedies. Mildred, Mozelle, and Bernice all remember a serious health scare involving their sister, Era. Mozelle begins[22]:

One day we were raiding the garden, something that Papa also did. I was eating green beans, my favorite. Era got sick from eating the hot cucumbers. It was fortunate that Papa was home on this day, for he realized that Era was very ill and flagged down a car headed for town on the highway. Soon an ambulance came and took Era to the doctor. Era had her appendix taken out in the doctor's office. Era described the procedure used as being given chloroform and the doctor performing the operation. I do not know if Era decided to become a nurse because of this experience, but she did decide she wanted to be a nurse and became one later in her life.

Bernice also remembers[23]:

It was a hot summer day in Texas and Papa was home. Era kept regurgitating. We had been eating tomatoes and other food from the garden. Era got sick and an ambulance came. Era begged Irmagene to go with her, but there was no space. The ambulance couldn't take Era to a hospital. Hospitals were only for White folk. They took her to a house and they operated on her on the dining room table. Era told me. She was gone for about a month. In those days, you could stick out your thumb and get a ride, so Papa got a ride to Longview to be with Era.

Mildred also remembers this incident[24]:

We also had access to several of President Roosevelt's "alphabet programs,"[25] which provided some food and clothing, as well as free medical care. If any of us became ill, there was a clinic a few miles from us. We would walk there and sometimes hitchhike a ride, which was safe in those days. During our stay in this house, several of us became ill. I had several spells. My sister Era always seemed to have been ill with some ailment. We resented the fact that the illness kept her from working in the fields most of the time. Some of the siblings thought she did this deliberately to avoid working. As I became more mature, I realized that she really was ill. I recalled that while we lived in this area, my sister Era, then a teenager, became seriously ill and required a doctor. We learned that her appendix had burst and she almost died. After that incident, my mother became very partial to her. Era was mean and was always fighting us, but mother always took her side.

These are some of the medicinal and health care practices used when I grew up in Texas[26]:

- Putting Epsom salts in hot water to soak tired or swollen feet.
- Placing salt pork on a boil to draw the pus from the boil.
- Mixing lye soap, salt, and sugar and placing it on a boil to bring it to a head.
- Mixing kerosene, sugar, and turpentine and drinking it to cure colds.
- Boiling hog jaws in water to a grease and mixing it with turpentine to rub on the body for fever.
- Boiling cow chips (manure) in water as a tea and straining it through a rag, then mixing it with sugar as a drink for pneumonia.
- Eating garlic for high blood pressure.
- Mixing castor oil and lemon juice, then drinking it for sore throat.
- Rubbing turpentine on stomach for a stomachache.
- Binding jimson weed to the legs with a cloth to relieve swollen legs.
- Boiling sassafras in water as a tea to drink as a spring tonic for measles and whooping cough.
- Using old rags for menstrual protections.
- Applying fat back (pig's fat) for scars or swelling.

- Using castor oil, Vicks salve, heated sugar, and whisky for colds.
- Drinking Epsom salts and black draught for a stomachache.
- Using quinine snuff for injuries.
- Drinking wine for swelling and boils and using potatoes to take out pus.
- Using Vaseline for beauty aids.
- Using baking soda for brushing teeth.
- Boiling hog hoofs in water or slightly baking hog toenails and making a tea from them to drink or rub on the body to treat colds.[27] The hog hoofs could also be used for whooping cough.
- Making small balls of asphidity, using a needle and thread to string them as beads, and placing them around a child's neck to treat worms and nosebleeds. It protects the child from influenza and relieves teething and fever. For medicine, Mom would not permit us to wear these stinky, horrible affinity beads as other children wore them—they stank![28]

Black Housing

Mildred describes her last housing experience in Texas[29]:

The last place that we lived before I left for college and our family's departure for the North was very adequate. It was not a sharecropper situation. The house was about three miles from the White's house. It was much smaller than the White's house, but it was quite adequate for us. Mom's friend, Mrs. Denson, allowed us to live there rent free. The Densons were Black people who owned oil fields and were doing fairly well. They liked my mother and helped us.

We had many friends in this small, rural community where there were a couple of White-owned general stores. The Baptist church and elementary school were within walking distance. The high school was some distance away, and we had to take the bus to get there. The majority of Blacks owned their homes. Some had oil on their property and lived quite well. My mother, my two older sisters, and I all worked as maids. My mother was employed by two White families nearby.

The house where I lived before I left for Kansas City, Missouri, was a six-room, unpainted wooden house. It had no wallpaper, so we put newspaper on the walls. There was a large yard with trees, a garden plot, and an area for laundering, with a black pot iron for boiling the white clothes, a clothesline, a wooden table, and a scrub board. There was also a wood pile for the cooking stove, heater, and wash pot.

An outdoor toilet about a half block away was only used by my family. We used Sears and Roebuck catalog paper for toilet tissue. There was a bedroom for the four older girls, a bedroom for the two boys, a living room (or parlor) only used on Sundays, a dining room, a kitchen, and a room for my parents. Only two of the six rooms were heated: the kitchen and Mom and Pop's room. During winter, we spent most of the time in our parent's room. I recall that we ate well and hauled water in buckets from our neighbor's spring about half a mile away. When my brothers left for World War II, their room became the bathroom, which consisted of a metal washtub for bathing and a wash stand.

With respect to life in general, it consisted of school, church on Sundays, courtship for my older brothers and sisters, and entertaining evenings at Mrs. Denson's family home. At the Denson's place we spent countless hours—snacking and listening to her ghost stories that scared us so much that we were afraid to walk across the street home! Mrs. Denson's teenage grandsons walked us home.

Mozelle remembers this time with the Densons[30]:

This house we moved to was across the road from a sweet old lady named Mariah Denson. Clyde and Lowell shared a room—the room opposite the kitchen. Mama and Papa had the middle room, but Papa was away so often that Ruby slept with Mama. Opposite Mama's room was the dining room. Then beside Mama's room was the girls' room, where we shared a bed. Opposite the bedroom next to the girls' room was the living room.

Mariah Denson lived with her two daughters, a daughter's husband, and the daughter's children. The daughters were Cora and Rosie [Jackson]. Mrs. Rosie's husband was Mr. Nug. The children were J.C., Myrtle, Benny, and Bruster. We called him "Bru." The other children were Delois and Phyllis. We called Delois "Dee." The older children were schoolmates of my older sisters. Dee went to school with me. Phyllis was too young to go to school, as was my sister Ruby. Dee, Phyllis, Ruby, and I had fun playing all sorts of games: hopscotch, hide-and-seek, and sock ball. All of us got whooping cough one summer, and it was hilarious to hear us all whooping and coughing at the same time.

Dee and Phyllis called their grandmother "Mama Denson." Mama Denson was a character. She loved to scare the daylights out of us kids by telling scary stories. In fact, she seemed to wait and tell her stories on the darkest of nights when there was no moon. One of her favorite stories was about the "Tennis Shoe Man" who would come and yell, "Booooo!" at people through their windows, sneaking up on them in his tennis shoes. In those days, we thought tennis shoes were funny because they only came in a high-topped style, and anyone who wore them got themselves laughed at. But after Mama Denson's stories, going back home across the tar road on a pitch-black night and expecting the Tennis Shoe Man catch us at any time was not funny at all. Despite being frightening, we continued to listen to Mama Denson's stories. Mama Denson could cook beans and cornbread with brown and crisp edges. I liked her beans better than Mama's. Mrs. Denson would sit us kids down on the floor on newspapers with our tin plates, and we would put away [eat] beans and cornbread. They were best on cold winter days.

This is the longest period I remember Papa staying at home. Irmagene was fond of a boy who was a nephew of the Densons. She was in her teens and was a majorette at school. She had just acquired a pair of white-tassled majorette boots. Irmagene was entertaining her beau in the living room one day. The door to the living room was open, for it was not allowed to be closed while entertaining one's beau. I also recall Papa prompting the girls' boyfriends that it was time for them to go home by clearing his throat loudly. "Harrumph!" he'd say, and the boys would go home.[31] This was a nice boy, but Mama did not like him. The boy went into the Army and before he returned, Irmagene had gotten married.

Before getting married, Irmagene worked in Dallas while attending Beauty Culture School. On some weekends she came home and would take me to the nearby town of Longview to shop and have her hair fixed. I really enjoyed these trips. We'd go to the 5- and 10-cent store, and she would buy me paper dolls. I recall we had to buy our glasses in order to get water from the store's only water fountain. This was one of my first experiences with Jim Crow.[32] Irmagene also took me to the movies, where we saw Roy Rogers and his horse. This was the most thrilling experience for me; there were tears in my eyes, I was so happy. Then, we'd go to the White's house, the people who owned the house where we had once lived. There, Irmagene would get her hair fixed while I played with my paper dolls.

Papa and his cronies liked to argue politics. They also sang and Papa would set the tone by singing, "Do, Do, Re, Me, Fa, Fa, So." Papa also brought the newspaper home on weekends. I got the newspaper when he finished with it and read the funny paper and did the crossword puzzle for children. I read everything I could find. When I ran out of reading material, I would make up word games for myself. I learned to spell "Mississippi" backward. I also learned to count backward but was never good at arithmetic.

Bernice and I were assigned the duty of getting water and were the ones who fetched the water. We got water from Mrs. Denson's spring and Mrs. Edna's well. Sometimes we would go to the little brook back in the woods behind Mrs. Denson's house. When going through the woods, we would often run into a snake, usually a cottonmouth. We'd run back and tell Mama, who would get a rake or hoe and go and kill it.

These were beautiful woods full of pine trees, blooming dogwoods, and crystal clear water. Our house once had a well, but for some unknown reason had been filled in. We also got water from the neighbor's well. Mrs. Edna lived up the road past a large magnolia tree. Bernice and I would stop in the shade of this tree. Bernice had learned that by swinging her water bucket over her head very rapidly, there would be no water spilled. She taught this trick to me. We would stand in the shade of this big old magnolia tree, swinging our buckets. Down the hill from the road lived Mrs. Ada, who would see us and call out, "If you young'uns don't quit that and get home, I'm going to tell your mama!"

Sometimes I would go fishing with Mama and her friend Mrs. Ada. I was not fond of fishing and did not like being the only kid there.[33] There was nothing to do but listen to Mama and Mrs. Ada talk, but I liked when they caught a fish because I really enjoyed eating them. Mama made us believe that fish bones were poisonous and was careful to not let us swallow a bone. She would chew the little kids' fish first before handing it to us to eat. I liked fish so much that I did not care. Mama also made croquettes from canned salmon which was really great with biscuits and syrup.

In Texas there were many different kinds of plants. In times of hunger, we kids sometimes ate these plants or the fruits that they produced. In summers we ate lots of plums and during the fall we ate lots of persimmons. I remember staring at a blooming plum tree in the spring and wondering how those blooms could be so beautiful and offer no immediate food. But fruit soon came, and we ate of it abundantly. In the fall the persimmon trees began to bear fruit, and we ate voraciously. Sometimes we got fruit that was not completely ripe. This puckered our mouths, and we'd laugh at each other. We would open the persimmon seeds and observe objects shaped like knives and forks and spoons. There were many wonders in the country, and I loved to see the sun come up and shine on the dewy grass. It looked like jewels and diamonds.

I can recall berry picking in the summertime with Bernice. Somehow we never seemed to gather many berries; either out of fear of snakes or because of the ones we collected. Bernice would play some trick on me and end up eating them all. I never learned. There were stray cats around the neighborhood, and many stayed around our house because I fed them. I liked the cats, and they soon began to follow me everywhere. I was happy with their company because I was often alone. One day I got the notion that I would introduce the cats to Mama and led them into the kitchen, hoping she would offer them a bowl of milk. Without as much as a "How do you do?," Mama pitched me and the cats outdoors. The cats ran up a tree and I was unable to follow them. I later developed what Mama called ringworm on my face. She said that it came from playing with the cats. Mrs. Denson put me on her formula for cure after Mama's failed. Between our house and Mrs. Denson's was a tree stump filled with rainwater. Mrs. Denson told me to rinse my face in this water each morning. I did, and soon the white, patchy lesions disappeared.

Unlike me, Bernice did not like animals. Bernice liked chasing banty roosters and tormenting cats and many other critters. Everyone recalls the time when Bernice murdered a cat and brought it home on a forked stick—as if it were a trophy. Once she got into a fight with a banty rooster; banty roosters are fighting roosters. I think Bernice felt she was that rooster's equal.[34]

Key Lessons

The 1997 Simon and Sirls Family Reunion book summarizes the sharecropping lifestyle of the 1930s and 1940s and the values and culture of African-Americans that were instrumental in their survival.[35]

What we want future generations to remember about Henderson, Texas:

- Our families loved each other.
- Our homes were happy because all worked to keep it that way.
- The Bible in the house was to be read and lived, not under lock and key because of questionable content.
- We practiced hospitality and everyone loved to visit us.
- Saturday was a day to go trade. Today, this is known as shopping.
- Sunday was the happiest day of the week—one of which we all looked forward to because it was the day when we went to church together.
- Water was carried in buckets from the well for washing clothes. The clothes were washed on what was known as a "scrub-board" or "rub-board" two or three times and rinsed with what was known as "blueing," which brightened the clothes.
- THROWING AWAY FOOD WAS A SIN! Nothing was wasted…or thrown away.
- When you passed a house, you could tell what was cooking.
- On New Year's Eve, we went to the watch meeting to watch and pray the old year out and the new year in.
- Old people would go out and muddy up the road so that the fish would float up.
- A delicacy was a home-cooked meal of cooked and baked sweet potatoes.

Remember when:

- People wore little bags of asafetida [asphidity] around their necks when there were any contagious diseases in the vicinity.
- A weekly Saturday chore was to sweep the entire yard and under the house as far back as was visible, with a brush broom made from the dogwood tree.

- A sprig of grass that dared peep up in the year was attacked as though it was a rattlesnake!
- At hog- or cow-killing time, everyone would get a mess of meat.
- A cow tongue would stop a child from stuttering (talking bad) if slapped in the mouth.
- A weekly order of groceries always included a big bottle of Garrett's Snuff, Day Work and Prince Albert tobacco, and Kol-Oil (kerosene), peanuts, and rat cheese.
- "Sleeping at the Foot of the Bed" wasn't just a hillbilly song; it was a common practice in large families.
- The young man who didn't formally ask the parent for his daughter's hand in marriage was considered a no-good reprobate!
- It was the height of disrespect to call anyone, even someone just a few years old, by his or her given name without a "handle of some kind."[36]
- A loud throat clearing in the other end of the house was the signal for a beau to get going.
- Christmas for the kids meant big red apples, oranges, pecans, nigger-toes, ribbon candy, a few firecrackers, roman candles, sparklers (if any), hoghead cheese and plenty of other food, and, above all, thanking God for giving us our health, happiness, and a mind to continue to serve Him.
- Children really believed in Santa Claus.
- [A common phrase was] "Go out on the garret[37] and commence to eating."
- It was a token of love when someone visited another family, and when it was time to leave, a small token (food, flowers, clothing, etc.) was given.
- It was a custom that, when visiting a home, you were asked if you wanted to eat. If not, it would hurt the feelings of the lady of the house. [Her] reply: "I didn't ask if you were hungry; I asked if you wanted to eat!"
- Floured water would stop diarrhea.
- Sunday was a day of worship for everyone. Parents didn't ask kids if they were going to Sunday school or church…they knew to go!

Things remembered:

- When a cake was made, children fussed over who would get the spoon or the bowl. A sample of cake was made, and a piece was given to all.
- Nothing was done on Sunday other than washing dishes and taking a wash-off [a quick bath].
- Sunday morning was prayer time in the household at the breakfast table.

- Bottle dolls were pine straw with a stick in the top of the bottle to hold it in place.
- In those days, we had "Nigga in the Blanket Pie" made with fruit. Today it is known as fried pies.
- When teacakes were made, they were placed in a flour sack and hung on the wall until Sunday (for dessert).
- Quilts were made by hand from all kinds of fabrics.
- At wintertime when there was snow, it was mixed with butter, sugar, and flavor to make ice cream.
- Sulfur-8 hair grease was known as "dog mane" hair grease.
- Kool-Aid was referred to as "polly-pop" and "Sweet Lucy."
- Clothes were passed down from one child to another.
- A hole was put in a penny and tied around a baby's neck when he or she was teething.
- The milk from figs was rubbed on a dime and placed on ringworm.
- Sweet potatoes were roasted by packing them in ashes and coal.
- Lye soap was made from "hog lard" and "red devil lye."[38]
- Lunches were carried to school or work in syrup or lard buckets, with holes punched in the lid to keep the lunch from going bad.

As the next chapter illustrates, Mildred's experiences in Longview, Texas, were very challenging during her middle and high school years. Her fortitude, determination, pride, and personal self-worth would be tested as she encountered significant challenges.

Notes

1. (M. Pratt, personal communication, n.d.).
2. See also, Valk and Brown (2010, p. 47), for a similar strategy for dealing with hunger.
3. Bernice remembers: "I kicked them and started them to fighting. Mama would then call me to come to her. I did it on purpose" (B. Miller, personal communication, August 23, 2013).
4. For another reference to Sears Roebuck, see Taulbert (1989, p. 4).
5. "Gregg County, Texas." For more about Gregg County Training School, see "Ned E. Williams School": "On this site (off [highway] 349 on [country road] 2953) in 1883, an all-colored school named Greenville was established in the Elderville Community School District by Ned E. Williams. This school was built to accommodate the children of the newly organized District No. 5 of Gregg County, which included Pleasant Green, Elderville, Greenville, Post Oak, and Easton. In 1918, the school's name was changed to Gregg County Training School. Mr. Williams became the first principal and upon his death in 1945 was honored by having the school named for him and his 57 years [dedicated] to the education of children."

6. For more about President Roosevelt's Alphabet Soup programs, see "FDR's Alphabet Soup."

7. Bernice remembers that Mildred had to repeat a grade: "I think it was 6th grade. I remember Mama was so mad, but there was nothing she could do. That was so unfair to Mildred" (B. Miller, personal communication, August 22, 2013).

8. For other references to honky-tonks, see Andrews (1990, p. 155); Taulbert (1989, p. 44); and Valk and Brown (2010, p. 76).

9. (M. Perry, personal communication, n.d.).

10. Bernice remembers: "Once when Mozelle and I were playing, my father said, 'Bernice, get some water.' I thought, *Why did he ask me and not Mozelle?* So I pushed Mozelle down the stairs and Papa beat me" (B. Miller, personal communication, June 13, 2013).

11. For more about truckin, see "Truckin."

12. Bernice remembers: "The man's name where we lived was Bob White. The Boarders called each other 'Nigger,' and they owned a juke joint. Mildred told Mama they liked Nat King Cole, and Mama said, 'Shut your mouth, youngun!' Mama said dancing was devilish and that the devil made you do it" (B. Miller, personal communication, June 13, 2013).

13. For a similar description of fireplaces, see Andrews (1990, p. 85); and Chafe, Gavins, and Korstad (2001, pp. 44–45).

14. Mildred remembers her mother using snuff: "I don't know where the practice began, but my mother and most of the other female adult women that I knew used snuff. It came in a small tin can, and the ladies would put it in their bottom lips. They would not chew it because it was a soft, brown flour-like substance. They would have to spit frequently. The spit was a nasty brown color. My mother dipped snuff all of her life. The men would sit around and chew tobacco. A few women would also chew tobacco. It was called chewing tobacco. There were some old ladies who ate clay. They could be seen on the roadside digging for eatable red clay" (M. Pratt, personal communication, n.d.). See also "American Snuff Company" and Taulbert (1992, p. 89).

15. For information about Camp Switch, Texas, see Long (n.d.) and Long and Allgood (n.d.).

16. Bernice also remembers the *Prose and Poetry* book: "When Lowell left his *Prose and Poetry* at home, Mama would read it to us. I remember one poem she would read to us all the time. It was called *House by the Side of the Road* (B. Miller, personal communication, July 13, 2013). See Foss, *House by the Side of the Road.* Apparently, this was a common poem taught to African-Americans in school.

17. For more about the history of *Love Story Magazine,* see "Newsstand 1925: Love Story Magazine."

18. (M. Pratt, personal communication, May 11, 2012; n.d.).

19. For other examples of cotton-picking, see Taulbert (1989, pp. 119–130); and Valk and Brown (2010, p. 29).

20. Mozelle remembers: "Papa slaughtered hogs in the fall and used the old iron pot in his preparation of the hog. I think only he and Mama liked the chitterlings. I know I did not. I would run away from the house when I smelled the chitterlings cooking. But I liked the fresh pork chops and sausage" (M. Pratt, personal communication, n.d.). See also Taulbert (1989, pp. 47–48), Valk and Brown (2010, p. 36), and Andrews (1990, p. 80), for a discussion of hog-killing time.

21. Gardening and canning were important survival skills during Jim Crow. See Chafe et al. (2001, p. 209), Valk and Brown (2010, pp. 20, 29), and Andrews (1990, p. 80).
22. (M. Perry, personal communication, n.d.).
23. (B. Miller, personal communication, November 26, 2013).
24. (M. Pratt, personal communication, n.d.).
25. For more about President Roosevelt's Alphabet Soup programs, see "FDR's Alphabet Soup."
26. See Pratt (1993), "Please Momma, Don't Give Me No More Cowchip Tea." For more medicinal practices, see Valk and Brown (2010, pp. 34, 37) and Chafe et al. (2001, p. 222).
27. Mozelle remembers the home remedies: "In the spring, Mama fixed teas for us. One tea was called hog's hoof tea. To me this was tasty. Anything with sugar in it was tasty to me. She also fixed some concoction with coal oil in it. She believed in the profits of castor oil. She'd mix the castor oil with orange juice and sugar, but I still hated it" (M. Pratt, personal communication, n.d.).
28. For more about asphidity bags, see Woods (n.d.).
29. (M. Pratt, personal communication, n.d.).
30. (M. Perry, personal communication, n.d.).
31. See Andrews (1990, pp. 208–209), for the use of throat-clearing to monitor courting.
32. For an extensive discussion of Jim Crow, see Robinson (2012).
33. Fishing was a common activity in the South for men and women. See Taulbert (1989, pp. 40–45).
34. Bernice remembers the cat: "Sometimes the cat would come and look. I did not like cats so I would say, 'Scat, scat.' It stepped across my playhouse, and the sticks went every way and tore my playhouse apart. I poked this cat and killed it, then took it into the house hanging on the stick. Mama screamed, 'Get that thing out of here!' My sister Era had to take the cat out and bury it" (B. Miller, personal communication, n.d.).
35. (M. Pratt, personal communication, n.d.).
36. A handle refers to Mr., Mrs., or Ms.
37. "Garret" was another word for porch. See Taulbert (1992, p. 130).
38. See Chafe et al. (2001, p. 65), for another reference to "red devil lye."

References

"American Snuff Company." *Wikipedia, the Free Encyclopedia.* Retrieved June 26, 2013 from http://en.wikipedia.org/w/index.php?title=American_Snuff_Company&oldid=544847876

Andrews, R. (1990). *The last radio baby: A memoir.* Atlanta, GA: Peachtree Publishers.

Chafe, W. H., Gavins, R., & Korstad, R. (Eds.). (2001). *Remembering Jim Crow: African Americans tell about life in the segregated South.* New York, NY: The New Press.

"FDR's Alphabet Soup." *U.S. History.* Retrieved September 1, 2013 from http://www.ushistory.org/us/49e.asp

Foss, S.W. "House by the Side of the Road." *iPoet.* Retrieved September 1, 2013 from http://www.ipoet.com/archive/original/Foss/House.html

"Gregg County, Texas: Public School Districts." *Online Directory of Texas*. Retrieved September 1, 2013 from http://www.greggcountytexas.us/PublicSchools/PublicSchoolsDistricts.htm

Long, C. (n.d.). "Camp Switch, TX." *Handbook of Texas Online*, June 12, 2010. Retrieved September 1, 2013 from http://www.tshaonline.org/handbook/online/articles/hrc18

Long, C., & Allgood, C. (n.d.). "Shiloh, TX (Gregg County)." *Handbook of Texas Online*. Retrieved June 15, 2013 from http://www.tshaonline.org/handbook/online/articles/hrsjg

"Ned E. Williams School." *The USGenWeb Project*. Retrieved September 1, 2013 from http://www.rootsweb.ancestry.com/~txgregg/School/WilliamsSchool.html

"Newsstand 1925: Love Story Magazine." *University of West Florida*. Retrieved September 1, 2013 from http://uwf.edu/dearle/enewsstand/enewsstand_files/Page3128.htm

Pratt, M. (1993, March 17). *"Please Mama don't give me no more cowchip tea": African-American folk remedies and their implications for medical care personnel*. Presented at Black Family Summit, College of Social Work, Columbia, SC.

Robinson, A. (2012, April 30). A museum teaches tolerance through Jim Crow. *WCMU Public Radio*. Retrieved from www.npr.org/2012/04/30/151697195/a-museum-teaches-tolerance-through-jim-crow

Taulbert, C. L. (1989). *Once upon a time when we were colored*. Tulsa, OK: Council Oak Books.

Taulbert, C. L. (1992). *The last train north*. New York, NY: Penguin Books.

"Truckin." *Street Swing Dance History Archives*. Retrieved September 1, 2013 from http://www.streetswing.com/histmain/z3truck.htm

Valk, A., & Brown, L. (2010). *Living with Jim Crow: African American women and memories of the Segregated South*. New York, NY: Palgrave Macmillan.

Woods, G. "Asphidity Bags: A Student's Guide to Ethnocentric Healthcare." *Samuel Merritt University*. Retrieved September 1, 2013 from http://www.samuelmerritt.edu/president/news_room/apr_2012/asphidity-bags-students-guide-ethnocentric-healthcare

CHAPTER SIX

Black Girlhood

Mildred would experience some significant family challenges as she moved into her teenage years. They included the betrayal by a brother, the death of a sister, and extreme poverty. Mildred also had to navigate the complex issue of skin color and beauty as a dark-skinned girl. While Mildred's high school years were challenging, she was able to persevere and overcome significant obstacles, graduating as class valedictorian, even though the senior class teacher chose to award the associated and related designation of class president to a boy. Mildred's experiences deepened her commitment and belief that education and academic achievement would help her make a way out of no way. The Sirls family would also begin their migration out of Texas, with the brothers going to war, the father going to California, and the sisters and mother going to Kansas City.

The Secret

Both Bernice and Mildred remember a particularly painful experience involving their brother Clyde. Mildred shares[1]:

I'm going to tell you [Menah] about this since my brothers are dead. But this should be told. My brother Clyde took me out into a field adjacent to our house and he raped me. I knew he was doing something that wasn't a game. I knew it was something wrong. I don't know if I told my mother because he told me not to tell.

He said we were going to play horse. I think I was between 11 and 12 years old. He told me to pull my panties down, and I knew that wasn't right. He was around 16 or 17 years old. If I told my mother, what would she say?

Bernice told me later when we were adults that she knew and that he had promised her money to keep her quiet. It made me feel just plain mad, and I did everything I could to avoid him. At that time, my mother spent many hours away from home working and cleaning houses. It never happened again. I don't know if it ever happened to Era.

Bernice also remembers this incident[2]:

It happened at Greenville when we were [living] in one of Bob White's houses. Papa was in jail and Clyde molested Mildred. I saw him "do" Mildred. Back in those days, the government would come out to the farm and tell you to let a part of your farm land "rest." They would build a high mound over it. One day Clyde told me to go home and not Mildred. I didn't understand why he wanted me to go home, and I wanted to know why she had to stay "put" and I had to leave. I pretended to leave but I didn't. I saw him take Mildred under the mound, beat her, and make her submit to him. I bent down and peeked and saw him rape Mildred. Clyde didn't like Mildred.

Mildred and I were talking one day when you, Menah [Mildred's daughter], were at college. Mildred said that Clyde had a child who was bright but lost his mind. I told Mildred I knew why the boy lost his mind. I told her that his sister told me that her father was "doing" her brother. Mildred wasn't believing me. She didn't think I knew stuff. So I told Mildred that I knew that Clyde was "that way" before we left Texas and that I knew what he did to her. She almost fainted. Mildred asked me if he had done it to me. I told her I didn't know. I do remember he took a hot poker and burnt my face with it and told me not to tell. To this day, I don't remember what I wasn't supposed to tell. He burnt it out of my brain. I didn't tell Mama because I didn't have the words for it. I would have told about the rape if I had words. I didn't. I left it alone. Mildred was the first person I ever told.

Clyde married his wife, Betty, when she was 15. Over the years Clyde [repeatedly] raped his son, Clyde Jr., from before he could crawl until he was grown. Clyde threatened to kill his son's mother if he ever told. He believed that his father would do harm. After Clyde and Betty divorced, Clyde Jr. told his mother. His mother, Betty, got a gun and went to ask Clyde who admitted his behavior. Yet later, the son began to hate his mother for telling his daddy since Clyde Jr. had made her vow not to tell. His sister knew but couldn't tell her mama. Who would have believed her?

I think Papa might have caused Clyde to become a sexual predator because he would take Clyde with him into town when he went on his jaunts looking for women. Another family member later told me that Clyde had been arrested more than once for "doing" [molesting] children. He said that my brother George knew because he was always getting Clyde out of jail for messing with children. Those kind of people have a way with people. They can act so loving. He had a personality that would charm a snake.

I had trouble liking Clyde. He could do mean things. I remember he would grab my chicken leg and tell me that I couldn't eat it because it had a bone in it, and then he would eat my chicken leg. I also remember once when I was in Los Angeles with my two children, he took me to see a movie. It was a dirty movie. It was a terrible thing for him to do. I just tried not to look.

A Sister's Death

All three sisters remember the tragic early death of their sister Ruby in 1944. Mildred shares[3]:

My mother had a child whom she named Ruby. I recall my mother being excited about this child, who became seriously ill and died within a few days after her sixth birthday. We never learned what caused her death. I do know that her death caused my mother great pain and extreme sadness. She expressed her agony by going out in the garden or the cotton field, sitting on the ground, and crying for hours, for several months—even in the cold—and we had no idea how to console her.

It was not until I had my own children that I really understood her pain. She doubtless felt tremendous pressure and very alone in her efforts to take care of her family. I do not know how we would have managed without the support of Mrs. Denson and her extended family. We had no relatives nearby, and they were in fact our furtive kin.

Mozelle remembers Ruby's death[4]:

At this time Ruby died from an illness we both had consisting of upset stomachs. We would vomit up everything we ate. We had high fevers. The doctor did not know what the sickness was, so he could not treat us. He suggested giving us tomato juice. I disliked tomato juice for a long time. I did gradually get better, but Ruby continued to be sick. I was in the room with Ruby, sitting in a chair by her bed, while Mama was in the kitchen cooking when she died. I saw the change in her little face and ran to call Mama.

Mama had a hard time accepting Ruby's death. She began to have screaming spells. Mama dipped snuff and money was scarce. Bernice and I would search the house for enough coins to buy Mama her snuff, for this was the only thing that soothed her. We went hungry for a while, and Mama sometimes kept us home from school because we had no lunch to take. Mrs. Denson and her family helped us out when things got too bad.

Bernice also remembers Ruby's death[5]:

Ruby was pretty like a little doll. We loved to play with her. Both Ruby and Mozelle had fevers in bed. Mozelle got well, but Ruby stayed sick. Mozelle was looking at her when she stopped breathing. By the time I entered into the room, the clock had stopped. (That is what happened when people died). Mama had ran across the road to Ms. Denson and left Mozelle alone with Ruby. Mozelle told me she was so scared to be alone with Ruby. Mama shouldn't have done that.

I remember when the man [undertaker] came to get Ruby's body. He was laughing and joking. I thought it was so ugly for him to be laughing while I was so sad. We belonged to the Sabine Valley Baptist Church, but Ruby was buried at the Center Graveyard near the Methodist church. Mama marked her grave with a platter that had belonged to her parents.

After Ruby's death, Mama realized that the only picture she had of Ruby was taken in the casket (see Figure 6.1: Photograph of Ruby Sirls in casket, age 6, 1944). Mama vowed that Ruby would be the last child whose only picture was taken that way. So, she said that everyone was going to go get our pictures taken. Mildred practiced her smile for days, only to decide the day of the event that she was not going. Mildred was very stubborn. She was so stubborn sometimes that she could override Mama.

Mozelle shares her recollections of the family photo[6]:

One day after Ruby died, without having a picture of her made and the only photograph of her taken in her casket Mama decided to get us together and go to Longview and have our picture made. We got together—Mama, Papa, Era, Bernice, and me. The others were away from home. Mildred was there, but she refused to go. In the picture Mama sits by Papa, with me on Mama's side and Bernice on Papa's side. Bernice and I look so skinny. No one smiled except Papa and Era, who seem to wear slight closed-mouth smiles (see Figure 6.2: Photograph of Mozelle, Eula, Era, RP, and Bernice Sirls, 1944).

Clyde and Lowell sent us pictures of themselves in uniform. Clyde was good-looking and Lowell was tall and handsome. Lowell looks like my Uncle Booker and Grandpa George (see Figure 6.3: Photograph of George Sirls, age 21, 1943). Clyde favors a second cousin of ours, tending to be overweight. Irmagene was a beauty and had fine features like our parents (see Figure 6.4: Photograph of Irmagene Sirls, circa 1940s). Era looked like Clyde (see Figure 6.5: Photograph of Era Sirls, circa 1940s). Bernice favors both Mama and Papa. I look like both Bernice and Grandma.

I once visited Uncle Griff [RP's brother] with Bernice and Mildred. Uncle Griff was aged and ill, but he arose from his bed to a sitting position, stared at me, and said, "You look just like my mama." Mildred favors Mama in build but looks

like Papa in features (see Figure 6.6: Photograph of Mildred Sirls, age 16, 1944).
I think Ruby would have favored Mama and Irmagene had she grown up. Mama
looked young for a long time. One day when she was sitting at a window in one
of the many houses where we lived, a neighbor passed by and, seeing Mama surrounded by her children, asked her, "Little girl, is your mother home?"

"Mama's Little Black Girl"

*Mildred, like many young Black girls, remembers another painful childhood experience
involving her skin color[7]:*

In the period in which I grew up, skin color was very important in the Black
community.[8] Color as an issue in human relationships in the United States began
with slavery. The slaves who were brought to this country were Black and the slave
owners were White. The slave women not only worked in the fields but also served
in their master's home, performing a variety of functions: cooking, laundering and
ironing clothes, waiting on their mistress's hand and foot, dressing her, preparing
her bath water, cleaning the house, and meeting the master's carnal needs.

Many of the offspring from these liaisons were of course light-skinned. Some
of these mulatto people were treated with deference. Many of them were educated
up north, and some even passed for White; and, thus avoided the horrendous
burden of being enslaved. After slavery, the concept of miscegenation was coined
to account for society's preference for lighter skinned African-Americans. For
decades, even African-American sororities behaved as though "White was right"
and only selected the lighter complexioned Black women for membership.

It was particularly important that girls have a light color. I did not. In those
days, if you were dark-skinned, you were not desired as a woman.[9] And I felt this
within my home. My mother, a light-skinned lady, had long hair and had married
a Black man. My father was typically Black in all his features. I was the darkest of
six girls and felt that my mother saw me as less desirable than her other children.
Both of my brothers were dark-skinned, but only Lowell was as dark as me.

I always felt that I was the lowest on my mother's admiration scale. I always felt
that my mother regarded me as less desirable than her other children. My mother
called me her "little Black girl." I resented it and felt this meant I was ugly, for
somehow I felt that she preferred my other sisters over me. As an adult in my 60s,
I raised the issue with Bernice who said it "was a term of endearment." I retorted
that I never felt that; indeed, I felt that I was the literal "Black sheep" of the family.

My mother's decision to call me her "little Black girl" was not a positive thing
to me. I never felt good about this because Black was not considered beautiful until

the late 1960s in this country. I also knew it wasn't good because of how much better she treated the other girls in the family. In many situations she would assign me to do the most menial tasks. I never liked this but could do nothing about it. I was the only one she called "my little Black girl." The name had meaning because she was less kind to me. I was very studious and had no boyfriends. Mom did not want me to go to my prom. I don't know why.

Bernice remembers her mother calling Mildred her "little Black girl"[10]:

Mama did call Mildred her "little Black girl." I also remember her saying, "my pretty little Black girl." I didn't know Black wasn't beautiful. When we were adults, Mildred told me what Mama called her upset her. I couldn't dig Mama out of the grave to get her to explain that she loved us all. But I knew Mildred was pretty. I also had a very pretty older sister, Irmagene. Irmagene was gorgeous, but she didn't know it. I also knew that I was ugly. I was skinny with red hair and freckles. When I grew up, I dyed my hair black and hid my freckles with makeup. This did not make me pretty, but I thought it did. We were all the colors of the rainbow and Mama loved us all, but I was always vying for attention to be number one. I was the type of child who had that personality that said, "Whether you like it or not, you gonna love me!" I wasn't right, but that's how I was then, and I got Mama to give me the attention I wanted.

Mildred shares a decision that she made as a result of her family situation[11]:

Because I was acutely aware that my dark skin was unpopular, I decided that I would do whatever was legally necessary to get as much education as possible.[12] I was determined to get out of that situation as quickly as I could. I believe this accounts for my unusual desire to achieve, even though my mother at no point ever encouraged me. Is this a condemnation of my mother or lighter-skinned siblings? No, for my understanding of the slave era tells me that such attitudes were remnants of the slave culture. Intellectually, I now understand, but emotionally, forgetting is still difficult.

Fortunately, I was strong enough to respond in a way that was not injurious to me. The rejection became the factor motivating me to achieve because I reflected a great deal as to what I wanted for my life. My mother never knew the extent to which her actions spurred my decision to prove to all of them that I would make Black beautiful by educating myself.

Education, then, would be the way to go and I increasingly felt the need to prepare for my future. I always liked to read. I had a love of learning, a healthy curiosity, and I was rather bright. Since my skin color would not open a door for me, I convinced myself that my brain and determination would. I further convinced myself that if one door closed in my face, I would keep knocking until one opened wide enough so that I could squeeze through. Having no other sources for funds except through my own efforts, I increasingly felt the need to prepare myself. I did this at a time in our country when legal segregation and discrimination were commonplace. Regardless of whatever obstacles racism might present, I realized early on that my color would get me nowhere in my family or anywhere else, so I learned to use my brain. No one could see that color!

So, I decided to go it alone. I think my birth position within the family gave me a proclivity for spending time alone. I do believe this position was functional for my development. I was the middle child in the family with four siblings older than me and three sisters younger than me. My mother, who was an only child, pushed the idea that we should have a buddy system or a partner-sibling: Irmagene and Era a pair, Bernice and me a pair, Mozelle and Ruby a pair, and my two brothers a pair.[13]

In the first place, I did not like the idea. I consulted with my ego and decided this would not work. I had a predilection to be a loner, and if I did have a buddy in the system, it definitely was not Bernice. Bernice, light-skinned, was my mother's favorite, and her pet. In fact, the only buddy system that did not work was Bernice's and mine. Although Bernice was smart, she was rather silly. She was not as studious as I was. I worked hard. I was always a studious person, and my siblings tell me that I spent most of my free time at home reading. She laughs now when I tell her this, but Bernice would always yell anytime she thought it would cause my mother to excuse her from doing chores. She also chronically wet the bed and kicked while she slept, and so much so that I chose to sleep on the floor rather than sleep with Bernice. I decided, "I don't care what these people do. I'm getting out of here."

High School

Mildred shares some challenges she experienced at Shiloh High School[14] as a Black girl in the 1940s[15]:

School for me had its problems. I recall my senior year at Shiloh High School for reasons other than graduating with my diploma. During this particular period, we experienced severe economic problems and found that we had to "make do" rather frequently. I didn't have many clothes, but the ones I had were clean clothes with patches. My mom insisted that we "make do" and never permitted us to leave home in dirty clothes. My mother always insisted that we bathe ourselves and she combed and braided our hair every day. She always said, "Cleanliness is next to godliness."[16] My mother made all of our clothes, making her own patterns. When we became old enough, she taught us how to sew. We had no sewing machine, so all sewing was done by hand with needle and thread.

Many times the flour and cornmeal sacks were used, as we could not afford to purchase the material.[17] Mom made bras, panties, dresses, and nightclothes. She did a great job. My mom made my bra to flatten the breasts to avoid what she knew happened in slavery between Black women and White men. My mother made all of our clothing except shoes and coats. My shoes had been patched with cardboard. Our coats were hand-me-downs given to my mother by the White family for whom she worked as a maid.[18] I will never forget the day when my history teacher, Mrs. Thompson, who also rode the bus with us, insulted me because of my coat.

In the rural area of East Texas, schools were segregated and Black students had to take a long bus ride to school. The nearby schools were reserved for White students. We always lived in rural areas, and school was generally a long distance away. We had to walk until my junior year of high school when we took a bus. Some faculty members of our school also rode the bus.

One day, I was wearing my only coat—a hand-me-down boy's gray, woolen suit coat. The coat was quite worn with patches on the sleeves and many torn places. My mother could not afford money for a new coat and had patched my coat as much as she could, but it still was not sufficient to cover the many holes in my coat. The teacher, Mrs. Thompson, looked at the coat, made a disparaging remark about it, and laughed, and so did the children on the bus. I kept quiet as I tried to hold back the tears. I bore this humiliation quietly, masking my anger and my tears.

This same teacher, Mrs. Thompson, did something else to me when I was a senior. In addition to being my history teacher, Mrs. Thompson also served as the sponsor of the senior class, and, as sponsor had the very important role of selecting the president of the senior class. The policy stated that the senior with the highest grade point average should be president. The person with the highest grades in my class was me. I was the class valedictorian (see Figure 6.7: Mildred Sirls, Shiloh High School, 1946).[19] But, Mrs. Thompson refused to appoint me to be class president. There was a light-skinned boy who tried to answer all the questions in class, but I had the highest grade point average. The records were there, yet Mrs. Thompson selected this boy to be class president. She just changed the policy—like that.

When I dared to protest by questioning her decision, Mrs. Thompson informed me that *a boy, not a girl,* should be president. I did not protest further. In retrospect, I still get angry at myself for not protesting more. I had learned even at that age to select my battles carefully. This gentleman married my best friend, and my sister informed me that at a school reunion she attended in the 1980s, he told her that he was sorry that he had insisted on being class president. I never attended any reunions.

Another challenge at Shiloh High School was my home economics teacher. She made me take the stitches out of my dress to change it so many times that it became filthy. When she insisted that I take the stitches out a fourth or fifth time, I sassed a teacher for the first time in my life.[20] Recalling that my mother was a great seamstress and made all of my clothes (by hand) and did a great job, I refused to remove the stitches. At my wit's end, I told this teacher that if she wanted the stitches taken out, she should do it herself. I passed the course. My generally mild behavior turned sassy and shocked her.

Mildred shares how college became a reality for her[21]*:*

I never thought about college until my senior year in high school. I did not perceive that attending college was a realistic goal for a child from a sharecropper family. In the 1940s, the perception that I could attend college was unrealistic for me. While my older brothers and sisters had completed high school, only Lowell had attended college. He spent a semester at Prairie View in Texas before being drafted into the army to serve in World War II. To my knowledge, no member of either my mother's or father's immediate family had graduated from college.

Neither of my parents finished high school, but my mother placed a great emphasis on education[22] and learning survival skills. I was fortunate to have a mother who modeled for her children the value of education and how to cope in a separate and unequal social and economic system. For example, while we were surrounded by people in rural Texas who spoke "Black English," Mom discouraged us from doing so. Even my father always tried to speak "proper"—a term used by Blacks during my childhood—though he could not. In attempting to speak "proper," he would say, "Oh yes, I are going to take care of it." My mother insisted that we speak proper English, use proper grammar, and enunciate well. She was a bright lady who read, recited, and enjoyed poetry. She encouraged us to do the same. But while my mother believed in education, her concept of education was limited to grade school and high school, and not to college.

Inasmuch as our education was separate and unequal, many of our Black teachers were relentless in their teaching. I had some great teachers who believed in children learning.[23] I believe that every student needs at least one teacher in their corner. Ms. Ira Henry, who taught literature and French, was my best teacher; she took great interest in me. She encouraged me. She was a brilliant woman who cared deeply about all of the students, but took a particular interest in me and my school-work. Ms. Henry taught at Shiloh High School which was located just outside Longview and Gladewater. She lived in Hawkins, Texas, where her parents were well-to-do mulatto African-Americans. She was a beautiful, tall, heavy mulatto woman who displayed the demeanor of pride and elegance. She had a pleasant smile and she walked with dignity. Her hair fell in ringlets around her shoulders (see Figure 6.8: Photograph of Ms. Ira Henry, Shiloh High School, circa 1940s).

Ms. Henry saw me as a good student and became my guardian angel. She took me under her wings—ragged clothes and all. Ms. Henry taught me to enjoy reciting poetry and gave me some special opportunities to do so at the school. She would give me special assignments where I had to read poetry to the entire class.

Perhaps the most significant impact she had on me was pointing me in the direction of college. She introduced me to the idea that I should and could go to college. And, throughout my senior year she sought me out to ask what I planned to do after graduation, and I recall telling her that I assumed that I would take a job as a maid. I did know, however, that I did not want to spend all of my life hoeing, plowing, picking cotton, carrying water in buckets, bathing in a washtub, and going to the toilet at night in a bucket and during the day in an outhouse. I did not want to chop wood, milk cows, churn milk, and wash clothes outdoors in a big kettle and tub. I also knew that I didn't want to spend my life working for White people as a maid.

Living near Jarvis Christian College and having graduated from the college herself, she talked with me about attending there. Knowing that mine was a poor family, Ms. Henry told me about a special program at Jarvis where students could work one year at the college and attend two years, then work another year and complete the last two years of college.

I was overjoyed having never thought college was possible for me. I was ecstatic, but when I told my mother, she was not so sure. At this point, her emotional and economic condition was so vulnerable that she could only focus on one thing: I should get a job and help the family. By now, there were only four of us in the home (my mother, along with Bernice and Mozelle—both in grade school). Our family structure had changed drastically. The only income and support came from her earnings from working as a maid, help from neighbors, and income I earned working as a maid on Saturdays and weekends.

While I was in high school, I don't know how we learned about these places where White people needed workers. We traveled those narrow streets in the country, and when I look back, I'm surprised that I could walk such great distances. For one nice lady, I cleaned house, washed dishes, and cleaned clothes. For another White lady, I remember doing maid work in a motel. There my job was to clean cabins which was a rather risky job since the motel served truck drivers and traveling salesmen. I was so afraid of being raped. Fortunately, that never happened. I also was able to keep most of the money I earned, except what I contributed to running my household.

World War II had started and my brothers had to sign up for it. My father had pretty much left us. We rarely saw our father, but as I recall his financial contribution continued to be negligible. We were barely able to manage, as my father had moved to California. Many Blacks were leaving Texas for California, especially those who did not join the armed services. My mother refused to go with Papa. She said, "I'm not going. You go." He promised to send for us, which he never did.

My two older sisters also had graduated from high school. When Irmagene finished high school, my mother refused to permit her to marry a good man, who I believed was college-bound, because his mother did not keep a clean house. Irmagene left for Dallas to study cosmetology. She soon married and moved to Boston where she had children. The last time I visited her, she did not recognize me. She was a beautiful person, but could not take care of herself and died early.

My next older sister, Era, left for Kansas City, Missouri, through the help of the Densons, to live with Uncle Booker. He got her a job as a dishwasher in restaurants and then later as an elevator operator. Era spent most of her adult life married to a man who suffered from madness resulting from his service in World War II. Somehow, he never learned this and got no care.

While I was reluctant to leave my mother alone with two young girls, I knew I had to do so. By the time I graduated from high school magna cum laude, Ms. Henry had already helped me gain admission to Jarvis Christian College (see Figure 6.9: Mildred Sirls, Shiloh High School graduation, 1946). Our family would soon be headed to Kansas City, and I would be going to college—something that I had never thought possible.

Kansas City

Mildred remembers her experiences in Kansas City, Missouri[24]:

It was just after my high school graduation that I had a plan to follow my two older sisters' paths—to go to Kansas City and live with Uncle Booker and his wife, Aunt Jessie, while I worked to earn money for college. I recall that I'd saved some money but did not have quite enough for my one-way bus ticket to Kansas City. By now Mom accepted my intention to attend college and did whatever she could to help. She said she would try to manage without me. Mom gave me a few dollars and borrowed the balance from our neighborhood friends, Mrs. Rosie and Mrs. Denson.

I took my first ride out of Texas by Greyhound. My Uncle Booker and his wife offered to rent me a room for the summer. My first job when I arrived in Kansas City was as a dishwasher and busgirl at a Kresge Drug Store. I took the dirty dishes from the table and washed them. For the first time in my life, I knew that I could not eat in a restaurant.

Growing up poor in Texas, we did not have an occasion to ever think about eating in a restaurant. In the drug store, the busgirls were all Black and the waiters were White. No Blacks could work as a waitress or in any other capacity except as a janitor or dishwasher.[25] While I worked at Kresge, I was permitted to eat lunch for free. However, the discrimination policy prevented me from eating at the restaurant tables. The Black workers could only eat in a small closet-like room reserved for Blacks adjacent to the toilet. The White employees, however, could sit in the restaurant to eat. Incidentally, the buses and streetcars of Kansas City were segregated. While aware that this was humiliating, I did not complain but kept my eyes on the prize—higher education.

Each summer break that I was enrolled at Jarvis, I went to Kansas City, Missouri, and lived with my uncle and his wife. I paid him rent for a room and cooked my own food. They had a nice house but gave me a very small room with no toilet. Neither Uncle Booker nor his wife treated me as a relative. Rather, they treated me like someone whom they were helping out by providing me with a room for which I paid them. I paid my uncle a small fee for rent and saved most of my money for college. My mother saved it for me in the post office. She did not trust the banks.

For a couple of summers, I worked as an elevator operator at the Board of Trade building in downtown Kansas City. I had heard that a job was available as an elevator operator in a large business (where my sister Era had once worked). I applied and got accepted. It paid more money than Kresge where I had worked. One of the several Black elevator operators taught me how to work the old elevators with both hands. I was required to stand up. Even though there were seats in each of the elevators, I was told that it was unacceptable to sit—and so I did not. This made operating the elevator a horrible job as it was quite a demanding job and physically very painful.

There was a special room in the building for the Black elevator operators to rest and eat. The area contained a restroom, several chairs, and a couch. All of the ladies with whom I worked were much older and experienced than me. They formed huddles that excluded me. All of my coworkers were African-American women ranging in age roughly from their 30s to 60s. Most were married or divorced. In any event, they were all very experienced in the ways of the world.

The ladies spoke freely—about their love life, the other workers, the supervisor, etc. They were generous with foul language, but in deference to me and my innocence, they would remind each other to be careful when I was around. Some regarded me as a person to be protected and admired for being a college student, while still others sort of resented me. Everyone knew that I was working to pay for my college and that this was only a temporary job for me. In the fall I would return to Jarvis Christian College.

In none of my experiences in Kansas City every summer working as an elevator girl or busgirl do I recall being called "Nigger" or suffer any other racial indignity. My only concerns were working, going to church, and saving money for college. Social life was not a part of my agenda.

Mildred's mom, Eula, decided that there was no way she could manage in Texas with two young girls. She decided to move to Kansas City, as well. Mozelle remembers this time of transition and Mozelle's poem, "Rumors of Wars," symbolizes the flux of these turbulent times in the 1940s[26]:

Wars, wars, somebody's wars.
When did they begin?
Where will they end?
Why must I
Fight this war?
Wars, wars,
Go away, go away.
Dance to another place.
Bring back the joy; bring back innocence;
Bring back the caring, the love. Bring back
Spontaneity, laughter, affection, living.
Bring back Freedom.
Wars, go away!

We never heard grown people arguing and cussing at each other in Texas. The only time we heard Mama and Papa arguing was about going to California. Papa was trying to get Mama to go with him to California. I'd hear them talking quietly through the night through the wall. Mama's argument was, "RP, you've taken us all over Texas. There are earthquakes in California, and I'm not going." They went on like this for a long time. By this time, Papa had taken off to California with one of his cronies, leaving us destitute again. He promised to send money. Papa also had promised to make a swing for me on the old Chinaberry tree, but he never got around to this.

It soon became apparent that we would have to move to Kansas City where Irmagene, Era, and Mildred had stayed with Uncle Booker and Aunt Jessie. Mildred says she had to pay Uncle Booker and he gave her a rather hard time. Uncle Booker was close to Papa in age. Mildred had also worked when she was still at home, and the money she earned went to help the family. Mildred began to give her money to Mama to save for her. Mama saved her money at the post office soon after moving to Kansas City and obtaining a job at a bag factory, where she worked until she retired after 15 years.

While Bernice and I cut our shenanigans, Mildred worked in Kansas City for a while. Mama did not want Mildred to go to college because we needed money that she could earn at home. Irmagene, Mildred, and Bernice worked for White families to supplement the funds for our food. We also received money from Lowell and Clyde when they first joined the Armed Services, but they soon got married and had to support their own families. This was at the time the war ended. Irmagene and Era got married soon after.

This left the three of us—Mama, Bernice, and me—almost destitute. So Mama decided to go to Kansas City. This is how we came to live there. Mama could not earn enough money working sporadically for the White families. The people Mama worked for gave her hand-me-down clothing, which we were glad to get though her income from the job was meager. Mama sold our household furniture (whatever little we had), and sent Bernice to Gladewater, Texas, a small town some miles away, to buy our tickets to Kansas City. This was a long walk for Bernice.

Bernice remembers this trip to Gladewater and the move to Kansas City[27]*:*

One by one, they all left home—the two boys to the Army and Navy, my two older sisters to Dallas for higher schooling, and then the one next to me, leaving me the oldest child at home. I was very small for my age at 14; I looked nine. Papa left us. The youngest child died at six years of age. There were only three of us left at home: Mama, me, and Mozelle. Mama didn't want Mildred to go to college, but Mildred was determined to go. Mildred said, "I'm going to college, and nobody's going to stop me."

Mama was sad about it because we needed the money that Mildred was making from working. There was no food and no money. I found a job cleaning and babysitting for a family. This money fed us for a few weeks. Then, Mama began to sell everything so that we could move to Kansas City. This was where one older sister and my two brothers lived.

One very hot day in the summer, Mama said, "Bernice, I want you to go to Gladewater and get one grown-up train ticket and two children's tickets to Kansas City."[28] I looked at her and wondered, *"What is wrong with her? Doesn't she know I have no idea what or where this place is?"* I took the money in a wad. She told me to walk on the path to some place and then turn left and walk until I got to Gladewater. She also told me that it would be on the left side when I got there. Truthfully, I had no idea where this place was or what it looked like, but Mama said, "Go," and I went. I walked out of the house; I remember walking past the magnolia tree and the thinking how hot it was. We would say that you could see monkeys in the air when it was so hot.

The next thing I remember, I was walking into the train station and it was my first experience with an angel. Someone was standing by the window. I did not see anyone, but I felt the presence and somehow knew it was a man. I cannot remember if he was White or Black. But I could feel the kindness, because without him I would not have known what to do. He walked away from the window, stood back, and watched me. I asked the White woman at the counter, and she gave me the tickets. I was so short that I could not see the top of the counter, only the top of her face. I remember turning around to walk out. The person I had felt was not there. The next thing I remember, I was [back] in the house giving Mama the tickets. It was very hot outside, but I was not sweating and my feet did not hurt. "No God, no angels," some say. No one can tell me this, because I rode in the arms of an angel. God moves my life still. I got those tickets, and we went to Kansas City and we were never hungry again.

Mrs. Denson helped Mama to come to Kansas City. Mrs. Denson's relative, Ms. McDonald, had a room, which is how it worked in those days. Black folks had to rent rooms to other Blacks.[29] Mama sold everything and the most money she got was from the gun Papa left. We were on the train and mama had Mozelle and me in her arms and Mama said, "Hey kids wake up and see the Red River." I was too tired to care about the Red River. All of a sudden we were in Kansas at Ms. McDonald's house. Ms. McDonald was the daughter-in-law of Ms. Denson. Ms. McDonald lived on Everett. Alex Haley's cousin lived across the street from Mama in Kansas City on Everett. She worked for Bemis Bag Factory[30] and got Mama the job. Once Mama got the job at Bemis Bag Factory she was happy.

We all lived in one room upstairs in the big house. In the house there was also a man who gathered prostitutes and the man was acting funny around me. So, when my brothers, who both lived in Kansas City at the time, came over to visit, Lowell decided I needed to stay with him and his wife. I got to come to Mama's every weekend where there was plenty of food and there was food that we liked. We didn't even think about Papa. We didn't even talk about him. I started tell people he was dead. I was just ashamed of him.

After about a year, Mama moved from Ms. McDonald's to Bit Warbington's house. Bit was my sister Era's husband's aunt and she provided a place for us to stay. The house was across the street from Era. I lived there with Mozelle. I was able to get a good job after I quit high school. I knew how to fix myself to look like a lady and I knew how to talk like a lady. I knew to look adults in the eye and I had good manners. I was at Whitehead Studios where I learned the etching trade.

During that time, Mozelle was acting up; she was acting terrible. She was acting a fool because you cannot make a dumb person act a fool. Mozelle was very bright but she started going with old married men and running away from home. She was in junior high school. I went to the movies and I caught Mozelle out with one of those old men in their 40s and 50s. After talking to Papa, Mama decided to send Mozelle to California to be with him. RP had married again and he was living with his new wife and her sister in their home. Somehow, he had gotten his name on their house and ended up with their house. He was just a scoundrel like that. Mozelle was very unhappy out there and she wanted to return to Kansas City. Papa sent her back to Mama after only a few months.

Alcoholism runs in the family on Mama's side and Mama would always say, "Don't start drinking because alcoholism runs on my side of family." Mozelle was an alcoholic. When Mozelle finally got a job, she did medical transcription work. She told me that she would drink gin every day and the folks at work thought it was water.

Mozelle also had mental illness and so did Irmagene. Mental illness runs on Papa's side because of Papa's mama. Life was tough for my sister, Irmagene. It was also tough for Era. I do remember when Era died in Kansas City. She was so weak, and it took all her strength to say, "Lord, have mercy, help me." I remember that's all she kept saying, "Lord, have mercy, help me." As I was getting ready to leave, she held her breath long enough to blow me a kiss. She barely had breath to breathe, but yet, she blew me that kiss. I'll never forget that.

Mozelle remembers her time in Kansas City[31]*:*

When we got to Kansas and Mama had obtained a job at a bag factory, Papa sent one small sum of money to us, and that was all. But we did not blame him too much because we were used to his neglect. He never beat any of us, except for Lowell, and that was because of his strong dislike for Lowell. Lowell suffered much from Papa's abuse, but never did Papa abuse the rest of us except from neglect. I believe this was because Lowell was named for Mama's Papa, George.

After our train ride to Kansas City, the cab drove up to a two-story house and stopped near 5th Street on Everett. This was to be our dwelling. I had a vision of a fine house; I'd seen pictures of fine houses in magazines. This was not quite what I expected, but it would do because it had an indoor toilet with a bathtub.

Our landlady, Mrs. McDonald, was a relative of Mrs. Denson. Mrs. McDonald rented us a room on the second floor. I was in awe of what I considered a big city. I would go down to the corner of 5th and Everett and look up the hill at the bright lights of downtown. The rest of the family lived across the river in Kansas City, Missouri, although Mildred was in college at Jarvis Christian College in Texas, and Irmagene was in Dallas with her husband. Era was about to be married. She got married our first year in Kansas City. Bernice lived with Lowell and took care of his children while he and his wife worked and Bernice attended school in Kansas City, Missouri.

Mama carried us with her to church on Sundays. We had to ride the streetcar because the church was quite away from home, but it was near Uncle Booker's, where we stopped sometimes afterward. Mama did not holler and stomp like some Baptists do. The most I saw her do when she was moved was shed a few tears, wiping them with her crocheted handkerchief. Mama was of a quiet nature, but people were drawn to her because of her honesty and being a real Christian. At her funeral years later, there were many people there.

Mama enjoyed crocheting and made beautiful tablecloths, bedspreads, and lace for pillowslips and doilies. She made our meager furniture in Texas pretty with her crocheted doilies. In the city, Mama still quilted and made our clothing, but not so much as she had in Texas. We got some store-bought clothing. Mama sometimes sent things down to Mrs. Denson because she remembered her help through the hard times. Bernice and I made our own skirts and blouses in the summer. We liked to make the then-fashionable wide skirts and equally wide under slips consisting of ruffles and lace.

Mildred came home periodically. Often she offered to pay my tuition to college, but to my great regret, I declined. I did not want to disappoint her. I was having a bad time at home and was planning to leave.

Key Lessons

1. *Young Black girls were vulnerable to rape. Mildred's rape by her teenage brother and the accompanying silence by both Mildred and her sister, Bernice who witnessed the rape, reflect a little discussed reality of life.*

2. *The value of community and supporting each other was important for Black family survival in the segregated South. The Densons, as a fairly wealthy African-American family, provided support, financially, emotionally, and socially to the Sirls' girls and their mother. Church and religion continued to be an important bond connecting families in the small rural community.*

3. *Life remained difficult for Mildred's mother, Eula, as a Black woman raising children with little financial means. Working as a maid was often the only option for gaining income. Mildred's role in supporting the family through her work as a maid made it difficult for her mother to encourage her education.*

4. *Medical care was scarce and children often died young, as reflected by Ruby's death.*

5. *Skin color affected many in the Black community. The preference for lighter skin made it difficult for many darker-skinned girls. It was particularly painful within families. For Mildred, it became part of what motivated her to achieve.*

6. *Mildred experienced sexism in high school from the teacher who refused to name Mildred as the class president. The teacher said that a boy—not a girl—should*

receive the honor. This experience, combined with the same teacher's mocking of Mildred's poverty, evidences the challenges of race, class, and gender for Black girls.

7. *The necessity for advocates, mentors, and supporters is reflected by Mildred's story about her teacher, Ms. Ira Henry. Ms. Henry encouraged her to attend college and explained how it could be possible. This is a legacy of the Black community's commitment to education, including the important role of Historically Black Colleges and Universities.*

8. *Families moved and migrated. It was necessary to move and live with other family members. Extended family and close friends played a critical role in ensuring the success of migration, as when Mildred's family moved to Kansas City. Given the role of segregation, it was often necessary to have existing family and friends in the new community. Kansas City became a place of opportunity for the Sirls' women as Eula was able to be employed and begin a new life—out of poverty.*

9. *Mildred, with Ms. Henry's assistance, would be starting the first step of her journey into the academy. She would begin at Jarvis Christian College in Hawkins, Texas. Jarvis was the first stop on her long journey into the academy.*

Photos

Figure 6.1: Ruby Sirls (deceased), age 6, 1944
Source: M. Pratt.

Figure 6.2: From left, Mozelle, Eula, Era, RP, and Bernice Sirls, 1944
Source: M. Pratt. Permission received from Bernice Miller, 2017.

Figure 6.3: George Sirls, age 21, 1943
Source: M. Pratt. Permission received from Pat Sirls, 2017.

Figure 6.4: Irmagene Sirls, circa 1940s
Source: M. Pratt. Permission received from Bernard Hogg, 2017.

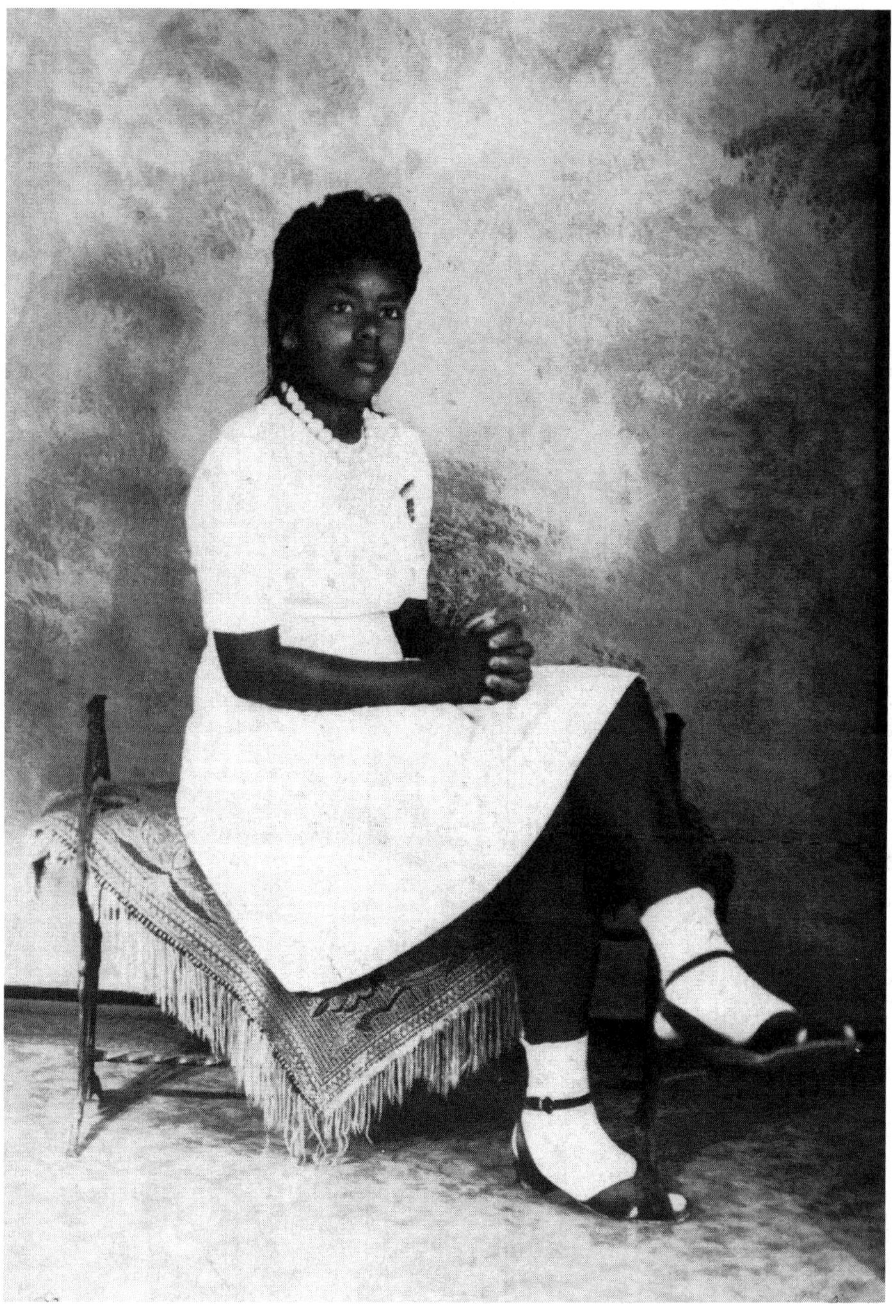

Figure 6.5: Era Sirls, circa 1940s
Source: M. Pratt. Permission received from Cecil Hickman, 2017.

Figure 6.6: Mildred Sirls, age 16, 1944
Source: M. Pratt.

Mildred Inez Sirls Is Valedictorian

Sirls, Mildred Inez, better known as "Smartie" has been a very studious young lady and served as vice president of our class during the junior and senior years. She is valedictorian of the class. She played the role of Aunt Hester in the senior play. She plans to be a missionary.

FRESHMAN CLASS NEWS

By LUCILLE STEPHENS

As we know it is about time for school to close, and we have enjoyed the second semester to the highest. Just before Easter the freshman class gave an Easter egg hunt. All had lots of fun. We are now looking forward to the semester exam. All of us hope to pass. We did enjoy our freshman year in dear o

Figure 6.7: Mildred Sirls, Shiloh High School, 1946
Source: Shiloh High School Student Newspaper.

MISS I. C. HENRY

Miss I. C. Henry is the High School English Instructor and Music Director of Shiloh High School. She has a very pleasing personality and exercises her hobby which is "going places."

During the past two years she has directed many outstanding intellectual programs.

Although she is a very busy person, she always finds time to smile and help others.

Who is the sponsor of the Campus Register? She is.

Figure 6.8: Ms. Ira Henry, Shiloh High School, circa 1940s
Source: Shiloh High School Student Newspaper.

Figure 6.9: Mildred Sirls, Shiloh High School Graduation, 1946
Source: M. Pratt.

Notes

1. (M. Pratt, personal communication, May 11, 2012).
2. (B. Miller, personal communication, June 13, 2013).
3. (M. Pratt, personal communication, May 11, 2012).
4. (M. Perry, personal communication, n.d.).
5. (B. Miller, personal communication, June 13, 2013).
6. (M. Perry, personal communication, n.d.).
7. (M. Pratt, personal communication, n.d.).
8. For more about issues of skin color in the Black community, see Keith and Herring (1991).
9. See Valk and Brown (2010, pp. 22–23, 71) and Chafe, Gavins, and Korstad (2001, p. 158) for discussion about skin color and gender.
10. (B. Miller, personal communication, July 21, 2013).
11. (M. Pratt, personal communication, n.d.).
12. Education was often seen as an escape from current circumstances (Valk & Brown, 2010, p. 22, 51).
13. Bernice recalls: "I just remember that for no reason Era and Irmagene disliked each other with a passion" (B. Miller, personal communication, November 25, 2013).
14. For a history of Shiloh schools, see "East Texas Educator" (n.d.) and "Online Directory of Texas" (n.d.). Shiloh School, in Gregg County, White Oak Texas, was located four miles northwest of Longview. The high school closed in 1949. As the historical marker at the site notes, "The newly freed African Americans of the Shiloh Community established a school for their children shortly after the Civil War" (Gobble, 2010).
15. (M. Pratt, personal communication, n.d.).
16. See Valk and Brown (2010, p. 76) for another example of this phrase.
17. See Valk and Brown (2010, p. 57) for another example of using flour sacks for clothing.
18. The use of hand-me-downs was common (Valk & Brown, 2010, p. 28, 47).
19. The high school newspapers states: "Thomas, Darnell D., better known as 'Donald Duck' is president of the class. ...He is a studious young man and is Salutatorian of the class" (M. Pratt, personal communication, n.d.).
20. Sass is often a tool for Black women to regain self-esteem (Braxton, 1989, pp. 30–31, 158).
21. (M. Pratt, personal communication, n.d.).
22. Education was an important value for many Black families (Andrews, 1990, p. 144; Chafe et al., 2001, p. 237).
23. Black teachers played an important role in the community (Coats, 2010; Taulbert, 1989, p. 35).
24. (M. Pratt, personal communication, May 12, 2012).
25. Dishwashing was a common job for Blacks (Taulbert, 1992, p. 81).
26. (M. Perry, personal communication, n.d.).
27. (M. Pratt, personal communication, n.d.; B. Miller, personal communication, June 13, 2013, and August 23, 2013).

28. Black migration by train was common (Taulbert, 1992).
29. Family members played a critical role in ensuring successful migration experiences (Taulbert, 1992, p. 13).
30. (Bemis, n.d.).
31. (M. Perry, personal communication, n.d.).

References

Andrews, R. (1990). *The last radio baby: A memoir*. Atlanta, GA: Peachtree Publishers.

Bemis. (n.d.). *Bemis Company History*. Retrieved September 1, 2013 from http://www.bemis.com/overview/2/history/

Braxton, J. M. (1989). *Black women writing autobiography: A tradition within a tradition*. Philadelphia, PA: Temple University Press.

Chafe, W. H., Gavins, R., & Korstad, R. (Eds.). (2001). *Remembering Jim Crow: African Americans tell about life in the Segregated South*. New York, NY: The New Press.

Coats, Linda T. (2010). The way we learned: African American students' memories of schooling in the segregated South. *The Journal of Negro Education, 79*(1), 6–17.

East Texas Black Educator Hall of Fame. (n.d.). *Black Schools*. Retrieved August 5, 2013 from http://etexeducator.com/3/family.htm

Gobble, M. (2010, December). Shiloh School. *Texas Escapes Online Magazine: Travel and History*. Retrieved June 1, 2017 from www.texasescapes.com

Keith, V. M., & Herring, C. (1991, November 1). Skin tone and stratification in the Black community. *American Journal of Sociology, 97*(3), 760–778.

Online Directory of Texas. (n.d.). *Gregg County, Texas: Public School Districts*. Retrieved September 1, 2013 from http://www.greggcountytexas.us/PublicSchools/PublicSchoolsDistricts.htm

Taulbert, C. L. (1989). *Once upon a time when we were colored*. Tulsa, OK: Council Oak Books.

Taulbert, C. L. (1992). *The last train north*. New York, NY: Penguin Books.

Valk, A., & Brown, L. (2010). *Living with Jim Crow: African American women and memories of the segregated South*. New York, NY: Palgrave Macmillan.

Part II Sunshine

I am aware that the job of helping people to realize to the fullest acumen the capacities which God has given them is one which perhaps as few others draws upon one's spiritual reserve and upon his whole self. …Although I am young in the social work profession, I think that I can say without the least equivocation that [this] is one which perhaps of all professions of its type has its origin in the Judeo-Christian religion, which stresses social justice, charity, love of one's fellow man, not seeking one's own, not being easily provoked, being kind, and long-suffering. All of these qualities might be summed up in the term "acceptance"—acceptance of people where they are and helping them to move on to where they, God, and their fellow men want that they should go. The business of accepting people requires a spirit and a quality of a person whose soul is steeped in the well-springs of faith and belief in a God who is Love. These are some of the ideas which I know accepting this noble calling requires of me, and I pray God to make me equal to it.—Mildred Pratt, 1955[1]

CHAPTER SEVEN

A New Beginning

Mildred attended Jarvis Christian College, Butler University, and the University of Indiana during the late 1940s and early 1950s. She reflects upon her college experiences, as well as life after graduate school, in segregated America in Los Angeles, St. Louis, and Detroit.

Jarvis Christian College

Mildred writes about her experience at Jarvis[2]:

Jarvis Christian College (Jarvis) had begun as Jarvis Christian Institute by the Negro Disciples of Christ [Christian denomination] in 1904 to enable Blacks to get an education.[3] It became a college in 1928. Of course it was segregated, but it was one of the few colleges dedicated to educating Blacks at that time. Once I was there I was one happy soul because I enjoyed learning! I also was to be the only one of my siblings to obtain a college degree. I was the "seed of the coming free."[4] And, in my determination to be free, I decided to do anything that was legal to get my education.

I attended Jarvis from 1946 to 1951. I was fortunate enough to be able to pay for my education by working one year and taking courses the next year; and, by working part-time during the years when I took classes. Because of this system it took me about five years to complete my bachelor's degree.

I was so eager to obtain my degree, I did whatever work was assigned to me to pay for my education. In the spring and fall, I worked in the university's garden—picking up and shucking corn that was to be cooked for the students. I would take the corn from the stock and prepare it to be cooked in the kitchen for the students. The work that I did included preparation of the grape juice to be served at Jarvis' Sunday church services. My primary job was cleaning the dorm bathrooms and the hallways, but I also cleaned the apartments in which the professors lived. In addition, I served as the personal maid of the Dean of Women, for whom my duties ranged from cleaning her residential quarters in the dorm, to babysitting her son, to scratching the dander from her hair, to ironing her clothes. I especially enjoyed working for the Dean because she shared special food and some of her clothes which I badly needed.

I also served in an informal position as an assistant to the Dean, where I monitored students in the dormitory. I monitored the courtship parlor or sitting room where the boys and girls could be together on Sunday at designated times. I made sure that when the girls used the room reserved to meet their boyfriends they did not get too close to each other and did not go beyond a handshake and a kiss on the cheek. I had to make sure the door always remained open and to tell the Dean if something happened. I also was expected to ensure that the girls' lights were off at curfew. Despite being the campus tattletale, I had some really good friends. Truthfully, many times I joined the students in their follies. As I reflect upon my college years, I was often treated as though I were an older student, even though I was not. In my glorified maid position, the students called me Miss Sirls and showed me deference. If any professor wanted a responsible student to do something, I was always given the assignment. This perhaps accounts for the fact that I never had a boyfriend.

While at Jarvis, I tried to learn and do as much as possible. Jarvis had no nationally affiliated sororities, but there were social clubs. One of the criteria for membership was "bright" skin color. Dark-skinned girls were not permitted membership in the special social clubs. They discriminated against people of my skin color. Despite the color issue at Jarvis, there is one event that stands out as the highlight of my experience at Jarvis—my poetry recital. I gave my first poetry recital at Jarvis. My English teacher singled me out to make a presentation before the entire university. She was from Alabama, and she not only coached me but made me this fancy pink dress that went all the way down to my knees. I can see myself in that dress now. The dress was like a fancy prom dress. Then, she invited all the faculty and students to watch me perform. I had memorized enough poetry for an hour-long presentation. My performance was well-received and I felt really fantastic.

After this event, something inside of me suddenly wanted to do all that I could do and experience as much as I could. So, I said to myself, "*Why don't you join the choir?*" I tried to join the college choir but was promptly dismissed. I thought I was doing fine until the teacher, Eugenia Powell, took me aside and said that I'd have to leave because the students said I "messed them up" by switching between the alto and soprano voice. I did not know the difference as I had never heard those words before. This really hurt me. It was my first experience being kicked out of anything.

Interestingly enough, Eugenia Powell and I made a connection many years after this incident. I received a call from her on the occasion of my son Awadagin's classical music performance in Atlanta, Georgia, where Eugenia was living. She said he looked so much like me that she decided to ask him if he knew Mildred Sirls, to which he replied, "She is my mother." Our friendship was renewed.[5]

My life at Jarvis College was indeed insulated. Somehow through the fact that I was majoring in religion and planning to become a missionary, I was selected to attend A Camp Farthest Out in a beautiful wooded area in Texas.[6] I had never heard of this organization. It was an interdenominational religious group and rather informal. I first learned about it from Mrs. White, a wealthy White board member from Dallas, Texas, and chair of the Board of Jarvis Christian College. She told me about this conference and paid my way to go. I was the youngest person at the camp. In fact, the majority of the people were elderly and were from several different states.

My recollection is that I was the only Black person there. I suppose they assumed that every Black person could sing or had rhythm, because they asked me to conduct the music. There was a great deal of singing. I was shocked when I was asked to be the song leader. Fortunately, I did know a lot of Black church songs and slave songs. I think they assumed that I would know Negro spirituals, which was what they wanted.

This was my very first interracial experience, and it seems weird that I do not recall being surprised or having difficulty adjusting to it. Why was I not surprised with all of this? I suppose just the fact of being in college was so completely out of my sphere of imagination that anything else that happened to me was just not unusual. In any event, I maintained contact with the organization through much of my experiences in Indianapolis until my critical study of Christianity resulted in my decision to give it up.

When I was a senior at Jarvis, I was elected president of the college branch of the Young Women Christian Association (YWCA) at Jarvis. One of the greatest honors of serving in this position was that I got selected to attend the International YWCA conference at the University of Kansas in Lawrence, Kansas. Consequently, I got my first train ride out of the state of Texas—even though I had to travel in the Negro section of the train. The conference was integrated but I remember feeling isolated and lonely. My most positive memory of this conference was hearing the famous civil rights strategist Dr. Bayard Rustin[7] speak and seeing the movie *Cry My Beloved Country*.[8]

During Christmas holiday in the winter, Jarvis was closed and I didn't have any place to go. Usually, Mr. Bob Whites' family, the Black family that once hired my family as sharecroppers, invited me to stay at their home in Longview. Because I didn't have money, they would pay my bus fare. They had a big house, owned land, and operated a grocery store. Their wealth was rare for Black people. They also had a stunningly beautiful daughter who dressed fancy and attended Jarvis.

At the Whites' home, I slept in a little closet. During the daytime, I would shuck peanuts in their attic. Now, shucking peanuts was a winter activity wherein you would take unshelled peanuts from storage and then remove their hulls and shell them. The attic was large and covered with peanuts, which I shucked by myself. The Whites didn't pay me for this work, but I did this in exchange for them buying my ticket and giving me a place to stay and some food. I stayed with the Whites for three Christmas seasons and I shucked peanuts in their attic for my keep. I didn't leave until Jarvis reopened for the winter semester. I was willing to do whatever I could do that was legal to get my education.

When I was scheduled to graduate within a couple of months, I had no definite career path. Although I had majored in religion and considered becoming a missionary, nothing had been settled. But, as graduation approached, a miracle happened and another door opened for me. During my senior year, the college president had become involved in a love affair on campus and consequently was asked to leave. A gentleman from Indianapolis, Indiana, who had a connection with the Disciples of Christ headquarters, was assigned as interim president of Jarvis Christian College. The man was Dr. Cleo Blackburn. He was the Executive Director of Flanner House (a Disciples of Christ Settlement House) and a powerful Black man.[9]

Because I had been doing the housecleaning for the Dean of Women, Dr. Blackburn asked her if I could clean for him too while he was in the President's house. I was assigned to be his housekeeper. One day while I was cleaning his residence, he asked me what I planned to do after graduation. I replied, "I do not know," which was, unfortunately, the truth. He proposed a plan where I could live with his family in Indianapolis and perform maid duties for them in exchange for my room and board while I attended Butler University School of Religion for my master's degree in religion which would prepare me to become a missionary. He also promised to arrange for me to get a scholarship from the Disciples of Christ Missionary Society.

Until that time, I had been oriented to education and had not studied religion critically. I also was becoming aware that I would not be a pastor, but perhaps a missionary social worker. I had many questions and saw in Dr. Blackburn's offer an opportunity to critically study religion. Dr. Blackburn had opened another door for me. I entered this door determined to further develop myself and to make a contribution to society. So, of course I said, "Yes," because I was on a roll to get as much education as possible. Only later did I learn from other women who had been in a similar relationship with the Blackburns that Dr. Blackburn did not pay my tuition, but that Butler had awarded me a tuition scholarship. In 1951, I graduated from Jarvis with honors.[10]

Butler University

Mildred describes her transition to Indianapolis in the 1950s to attend Butler University and her experience as a live-in maid and graduate student[11]:

I spent my last summer as an elevator operator in Kansas City, Missouri, and earned enough money for my transportation to Indianapolis. I moved in with Mr. Blackburn and his teenage son, two daughters, and his wife. They lived where most upper-class African-Americans lived. The house had four bedrooms upstairs, a large living room, a dining room, and a kitchen. I shared a room with the Blackburns' eldest who was in high school.

This was the only time that I had lived in such a house and as a live-in servant. I cooked the meals, washed and ironed, cleaned the house, and got ordered around by both the children and adults. Among the most disgusting tasks I performed involved cleaning woodwork, windows, and frilly curtains, which normally took the better part of a morning. While I was not happy to be put in the position of a live-in maid, I contented myself by deciding to focus on my future rather than the present situation. I was a very busy person: working as a maid and studying for my Masters in Religion. I was one of two women in the program. I studied and worked hard with no time for any extracurricular activities.

At Butler University, I do not recall any racial problems, at least not manifest.[12] There was only one other Black student in the Religion Department, Effie,[13] and we became very close friends. She, too, had served as a maid for the Blackburns. So, we spent a great deal of time talking about the peculiarities of middle-class Blacks who had their own exclusive societies and tendencies to treat their help like southern Whites treated theirs.

While I lived with the Blackburns, I went with them on summer vacation once to Michigan. This vacation took place at a segregated vacation spot for Black high society. Again, I was taken along as their maid and treated by them as such, as well as by the other high-society Blacks. While I found this experience humiliating, I was at their mercy because at that time it was the only way that I could get my education.

When I had almost completed my work for a Masters in Religion and my thesis was well on its way to completion, I was beginning to question the historicity of Jesus as presented in the literature that I was reading.[14] As an unintended consequence of studying religion, Christianity, and the historicity of Jesus, I became a bit agnostic.

When Dr. Blackburn suggested that I take one year of study at the Indiana University School of Social Service before I began my missionary work for the Disciples of Christ, I was delighted. I was to work part-time at the Flanner House where Dr. Blackburn was Director and continue living with his family and working as a maid. More education? Sure, I'd do it. He arranged for me to get a scholarship from a missionary society to pay for my tuition.

Jamaica

Before Mildred began studying at Indiana University, she had the opportunity to travel to Jamaica. She shares about the segregation and discrimination that she experienced[15]:

Before entering the School of Social Services in 1951, I learned about a hurricane in Jamaica that had destroyed that island's Disciples of Christ Church building.[16] Dr. Blackburn suggested that I go there for the summer before enrolling in the fall. I was among 15 people selected to go to Jamaica as work campers sponsored by the Disciples of Christ National Headquarters to rebuild the church. In preparation for the work camp in Jamaica, the work campers were scheduled to meet in Florida for orientation. A White lady who had just graduated with me from Butler School of Religion and I agreed to take the trip to Florida by Greyhound bus. We both intended to be missionaries.

We boarded the bus in Indianapolis and sat together. The driver made a stop someplace in Kentucky for us to use the restroom and eat. When my White friend and I approached the door of the restaurant, I was told that I could not eat in the restaurant but would have to go to the back of the restaurant to a window, order my food, and eat outside. There was a sign posted stating, "No Negroes Allowed Inside." I complied, but not with a smile as I was of no mind to "go gently into that good night." While very disturbed by this, I did not feel comfortable taking any action, and I knew the other lady would not. When we reboarded the bus, the driver informed me that I would have to go to the back of the bus.

When we arrived in Tampa, Florida, where we spent the night, we picked up the other 12 to 15 work campers. We were an integrated group consisting of Black and White students from all over the country. We all assembled in the home of one church member and later went to the local church where we received briefings about our pending missionary trip. The camp director greeted us there and informed us about the program. I recall being told that the three Black participants would have to stay in a different hotel because the one that had been reserved would not accept Blacks. We all remained on the bus until a decision was made as to where we would spend the night. The planners spent considerable time deciding what to do. They eventually decided to have us stay in family homes.

During the orientation we learned that we would be taking a bus to the airport to board a plane to Kingston, Jamaica. We also learned that the three Blacks would have to sit in a special section in the rear of the bus, and the Whites would sit in the front. By this time, I had made friends with a White couple who were doctoral students from Indiana University. They were what in those days would be called radical.

Well, this couple and I became fast friends. The three of us organized a protest about the bus arrangements. We insisted that we would not ride on a segregated bus. My two friends and I insisted that this was unchristian and we stated our refusal to accept the plan. The other two Black campers refused to participate in the protest. I recall that there was quite a long discussion on the matter one evening that went late into the night and it became very heated. Eventually, the majority of the campers agreed that we must all travel as a group—integrated. We spent most of the night and part of the next day negotiating and trying to get a bus that we could ride unsegregated. Arrangements were made, and we all sat anywhere we wished on the bus.

A daily journal from one of the missionary trip organizers from June 16 to July 14 confirms the concerns around segregation related to the missionary trip.[17] The journal begins on June16th:

In the late evening, the first campers from the United States began to arrive at St. Petersburg, Florida. Weary and tired, each one of us was met at the Greyhound bus station by the smiling faces of the young people of Mirror Lake Christian Church. This church was a splendid host to the campers during our entire orientation session. Those who arrived this evening were Mr. and Mrs. Jed White, Mr. and Mrs. Bob Ruff, Mildred Sirls, Lucy Ann Hass, and Mr. and Mrs. Lytt Noel. We spent the night at the church, and the army cots were as wonderful as Beautyrest mattresses.

The June 18 entry mentions the incident related to segregation[18]:

We covered a lot of practical problems that we needed to face—particularly our segregation while in Florida. … Here we go again, another bus ride—and all night, too! Once again we had to become segregated with much sorrow and confession of guilt—but from our weakness there came renewed strength.

On June 19th, they departed for Jamaica from the Pan American airport. It was Mildred's first plane flight. The group picture was taken just outside the plane by the Pan American Public Relations Department for release to various newspapers.[19] *Once in Jamaica, issues of discrimination continued to surface. Mildred shares an incident related to discrimination against the Jamaican camp workers who joined the American work campers and the protest that was organized in response to the discrimination*[20]:

Once in Jamaica, three male Jamaican camp workers joined us. We traveled about 15 to 20 miles per day in a truck to the rural mountainous area where the church was located to repair it. During our stay in Jamaica, another incident occurred related to the class system there. The Queen's representative was scheduled to visit Jamaica from England. The Jamaican government had planned a formal dinner for the Queen's representative and invited the work campers. However, the camp directors were informed that the Black Jamaican campers could not attend. This was because the Jamaicans were regarded by the British as lower class; and therefore, unwelcome at such an event. When the work campers, including me, learned of this we decided to protest. Again, I, along with my two radical friends and several others (who now made up our subgroup), insisted that if the Jamaicans could not attend the event, then we would not either. The other African-Americans refused to join the protest. However, a lady from Texas joined us. She spoke "real Texas." For several days there were several meetings held to try and get us protestors to relent. We did not, but the Jamaican officials did. We won. All campers attended the event.

I remember one other event that was rather embarrassing. The ladies in the work camp were doing some work digging up fallen tree limbs when we all felt the need to go to the toilet. We looked for the nearest tree that we could use for a toilet. That meant finding a tree that we could scoot around and not be seen. We found one, had removed our pants, and had just positioned ourselves to use the "toilet" when suddenly we heard giggling noise from our large tree. We looked up to find a couple of Jamaican boys laughing as they observed us trying to use our "toilet." We pulled ourselves together and ran away as fast as we could. We laughed almost all night about this incident (see Figure 7.1: Photograph of Mildred, Jamaica, 1952)!

University of Indiana

After returning to Indianapolis from Jamaica, Mildred enrolled at the Indiana University School of Social Service to begin her career in social work. Mildred describes her experience with discrimination at the Indiana University School of Social Service[21]:

When I had almost completed one year at Indiana University, I decided that I wanted to study for another year to get my Masters in Social Work. The School of Social Service had a history of discriminating in its internship program. The majority of social work agencies were segregated, and this was deemed acceptable by the social work community. Several agencies would not accept African-American interns, yet the Dean continued to send White students there. There were only two or three African-American students and they could only do their field instruction in African-American agencies. The only exception was the state agency for the mentally ill which did not discriminate. There was a YWCA for Whites and one for Blacks. I did my internship at the Black YWCA. There were separate settlement houses for Blacks and Whites. I worked at Flanner House for about two years. It was a Black agency. I know that the Jewish Community Center was open to Blacks because I participated in the folk dancing program.

I left the Blackburns to rent a room from a former school principal and his wife in Indianapolis—a prominent family in the city. It was within walking distance of the university. Making ends meet became rather difficult. Most of the White students had some kind of financial help. During my years at the university, I was unable to get one penny from the school. Some students had told me that the Dean had a special fund with which she would help students who found themselves in need of money. I decided to request money from her. One freezing day, I walked about two miles in deep snow to request a loan from the Dean. She said that she would see what she could do. She said she thought she could get help from the PEO (Philanthropic Educational Organization).[22] I waited several weeks, and I heard nothing from the Dean.

One Friday after all classes were completed, embarrassed, I went to see the Dean without an appointment. I asked her what she had learned, and I recall her coldly saying that the group could not help me. I remember thinking that this was a sad commentary on social work. Parenthetically, I have since learned that at that time there was no way the PEO would have granted funds to a Black student. I left her office in tears, and seeing my pain, the secretary inquired what the problem was. When I told her, she offered to loan me money, which she did. I recall that it was a small sum of money. Incidentally, this secretary had a history of helping other students in similar circumstances.

This experience of struggling financially in school led Mildred to start a small fund to help students in the same situation when she became a professor at Illinois State University. The website states, "Our Mildred Pratt Assistance Fund is an emergency-only student assistance fund that is administered by our School for BSW [Bachelor of Social Work] and MSW [Master of Social Work] students who unexpectedly find themselves in emergency situations. Typical financial assistance is for needs of $100 or less. Exceptions for this can be made on a case-by-case basis."[23]

The Director of the Illinois State University School of Social Work, Diane Zosky, describes how the fund has been used[24]: "The fund is used for emergency student needs. We have used it for such things as buying a textbook for a student or perhaps a gas card for a student who commutes. …Your mother's fund has been used for those highly individual emergency needs that come up for students…usually the…type of stressors that may…become the barrier in them finishing their social work degree. I think it is really quite poetic that although your mother was a professor, she was a social worker, and her fund is being used like a social worker would see fit—to help those who are vulnerable to become successful."

Mildred graduated from Indiana University in 1955. She was inducted as a missionary at Disciples of Christ and sent to work at their settlement house in downtown Los Angeles, California—the All People's Church and Community Center. Mildred's letter of acceptance of the position is below[25]:

I accept this position which is given me with Home Missions Division of the United Christian Missionary Society. And as I accept the specific job at All People's Christian Church and Community Center, I do so with a full awareness of the duties and the joy and hard work which are necessarily a part of performing the job. Therefore, my constant prayer is that God will keep me replenished with the sense of consecration and dedication which I now experience, that will make me equal to the task.

I am aware that the job of helping people to realize to the fullest acumen the capacities which God has given them is one which perhaps as few others draws upon one's spiritual reserve and upon his whole self. This being true, then, and in order to be able to continue to give, not only requires the constant sharpening of one's own knowledge and skills in working with and for people; but equally or more important it requires that such a person not only know, but that one be able to call upon God for spiritual nourishment for the soul, which is the person.

Although I am young in the social work profession, I think that I can say without the least equivocation that [this] is one which perhaps of all professions of its type has its origin in the Judeo-Christian religion, which stresses social justice, charity, love of one's fellow man, not seeking one's own, not being easily provoked, being kind, and long-suffering. All of these qualities might be summed up in the term "acceptance"—acceptance of people where they are and helping them to move on to where they, God, and their fellow men want that they should go. The business of accepting people requires a spirit and a quality of a person whose soul is steeped in the wellsprings of faith and belief in a God who is Love. These are some of the ideas which I know accepting this noble calling requires of me, and I pray God to make me equal to it.

Los Angeles

Mildred's move to Los Angeles connected her back to her family—her mother, her sister Bernice, and her brother George. She joined the Unitarian Church and remembers listening to Mamie Till speak about the lynching of her son, Emmett. Mildred shares about her experiences in Los Angeles and supporting her mother and Bernice[26]:

I was living in a one-bedroom apartment, and I gave my mother the bedroom while I slept in my living room. My mother had remained in Kansas City until her son [George] convinced her to come live with him in California and babysit his children. When Bernice was in trouble, as she was on many occasions, my mother expected me to take care of her. She seemed oblivious to the fact that Bernice did not change her behavior when I tried to help her. On one occasion when Bernice was in trouble with her husband, my mother insisted that I take Bernice and her two children in. I agreed if Bernice would "straighten up and fly right."

When my sister showed up with her two children, I found a duplex that had three bedrooms so as to have adequate space for the five of us. I told my sister that they could live with me (I'd pay the rent) if she took a job and went to night school to get her General Education Diploma. I helped her enroll in a typing class while we took care of her children at night. Well, I found out that instead of going to classes, Bernice was going to the honky-tonk with men. When I approached Bernice about the matter, my mother expressed her displeasure at me.

As soon as my mother began getting her retirement money and social security checks, I found her a nice but smaller apartment and told her that it was up to her whether or not she wished to keep my sister and her two children. Eventually Bernice was fortunate to marry into a family that owned land in Arkansas. They made considerable money from it. She lived quite well.

Bernice also remembers this time and the assistance Mildred provided[27]:

I remember when I took my first husband to meet my mother. My mother said, "Bernice, leave that man alone. He looks like someone who has been locked up somewhere." I didn't listen to her. I thought, *how would she know?* Later, I realized that Papa had spent about eight years in and out of jail. Mama knew "a monkey" when saw one. One day, I saw some papers and learned that my husband had gotten out of Fort Leavenworth Prison. I realize now people ought to listen to old people. We are not going to be right all the time, but we are going to be right most of the time.

I immediately picked up my kids and went to California. I showed up at Mama's with my two children, and I knew I was in a pickle. Mama was watching Lowell's kids, and everyone started discussing what was going to happen. Mildred was mad. I had two children, no job, and no money. Mildred could talk to George like no one else could. She told him that he needed to watch his own children and that Mama was going to watch my children. There is no way I would have survived. When I went to bed, I had decided that I was going to commit suicide. When morning came, Mildred woke me up and said, "Bernice, come eat breakfast." She had made a wonderful breakfast, and she had set the table immaculately. She said, "We will help you get a job, and Mama will take care of the children." After that, I knew everything was going to be fine.

Mildred did a lot of good in the world. Mildred was so good to Mama. She took care of Mama; she took Mama on cross-country trips because she had the job and the money to do it. She took Mama to Kansas City a few times, the Redwoods, the Rose Parade, and Las Vegas. Mama saw places she would never have seen because of Mildred. Mildred found a nice place for Mama to live. She furnished Mama's place with nice, expensive furniture, and Mama loved her apartment. She lived there until she died in April 1975.

Eula's service was held on April 24, 1975. Mildred's final note to her was sent on April 8, 1975:

Dear Mom:
It was my joy to be able to see you even though I know that you were in much pain and wanted so much to be strong enough to talk more, eat, and most of all get back to your lovely little apartment. I am afraid that I was not as clean as you are, but I don't think I damaged the apartment (smiles). You are a remarkable woman. I know that you feel quite pained and weak, but I do hope that you feel less pain now. How good that you had all of your children visit you. You see how important you are to us. We are all well and hope that you are feeling better. We all love you, Mom[28]

Bernice remembers the day of the funeral[29]:
Mama and I were very close. After her funeral, I went home to lay down in my bedroom, and my husband CJ was with me. I was not sleeping. I remember looking at the door, and I saw her [Eula] standing in the doorway of my bedroom looking at me. I knew she was dead. She was a ghost. She came to let me know that she was all right. I saw her turn and walk out. My husband heard the front door slam and

jumped up. I didn't hear the door slam, but I know it was her leaving. And I was all right after that (see Figure 7.2: Photograph of Eula Sirls, funeral program, 1975).

There were several defining events involving race that Mildred experienced in the 1950s in Los Angeles[30]*:*

When I arrived in Los Angeles in 1955, Emmett Till had just been murdered and hanged for allegedly whistling at a White woman.[31] I attended a church where his mother spoke shortly after his death in 1955. I recall later that when I was discussing this in a social welfare course and mentioned Emmett Till's mother describing his brutalized body in detail, several students challenged me that this was a lie, including the few Black students in my class. Fortunately, I had the *Jet Magazine* photo and article explaining the details of the murder. I made copies for the students to see.[32]

I think this incident had a great impact on me, and I became active in the Unitarian Church. During this time, the House Un-American Activities Committee was very actively looking for communists or communist sympathizers. I was now a member of the Unitarian Church (a very liberal organization) in which several people, including the minister, were being called before the House Un-American Committee. This was a dark period in U.S. history when one could easily be called before the committee. During that time, almost anyone who applied for a position was required to complete a form indicating if they were now or ever had been a member of the Communist Party. I hesitated to complete the form because of my involvement with the Unitarian Church in Los Angeles, which had been labeled communist by the House Un-American Activities Committee.[33]

When I lived in Los Angeles, I took a trip to Kansas City, Missouri, and Indianapolis, Indiana, in 1956. En route, I stopped at some place in Missouri at a restaurant for food. As I entered, all of the eyes of the White men stared at me, and the server said, "We don't serve niggers." Scared to death, I rushed to my car and drove like a racecar driver to get out of there.

On that same trip, I planned to stay in a hotel in St. Louis to rest. I'd decided that I'd better call before I arrived and make a reservation, because I thought that if I simply appeared at the hotel without a reservation I would be told that they had no vacancies. I called and reserved a room at a rather nice—and safe, I thought—hotel. Before I went to the hotel, however, I decided to check with another hotel near the one where I'd made the reservation. I parked in front of the hotel and got out of my car. As I walked to the hotel entrance, a uniformed Black man asked what I wanted. When I told him I wanted a room for the night, he responded, "Blacks are not allowed to stay here."

I got into my car and continued on to the hotel where I had a reservation. Upon arriving at the hotel, I parked and went with my luggage to the reception desk. I said I'd made a reservation and gave the gentleman the reservation number. Before checking, he said that he had no such reservation. I assured him that I had called a few hours ago and made the reservation. He asked me to wait until he checked. I waited about 30 minutes. There were no other people coming to check in, so I decided to approach the desk again. I knocked on the desk several times, and no one answered. Needless to say, I was scared now. I went back and sat in the lobby for a few minutes. Then, I went to the pay phone to try to find the National Association for the Advancement of Colored People and call their office. I tried several times but got no answer. I knew no one in St. Louis.

About to give up, I approached the desk once more and was given a room number and key. Relieved, hungry, tired, and scared, I rushed to my room and locked the door. I was starving, but did not dare enter the restaurant and instead ordered room service. Shortly afterward, there was a knock at the door and an African-American man entered, surprised to see a Black lady. He said he was surprised and inquired if I was the wife of a baseball player. He said the people at the desk must have thought I was the wife of a ballplayer, because they never permitted any other Blacks in the hotel. I smiled without answering—"Let sleeping dogs lie." Now I knew why they eventually assigned me a room. I hardly slept that night and quietly left as soon as I saw daylight.

Mildred's niece, Debbie (Era's daughter), remembers Mildred's visit. She shares that she was a young girl, about six or seven years old, when Mildred visited. Mildred took her to see a movie—maybe, Roy Rogers—and to a nice restaurant. She said that Mildred wanted to show her what was possible in the world so that she could have something to aspire to attain in the world. Debbie said, "That is just how Aunt Mildred was…. always wanting to help others be better"[34] (see Figure 7.3: Photograph of Mildred in Los Angeles, circa 1950s).

Detroit

Mildred lived in Detroit from 1959 to 1962. She describes her experiences with employment discrimination and housing discrimination. She also discusses her decision to apply to the University of Michigan to pursue a doctorate degree and her subsequent denial of admission, perhaps because of her race. As a result of the denial, she decided to apply initially to the advanced degree program—not the doctoral program—at the University of Pittsburgh and was subsequently accepted[35]:

After completing a year at All People's Church, I was not pleased with the quality of work and decided to take another job at All Nations Foundation in Los

Angeles. I found myself very involved in the agency, but organizational problems and lack of social work professionalism caused me to seek employment elsewhere.

Since I lived in dire poverty until I graduated from high school and essentially only saw the rural South, I vowed to take jobs in different states and cities to broaden my experience. I was living in Los Angeles, California, when I decided to seek employment in another state. I had decided that since I had limited experience in areas other than Texas and Missouri, where I experienced racism and discrimination rearing its ugly head, I would seek residence in other areas as a woman.

I had a very good friend in Detroit, Pat Pilling, who had encouraged me to come there. The position for which I applied was with the River Rouge Community Center in Michigan.[36] When I applied for the position, I had to write, "I am not now and never have been a member of the Communist Party." I wrote it and then scratched it out, hoping nobody would call the police on me. When I arrived for my interview, I was told that the position available was that of Director of the Ecourse Community Center, not River Rouge. I was soon to learn that the Ecourse Center was located in a Black town adjacent to River Rouge, a White town. I immediately knew what the situation was but had made a conscious decision not to get my dander up at this point. While I knew that the switch had been made when the board and director learned that I was Black, I simply accepted the position at Ecourse without protest. I'd decided to carefully select my battles. While I did not object to working with African-Americans, I objected to the obvious discrimination. I did not raise questions because I had prepared myself for a position there and accepted what I was offered.

I was asked to be a field instructor for the University of Michigan School of Social Work and was assigned Black students only.[37] I made no complaint. I knew what was happening. Since I had decided that I would only work a few years in a social work position, I settled down for two years. I was supposed to develop recreation programs which didn't satisfy me. I found the experience extremely unprofessional and a waste of my time.

I made some great friends in Detroit. I was active in the Unitarian Church and found life there satisfying in most respects. Most of my White friends were in the liberal-radical category. While in Michigan (living in Detroit), I became active in protest marches—protesting a major store that did not permit Blacks to try on clothes.

Mildred remembers her experience with discrimination and segregation while trying to go on vacation with her good friend, Pat Pilling, in 1962[38]:

I remember another trip—a vacation with my friend, Pat Pilling, an anthropologist I'd met in Los Angeles, and her children. We were denied many vacation places because of my color/race. We were both so shocked and angry about the discrimination that we decided to write a journal article about it.[39]

Pat shares in the article the challenges that they experienced based on race. The abstract states:

Finding suitable cottage accommodation for a week-long summer vacation is normally easy if one makes a reservation some months in advance. This situation, however, may be drastically changed when one of the party is Negro, as my friend Mildred Sirls and I found when we tried to obtain temporary housing in southwestern Michigan for ourselves and my three children in August of 1962. Somewhat naively, we had thought that it would not be too difficult to find a cottage or resort that would accept our interracial group in the North. But we were wrong.

The article notes that when Mildred and Pat shared their decisions to vacation together with their friends, both Black and White friends suggested that Mildred and Pat say that Mildred was the maid or Pat's children's nurse. Both Pat and Mildred chose to be authentic and honor their relationship as friends. To secure a resort, Pat and Mildred wrote separate letters to 16 resorts requesting accommodations. Pat's letter did not disclose race. Mildred's did disclose her race. In response to Pat's letter, 8 resorts indicated they had vacancies. None of those same resorts indicated a vacancy in response to Mildred's letter. Mildred and Pat eventually found a private cottage. Had they relied on public places, they probably would not have been able to vacation together. As Pat concludes in the article, "Discrimination in public accommodations in Michigan makes ease of travelling for Negro families still very remote" (Pilling, 1964, p. 201).

Mildred decided it was time for a transition and to continue her education. She shares about her experience applying to the University of Michigan and the University of Pittsburgh:

At some point in my life I had made a decision that I wanted to get as much education as possible. I enjoyed learning and being challenged. At that time, I had two Master's degrees and several years of social work practice. I sought information about admission to the University of Michigan School of Social Work. The application requested two pieces of information that I did not feel were relevant. The application form at the time included racial identification. Innocent me, I identified myself as Black. I checked "Negro." The form also requested information as to whether I was then or had ever been a member of a communist organization. The question was required by the House Un-American Activities Committee. I refused to answer it.

I received a letter simply informing me that my application was not accepted. No reason was given explaining why my application had been refused. This was despite the fact that I had a Master's degree in Religion from Butler University, a reputable university; a Master's degree in Social Work from Indiana University;

four years of social work practice; and was serving as a social work supervisor for the University of Michigan. I accepted my fate and did not protest or inquire as to why I was not accepted into the University of Michigan School of Social Work. I did not give up on my plan to enroll in a university to get my doctorate degree in social work. I sucked up the rejection, and it did not discourage me. I thought and thought, and then I realized, *Oh yes, I wrote "Negro" where the form included "racial identification." Was that the reason?* Undeterred, I decided that next time I would not identify my race even if the form required it.

At that time, I was a field instructor for several Wayne State University students also at Ecourse and had contact with a professor in their School of Social Work. I had a good relationship with her. She suggested I apply for the doctoral program at the University of Pittsburgh where she had received her Master's degree. I asked to use her name as a reference and filled out the application. I did not check race as the form required. I'd been bitten once and learned my lesson. Now having lost my confidence after being rejected by one School of Social Work, I'd lowered my expectations and applied for their advanced certificate/diploma program rather than the doctoral degree. I did not send a photo as they requested, feeling then that University of Michigan had rejected me because of my race. I thought I would not again give another university the noose with which to hang me.

I was invited to come for an interview. My friend invited me to ride with her to Pittsburgh for my interview. She said she would have offered me to stay with her, but hers was a large family and everyone would be home for the holidays. She suggested that I make a reservation for the Negro YWCA, as they rented rooms. The White YWCA did not rent to Blacks or permit them to become members and use their facilities. I also was told that White cab companies did not serve Blacks. I was instructed to contact a jitney (unlicensed) to get to the university for my interview.

As I was preparing for my interview, I was quite prepared to be rejected and was sure in my own mind that the person who would receive me would be White. When I arrived for my interview, the White secretary took me to the office of the Assistant Dean. To my chagrin, she was a light-skinned, freckled-faced African-American woman. She was a tall, beautiful, and kind middle-aged mulatto lady. Her name was Dr. Mary Ella Robertson.[40] I was to learn that she had received her doctorate from Pitt. She had a major impact on my development.

When I told her why I'd not sent my photo, we both laughed knowingly. She urged me to apply for the doctoral program rather than for the advanced degree, as my credentials suggested that I met the requirements. I lacked confidence and insisted on enrolling for the advanced degree program. Unable to convince me, she accepted the image I had of myself and said that at any time I could write a scholarly paper, which she would present to a committee for my acceptance into the PhD program. When I received my acceptance letter, I celebrated and began to plan for my next step.

Key Lessons

1. *College was rarely an option for poor sharecropping families who were barely surviving and needed income from every family member who could work. The quote below reflects the reality for African-Americans in the 1940s[41]:*

   In 1940 most black men and women lived out of common view in rural communities chiefly in the South. Approximately 90 percent lived in poverty (Jaynes & Williams, 1989, p. 277). Their annual earnings were less than half those of whites. The education they received was markedly inferior in quality. African American children in the South went to predominantly black schools in which (on average) pupil-teacher ratios were one-quarter greater than those in white schools, school terms were 10 percent shorter, and black teachers were paid half the salary of white teachers (Card & Krueger, 1992, p. 167). The median amount of education received by blacks aged 25–29 was about seven years (Jaynes & Williams, 1989, p. 334). Only 12 percent of blacks age 25–29 had completed high school; less than 2 percent could claim a college degree (U.S. Department of Education, 1997, p. 17).

   In the context of this reality, it was rare for Mildred to complete high school, yet alone go to college. Mildred's ability to go to college meant a difficult choice for her mother who recognized that it would be a hardship for her and her two daughters, Bernice and Mozelle. Milded's mom eventually supported Mildred and Mildred was able to attend Jarvis Christian College.

2. *Jarvis Christian College, as a historically Black college and university, played a critical role in Mildred's path. In fact, Historically Black Colleges and Universities (HBCUs) have provided undergraduate education for 75 percent of all African-Americans who have a doctorate degree (United States Department of Education, 1991). There were very few Black graduate students in the 1950s. Mildred's opportunity to pursue a master's degree at Butler and Indiana University as a Black woman was indeed pioneering. In the 1950s, only 2.4 percent of Black women had completed four or more years of college (Snyder, 1993).*

3. *The role of maids was an integral part of the experience of many Black women. They were not only maids to Whites, but also to Black families. Mildred's*

experience with the Blackburns reflects the reality that there were well-to-do African-Americans who had power, prestige, influence, and wealth. The Blackburns, however, provided a crucial opportunity for Mildred to continue her education at the graduate level and also experience Jamaica.

4. *Legalized discrimination and segregation in the United States in the 1950s was humiliating, confusing, and frightening for African-Americans. The inability to comfortably travel and sit on a bus, the difficulty of reserving hotel rooms, the inability to eat at restaurants, the maintenance of cross-racial friendships, the discrimination in employment, and the segregation of education were all realities of daily life. Ironically, the fields of religion and social work, including missionary work, were full of inconsistency. Despite a mission of serving and helping others, many community organizations and Christian organizations sanctioned racial segregation and its inhumanity. From the segregated bus trip to Jamaica, to the inability to receive scholarships from White organizations, to only being able to work in Black-only organizations, Mildred constantly faced barriers, even in the field of social work.*

5. *Every part of life had a barrier: education, housing, employment, and social relationships. Each act of injustice required a decision about whether to protest or accept. "Testing" was part of how African-Americans were able to prove discrimination and decide if they wanted to mount a legal challenge (Pilling, 1964). Testing required partnerships with Whites to prove that a White person was able to obtain access to opportunities that were denied to African-Americans. Mildred's vacation to Michigan with her friend Pat was an example of pushing the boundaries of the law and society in deciding to vacation together as an interracial group.*

6. *Mildred's acts of resistance and "community organizing" during her trip to Jamaica reflect her early efforts to speak out against injustice. Her decision to not send a picture with her application to the University of Pittsburgh was also another act of resistance. Mildred would continue to speak out against injustice as she pursued a career in academia.*

7. *Mildred was deeply loyal to her family. In Los Angeles, she continued to support and sacrifice for her mother—allowing her mother to have her bedroom while she slept on the couch in the living room. She took in Bernice and her children, and offered to support Bernice in obtaining her high school credentials.*

Photos

Figure 7.1: Mildred Sirls, Jamaica, 1952
Source: M. Pratt.

Figure 7.2: Eula Sirls, funeral program, 1975
Source: M. Pratt.

Figure 7.3: Mildred Sirls, Los Angeles, circa 1950s
Source: M. Pratt.

Notes

1. (M. Pratt, personal communication, n.d.).
2. (M. Pratt, personal communication, n.d.).
3. (M. Pratt, personal communication, n.d.). For more on the history of Jarvis Christian College, see Jarvis Christian College Facts (n.d.) and Jenkins (n.d.).
4. (Hughes, n.d.).
5. Eugenia Powell died in January 2013. For more about her life, see Dignity Memorial (n.d.).
6. For more about Camps Farthest Out and its founder, see "Glenn Clark" (n.d).
7. For more on the life of Bayard Rustin, see Singer and Kates (2003).
8. For more about Cry, the Beloved Country, see Korda (1951).
9. For more on Cleo Blackburn, see Cleo W. Blackburn (n.d.) and Indiana University-Purdue University Indianapolis (n.d.). For more on the Flanner House, see Flanner House (n.d.).
10. The *Crisis* magazine mentions "Inez Sirls" from Jarvis as the highest honors winner. The commencement exercises for Jarvis lists winners of awards and departmental certificates.

Mildred Sirls received the Scholarship Award, the Young Lady Religious Award, the Religion Department Certificates, and the V.L. Robinson Award given to the All-Around Work Student in Ida V. Jarvis Hall (M. Pratt, personal communication, n.d.). For more information, see Ivy (1951).

11. (M. Pratt, personal communication, n.d.).

12. For more about Butler University's School of Religion and its relationship with Disciples of Christ and African-American Students, see McCarter (n.d.).

13. For more on Effie Burford, see Global Ministries (2010).

14. See Mildred's thesis, Sirls (1952).

15. (M. Pratt, personal communication, n.d.).

16. For information on the Jamaican hurricane, see Clarke (2004) and Dealy and Dealy (2007). For more information on Disciples of Christ in Jamaica, see Holloway (2011).

17. (M. Pratt, personal communication, n.d.).

18. (M. Pratt, personal communication, n.d.).

19. (M. Pratt, personal communication, n.d.). Group photo is part of a 1952 newspaper article from the Jamaican Gleaner about the mission trip.

20. (M. Pratt, personal communication, n.d.).

21. For more about the history of the school and its name change, see Indiana University (n.d.).

22. For more on the Philanthropic Educational Organization, see P.E.O. International (n.d.).

23. (Illinois State University, n.d.).

24. (M. Pratt-Clarke, personal communication, June, 19, 2013).

25. (M. Pratt, personal communication, n.d.).

26. (M. Pratt, personal communication, n.d.).

27. (B. Miller, personal communication, June 13, 2013).

28. (M. Pratt, personal communication, n.d.).

29. (B. Miller, personal communication, June 13, 2013).

30. (M. Pratt, personal communication, n.d.).

31. For more on Emmett Till, see "The Murder of Emmett Till" (n.d.) and "The Face of Emmett Till" (2009).

32. Public Broadcasting Service (n.d.).

33. For more about the Unitarian Church experiences with the House on Un-American Activities, see Unitarian Universalist Association of Congregations (1961, n.d.).

34. (M. Pratt-Clarke, personal communication, n.d.).

35. (M. Pratt, personal communication, n.d.).

36. River Rouge Museum (n.d.) and Dowdell (1952).

37. University of Michigan Official Publication (1963–1964) lists Mildred Sirls as a field instruction supervisor from September 1961 to September 1962 at Rouge-Ecourse United Centers, River Rouge.

38. (M. Pratt, personal communication, January 16, 2002).

39. (Pilling, 1964).

40. For more on Dr. Mary Ella Robertson, see Williams (2010) and "Dr. Robertson Attains Goal" (n.d.).

41. (Bowen & Bok, 1998, p. 1; Hout, 2004, p. 263).

References

Blackburn, C. W. (n.d.). *Wikipedia*. Retrieved May 2, 2013 from http://en.wikipedia.org/w/index.php?title=Cleo_W._Blackburn&oldid=549343426

Bowen, W., & Bok, D. (1998). *The shape of the river: Long term consequences of considering race in college and university admissions*. Princeton, NJ: Princeton University Press.

Card, D., & Krueger, A. (1992). School quality and the relative earnings of Blacks and Whites. *The Quarterly Journal of Economics, 107*, 151–200.

Clarke, K. (2004). Hurricane Charlie revisited: August 17, 1951. *Jamaica Gleaner*. Retrieved September 1, 2013 from http://jamaica-gleaner.com/gleaner/20040811/lead/lead2.html

Dealy, M., & Dealy, M. M. O. (2007). Jamaican Hurricane. *The Ough Family Website*. Retreived from http://www.family-ough.co.nz/Jamaican_Storm.html

Dignity Memorial. (n.d.). *In Memory of Eugenia Sarah Powell*. Retrieved September 1, 2013 from http://obits.dignitymemorial.com/dignity-memorial/obituary.aspx?n=Eugenia-Powell&lc=4946&pid=162271172&uuid=8bfdd303-a5e9-41bf-bd4e-6f067176ed7b

Dowdell, D. (1952). *A history of the Rouge-Ecorse United Centers*. Detroit, MI: Wayne University School of Social Work.

Dr. Robertson attains goal of being a social worker. (1965, December 31). *Pittsburgh Post-Gazette*. Retrieved September 1, 2013 from http://news.google.com/newspapers?nid=1129&dat=19651231&id=251RAAAAIBAJ&sjid=kmwDAAAAIBAJ&pg=3727,4906864

Flanner House. (n.d.). *Flanner House: History as of 1946*. Retrieved August 5, 2013 from http://www.flannerhouse.com/about/History-1946/default.aspx

Glenn Clark: Founder of The Camps Farthest Out. (n.d.). Retrieved from http://glennclark.wwwhubs.com

Global Ministries. (2010, January 21). *Death of Effie Burford, Former Missionary and Board Member*. Retrieved from http://globalministries.org/news/losses/death-of-effie-burford.html

Holloway, C. (2011, July). *World Convention: Jamaica*. Retrieved from http://www.worldconvention.org/resources/profiles/jamaica/

Hout, M. (2004). Educational progress for African Americans and Latinos since the 1950s. In G. Loury, T. Modood, & S. Teles (Eds.), *Ethnicity and social mobility in comparative perspective* (pp. 262–297). Cambridge, MA: Cambridge University Press.

Hughes, L. (n.d.). *The Negro mother*. Retrieved August 5, 2013 from http://www.autodidactproject.org/other/Hughes-NegroMother.html

Illinois State University. (n.d.). *Mildred Pratt Student Assistance Fund*. Retrieved September 1, 2013 from http://scholarshipfinder.illinoisstate.edu/scholarships/Mildred_Pratt_Student_Assistance_Fund.shtml

Indiana University. (n.d.). *Indiana University School of Social Work: Program history*. Retrieved August 5, 2013 from http://socialwork.iu.edu/about_iussw/program-history.php

Indiana University-Purdue University Indianapolis. (n.d.). Blackburn House. Retrieved September 1, 2013, from http://www.iupui.edu/spirit/campus/blackburnhouse.html

Ivy, J. W. (1951, March). *The Crisis*. New York, NY: The Crisis Publishing Company, Inc.

Jarvis Christian College. (n.d.). *Jarvis Christian College Facts*. Retrieved September 1, 2013 from http://www.jarvis.edu/jcc-facts/

Jaynes, G. D., & Williams, R. (1989). *A common destiny: Blacks and American society*. Washington, DC: National Academy Press.

Jenkins, R. (n.d.). *Jarvis Christian College*. Retrieved December 31, 2013 from http://www.tsa online.org/handbook/online/articles/kbj06

Korda, Z. [producer] (1951). *Cry, the Beloved Country*. London: London Film Company

McCarter, J. (n.d.). Back to Their Roots: The Butler-CTS Partnership. *The Butler Collegian*. Retrieved December 26, 2013 from https://thebutlercollegian.com/2013/11/back-to-their-roots-the-butler-cts-partnership/

P.E.O. International. (n.d.). *Women helping women reach for the stars*. Retrieved September 1, 2013 from http://www.peointernational.org

Pilling, P. (1964). Segregation: Cottage rental in Michigan. *Phylon, 25*(2), 191–201.

Public Broadcasting Service. (n.d.). *The murder of Emmett Till*. Retrieved September 1, 2013 from http://www.pbs.org/wgbh/amex/till/filmmore/pt.html

River Rouge Museum. (n.d.). Retrieved September 1, 2013 from http://www.riverrougemu seum.com/1950SepOct.pdf

Singer, B. [producer] & Kates, N. [producer], 2003. *Brother Outsider*. [Film].

Sirls, M. I. (1952). *Some psychological and philosophical aspects of Christian prayer*. Indianapolis, IN: Butler University.

Snyder, T. (1993). *120 Years of American education: A statistical portrait*. Washington, DC: National Center for Education Statistics. Retrieved from https://nces.ed.gov/pubs93/93442.pdf

The Face of Emmett Till. (2009, May 14). *Daily Kos*. Retrieved August 5, 2013 from http://www.dailykos.com/story/2009/05/14/731205/-The-Face-of-Emmett-Till-UPDATED

The Murder of Emmett Till. (n.d.). Retrieved September 1, 2013 from http://www.pbs.org/wgbh/amex/till/filmmore/pt.html

Unitarian Universalist Association of Congregations. (1961). *Abolition of the House Un-American Activities Committee and the Senate Internal Security Sub-Committee*. Retrieved from http://www.uua.org/statements/statements/7976.shtml

Unitarian Universalist Association of Congregations. (n.d.). *Rev. Stephen Fritchman and the House Un-American Activities Committee*. Retrieved August 5, 2013 from http://www.uua.org/re/tapestry/adults/resistance/workshop9/workshopplan/handouts/182553.shtml

United States Department of Education. (1991). *Historically Black Colleges and Universities and Higher Education Desegregation*. Retrieved March 25, 2017 from https://www2.ed.gov/about/offices/list/ocr/docs/hq9511.html

United States Department of Education. (1997). *Digest of Educational Statistics*.

University of Michigan Official Publication, General Register. (1963–1964). Ann Arbor, MI: University of Michigan Libraries.

Williams, M. (2010, June 4). *Kent School of Social Work: Remembering Dr. Mary Ella Robertson*. Retrieved from http://kentschoolofsocialwork.blogspot.com/2010/06/remembering-dr-mary-ella-rob ertson.html

CHAPTER EIGHT

Pittsburgh and the PhD

Pittsburgh was the sunshine in Mildred's life from 1962 to 1969. It was where she met her husband, Theodore Pratt, in 1964; where she had her two children in 1966 and 1967; and where she received her doctorate degree in 1969 from the University of Pittsburgh School of Social Work. Pittsburgh was also a place very much reflective of the segregation, separation, and discrimination in America. Because Mildred had a master's degree, she held a faculty/instructor position in the School of Social Work. Thus, Pittsburgh was the start of her journey into the academy as a faculty member. At the University of Pittsburgh, Mildred continued to fight racism, sexism, discrimination, and segregation, including engaging in activism in response to the assassination of Dr. Martin Luther King, Jr., in 1968. As she stated in a letter relating to the role of race in public health matters involving her son, "Today it is no secret that questions are being raised daily about Negroes being denied their civil rights…in other words, being discriminated against glaringly or subtly."[1]

Marriage

Mildred shares her love story of meeting her husband, Theodore Pratt, in Pittsburgh from A Tribute to Love[2]:

One morning in August 1964, I crossed Forbes Avenue in Pittsburgh to take clothes to the cleaners. I was in a hurry to get to work at the University of Pittsburgh School of Social Work. At the small cleaners, I found a handsome African man [Ted] arguing in British English with a Chinese clerk who was arguing in Chinese-accented English about whether or not the pants Ted was asking to have cleaned were brown or green. An extremely animated conversation punctuated by hearty laughter was taking place as I tried to rush to get my clothes checked in. True to his form as I was later to learn, Ted brought me into the conversation to agree with him that the pants were green; I did not agree and as I hastily left, I thought, "What a nut." I was later to learn that if he was a nut, he was an extremely intelligent one as he was enrolled at the Carnegie Institute of Technology studying for a PhD in Nuclear Physics. I was later to learn that humor was a part of his character and he enjoyed sharing humor with others.

I hastily left my clothes to be cleaned and went to work clearly not expecting to encounter Ted again. In August 1964, I had an occasion to take a weekend drive to Indianapolis. Upon my return on Sunday evening around 9:00 or 10:00 p.m., I was hungry and walked across the street to a restaurant. Not many people were in the restaurant and I sat alone at a table a considerable distance from others. I had not observed that Ted was in the restaurant until I was leaving when I heard this familiar voice say, "Hi, what's your name? Where do you live?" I told him and went to pay my bill. (I think he had asked the clerk of the cleaners for my address and wanted confirmation). I observed that he was seated with an Indian, whom I later learned was his good friend, Roy, from India, also studying for his PhD in Physics.

I went about my business. Several days later, I received a phone call from this person [Ted], identifying himself as the person who had spoken to me in the restaurant. We spoke a bit about ourselves and he asked to visit me. He came for a visit and we saw each other every day up to our wedding date, November 24, 1964. I think he was attracted to me because he pursued me. I was attracted to his humor, hearty laughter, intelligence, and the fact that he was African and handsome. He also was quite a gentleman.

After our first meeting we had several meals in his one-room apartment where he had one pot and a few other kitchen supplies. He cooked great food, particularly fish stew. We both ate from the same pot, which I was later to learn was an important aspect of Sierra Leone culture. When we had meals at my house, we used separate plates, about which he made no comment. However, after our marriage, this became our first argument when he wanted to eat from my plate. It was a culture clash. You see, I grew up in rural poverty in East Texas in the depression in an atmosphere where, a sibling who dared take what little food you had from your plate, was in for a fight. With seven other siblings, each had to protect their food.

Anyway, this matter was resolved because the idea was not that Ted always wanted to eat from my plate but "sharing a plate" of food for him was a romantic interlude.

Our dating consisted of long walks in the evening after he'd graded his paper, sharing our home-cooked meals, and frequent long night parties with other African students. These were very festive occasions, albeit in small apartments. There was always great African food and drinks, along with African music and dancing. There was also laughter and heated discussion about politics in the various countries, spiced with plans to return home and improve conditions.

I attended his faculty affairs and he mine. I recall one occasion when we had just met and I was to attend a small faculty home party. One of the unmarried faculty members had asked me to ride with him. When I told Ted, he said, "I will take you and collect you!"

Almost every day we had lengthy telephone conversations when he was at the C.I.T. [Carnegie Institute of Technology] Nuclear Laboratory in Saxonburg, about a two-hour drive from Pittsburgh where he was conducting research for his dissertation. Other evenings he would visit me upon his return from the lab. We would talk at length about his work, problems, etc. Interestingly enough, we spoke little about our families prior to marriage.

I was now 36 years old and resigned to the fact that I'd never get married, because not only did I not have any prospects, but [I] had few real dates. I had been totally involved with my education (I now had three degrees) and had decided that if I were not married before I received my PhD, I'd go live in a country in Africa or in Jamaica (where I'd spent a couple of months on a project). Since I had always been interested in meeting new people and exploring new places, after graduation seemed the perfect time. Now, with my first real "steady boyfriend," it seemed that my life would take a new direction.

One evening in October or November, Ted came over in a more serious, less jovial mood. He suggested that we go for a drive. We drove around for about an hour, and he stopped the car on a street in Squirrel Hill. He suggested with not much formality that we get married. At this time he didn't know my age, nor I his, and I told him that I was 36. I had some idea based on what he'd told me about his education experience that he was younger than me. It turned out that he was 29. While he appeared surprised that I was 36 years old, he said that that did not matter to him. My concern was that if he wanted children, I might not be able to have [them] at my age. I, of course, accepted the proposal. We discussed marriage plans during the next few weeks. The length of time between our first meeting and the marriage proposal was one month.

We settled on…Thanksgiving weekend because we'd have relatively free schedules. He wanted only a ceremony in the courthouse. I convinced him that we should have something a bit more formal. I set about to find a place. Since neither of us were church members nor had no apartment large enough, it was difficult to find a place for the wedding. I had attended the Unitarian Church a few times and thought I could ask the minister to perform our marriage vows. There was a Jewish Community Center a block and a half from my apartment in the University of Pittsburgh area. I arranged for the wedding at the Jewish Community Center, and the Unitarian minister agreed to perform the marriage vows. Neither of us felt strongly about having relatives present, and, since we were not having an elaborate wedding, we invited a few close friends.

I spent a few hours shopping for my dress. We went to the Marriage License Bureau and Ted brought no money, so I paid for the license and never let him forget it! On the same day, he shopped for a suit. He insisted on going to the cheapest store in town for the cheapest suit he could find—the least of his worries. My colleagues and friends in the Social Work Department had a wedding shower for me, and we had a great time. Ted dropped me off and "collected" me.

The day of the wedding, November 24, 1964, was quite eventful. It poured rain all day. My friend from India came to my apartment to get me dressed. I called a cab two hours before we were due to leave to assure that we'd have one. With the pouring rain, cabs were in great demand. While the Jewish Community Center was only [a block and a half] away, taking my car was no solution, because there was no place to park near the building. We had planned to walk, but with the downpour of rain that wasn't not possible. At the time the cab was due, it had not arrived. We waited so long that I was afraid I would miss my wedding. I was desperate. I thought I might find an apartment dweller [leaving] the…underground garage…and we would hitchhike a ride—which, to the driver's chagrin, is just what we did. Everyone was there when we arrived with our story. Ted and his friend Kojo both laughed when we told our story. They were having fun in their apartment while we anxiously waited for a cab.

Honeymoon? What is that for two busy PhD students? We'd booked a hotel in a nearby town, but Ted spent most of the time studying for his exam. We were married for 32 years until Ted's death on October 30, 1996 (see Figure 8.1: Photograph of Ted and Mildred, Pittsburgh, 1964).

Mildred shares her memories of segregation, discrimination, and finding housing in Pittsburgh[3]:

As I reflect on some of the experiences at the University of Pittsburgh during the 1960s, I recall that life there often reflected the turmoil of society at large. Housing was a problem for African-Americans. We were directed to find housing (usually rooms) in African-American neighborhoods. When I first came to Pittsburgh, Dr. Robertson informed me that housing was segregated and gave me the name of a couple who rented efficiency apartments in their house. Dr. Robertson resided in a house that had an attic apartment. I would be living in a house next to hers, which was in the upper level of the famous Hill District. I lived in the Upper Hill District of Pittsburgh which was all Black. I was taking residence in a two-story house of a middle-class Black couple. The owners lived downstairs and I had an efficiency on the second floor, with another roomer on the same floor. I was only about five or six blocks uphill from the University of Pittsburgh. Black people couldn't live in certain neighborhoods, so you had to find Black people with whom you could live. I recall living there until I earned enough money to rent a small university apartment. I qualified because I was a PhD student and a part-time assistant professor.

I found it interesting how when I decided to seek other non-university housing, I was told that I'd have to go with an apartment in the Hill District or another area for Blacks. I can't recall that there were any desirable non-university owned apartments for African-Americans. I do have a memory of the visiting professors and students from other countries, including India, being perplexed in understanding why I couldn't find decent housing because of my color. I lived in the university apartment until I married.

Once I was married, I was told that I could no longer live there. So, Ted and I set out to seek housing. He was living in a one-room apartment. I do recall that we could live in an apartment owned by Ted's university. We lived there until we had two children and then it became too small. Ted had been awarded his PhD in Physics from Carnegie Institute of Technology and had taken a position as an Assistant Professor at Hampton Institute as a way of paying back since Hampton Institute had given him a full-time scholarship and assistantship when he first came to the United States from Sierra Leone. Ted made a deliberate decision to go to Hampton Institute. He only taught there for a year and decided that once I earned my PhD we would seek a university where each of us could get a position. As he was preparing to go to Hampton, Virginia, he thought we should move to a larger place within walking distance of University of Pittsburgh.

A White couple whom we knew told us that they were soon moving from a duplex in Squirrel Hill, a primarily White Jewish neighborhood. When they moved, we called the landlord to inquire about renting the duplex. The gentleman described the place to us and agreed to show it. My husband spoke with a British accent from Sierra Leone in West Africa. When we arrived to see the apartment and the gentleman saw our color, he immediately said it was taken without showing it to us. We left, not accepting the lie.

There was an organization in Pittsburgh that was actively fighting housing segregation. We made contact with this group. A campaign was launched to "test" the practice of housing discrimination, which was rampant in the city. They had several people call to ascertain if the duplex was vacant and if they could see it. Then we called the manager and informed him that we understood that the duplex was not rented. He now simply said that he'd rent the place to us. We got the duplex.

We were delighted to have a three-room, two-story house (4531 Forbes Avenue, #304). We only owned one car and Ted had taken it with him. I found a great babysitter to take care of the children. I managed most times, but during the winter, sometimes I had to take a cab for Blacks, called a jitney, or walk to take the bus. White cab companies would not serve Blacks. I used the jitney every Saturday to go to the laundry mat and other places. I also used the streetcar but usually walked to school on the great Pittsburgh cobblestone streets.

When I was in Pittsburgh, there were very few restaurants that Black people could go to. There were some people from India and China. I took them to a restaurant, and they said the foreign people could come in but I couldn't. The restaurant informed us that they did not serve Negroes. I was disturbed, but we left without being served. These friends just couldn't understand the crazy business. Then we found a restaurant that served all students, so that's where we went.

Children

Mildred talks about raising young children[4]:

When Ted and I were considering marriage, I told him that I was 36 years of age. At that time women were not advised to have children at that age because it was highly likely that they would be physically or mentally disabled. Ted told me that he did not think that was a problem and we'd cross that bridge when and if we got there. Well, it turns out that we had a healthy son and daughter—Awadagin and Menah. They were one year, one month, and one day apart, as they enjoyed announcing when we were together with friends. I recall that on one occasion we were having dinner with Awadagin's friends following one of his performances in Nashville, Tennessee, when they were asked their ages. They each said, "One year, one month, and one day apart." I didn't even have it down to that kind of precision.

Neither Ted nor I had anticipated the kind of logistics that would be involved in caring for infants while each of us worked for our PhD. He was a teaching assistant at Carnegie Institute, and I was a professor at Pittsburgh. It wasn't easy, but we managed with the help of a responsible babysitter and our flexible schedules.

Things went reasonably well with each of us working, conducting research, writing dissertations, and rearing two children.

Upon the birth of her son, Awadagin, Mildred and Ted were immediately forced to confront the issue of race. Mildred raised concerns about the racial questions involving her son in a letter dated May 10, 1966, to the medical clinic in Pittsburgh. In the letter, Mildred wrote the following[5]:

I wish to bring the following distasteful incident to your attention. It all happened when my husband and I decided to avail ourselves of the services of the Child Health Conference. My phone call was transferred from one person to another for a good half hour. Finally, upon my insistence that from my address, my call had been made to the right district office, I was then asked for my race. I handed the phone to my husband, and he questioned the importance of the race issue. The reply was apologetic; the race issue was dropped … other information such as names and ages of parents and baby were asked for and given by me, and an appointment [was] given: May 12th.

Two weeks later I was called, and the race of the baby was asked for and the appointment confirmed. My husband and I are particularly bothered about the race question and, in fact, feel insulted. Whereas we both pay taxes irrespective of our race, color, or creed, and whereas such a public service is offered without regard to race, color, or creed, we wish an official explanation about the importance of race in a health service which is in fact not curative but a preventive one.

Today it is no secret that questions are being raised daily about Negroes being denied their civil rights…in other words, being discriminated against glaringly or subtly. We have no choice but to wonder whether it is not immediately suggestive that our baby, who by chance happens to be born Black, is to be discriminated against in some form or other. This is not an oversensitivity on our part, except that we note with great concern that the race issue is so important as to warrant a second telephone call only for that.

This matter is considered very important to us as residents of Allegheny County, and we hope you will consider it important as to give it your attention and thus satisfy us in the process.

Sincerely yours,

(Mrs.) Mildred Pratt

The reply on May 19th emphasized the Health Department's policy of providing services without regard to race, color, or creed. Unsatisfied, Mildred sent another letter on May 31st, reiterating her concerns about the "rather distasteful subject of race."[6]

The Doctoral Program

Mildred reflects on her experiences at the University of Pittsburgh as both a professor and doctoral student[7]:

I was the only Black person in the advanced degree program, with one lady from India, one lady from Belgium, and three to four White males. All of us ladies were feisty. I had a little money that I'd saved and an assistantship from the Department of Housing and Welfare. I settled in and was performing so well that Dr. Robertson [the Assistant Dean who admitted Mildred] encouraged me to go for the PhD, and I did. I had to write a scholarly paper to be accepted and I was accepted for the PhD program. Dr. Robertson helped me in the doctoral program. She advised me about faculty and how to select dissertation members.

As a student in the School of Social Work at the University of Pittsburgh, I experienced racism and sexism. During a doctoral seminar on community organization when the class was discussing work as a community organizer, the professor said that women shouldn't get involved in community organizing; only males, since it required working with top company executive men.

I was assigned to perform my community organization work experience in an agency located in a large downtown building that housed several executives. I had called the agency director's secretary to set up my appointment. When I arrived at the building and presented myself to the desk clerk, telling her that I had an appointment with a gentleman in community organization in a particular office, she immediately informed me that I had no such appointment and no Black person was permitted in the building. I reported it to the professor, who called about the matter. The professor made other arrangements for me. I was assigned to an all-Black office and area to perform my community organizing practice. I did not complain, but accepted the assignment.

When I was hired to teach a course practicum, I learned that one agency would not accept Black students. In discussion of the matter with faculty, I proposed that if Black students were not accepted, then no students should go. The local YWCA had one agency for Blacks and one for Whites. The local settlement houses would not permit Blacks to swim in the swimming pool. We protested.

I recall one class, the History of Social Welfare, with Dr. Samuel Mencher, who was an eminent scholar in his field. It was widely held among students that this was the course with a latent motive of screening out candidates. In the first exam for which we all studied together, I made the only "A" in the class. "How did you do it?" they asked. I said I knew the strategy of taking an essay exam: "Focus the most time on the question you know well first." I knew I was not good at statistics.

I also had a course with a Jewish professor, Dr. Joseph Eaton,[8] and he disliked Black people. Among his more extreme views was his belief that Black women should not be anything. The lady from Belgium openly disagreed with the professor and even told him off. She would tell him what she thought. She wasn't afraid of him. I was unfortunate to have this professor assigned to be the chairman of my dissertation committee. On learning that this particular professor would serve such a role on my committee, another faculty member remarked, "Great, because he will be rough on you." What I understood that statement to mean was that he didn't want me to graduate. My dissertation topic was on social welfare system in selected African countries.[9]

Mildred remembers the difficulty of the dissertation process[10]:

My worst situation occurred when I was recovering from surgery [a hysterectomy] and my dissertation PhD chairperson set up an appointment for me to go to his house to discuss the second draft of my dissertation. I drove to his house in 12 feet of snow in Squirrel Hill to discuss the dissertation. He had red on practically every page. A more renowned scholar than he had had suggestions for changes, but nothing like this man. When he finished, I was livid.

As I was preparing to leave, he said, "By the way, will you take my son to the university?" This was in spite of the fact that I had just been released from the hospital for surgery and had my own young children with the babysitter at home. It was in spite of the fact that the snow was 12 feet deep, I'd have to drive up and down Pittsburgh hills, and he had put red marks on practically every page of my dissertation. At that point there was nothing that he could have done to me to deter me from getting my PhD. He had got my dander up! As soon as I got home, I called Ted to tell him about the situation. He told me just to go ahead and make the changes. I swallowed my pride and got to work. Quickly, I did what my chairperson wanted, had the paper retyped, and hid three copies in different places.

I had learned from someone that I should always keep several copies of my dissertation in various places, because both he and I knew of situations in which student's dissertations were deliberately discarded. In fact, I was at a particular office in Illinois State University where a secretary showed me a dissertation in her desk. A professor had deliberately placed the dissertation there, insisting that the student had never submitted it.

I made all of the corrections and prayed that it would be accepted. When I got it back to my chairperson, he approved it. Others thought he was stupid to do these things, but he was in charge. I wanted to write a nasty letter, but my husband said, "No, you got what you wanted," so I didn't do it.

Mildred remembers preparing for her dissertation defense[11]:

The Dean was on my dissertation committee. Ted suggested that I invite the Dean and his wife for a Sierra Leone lunch with us. He came to our house with his wife to meet with me to discuss and hopefully approve my dissertation. We all sat down for a lunch with several Sierra Leone dishes and great wine. After the lunch, the Dean and I sat down, and he examined my dissertation. He approved. Fortunately by this time, all of the other three members had read it and approved.

The final dissertation hearing was held in the Dean's office with me in the hot seat. The committee included my chairperson, a professor of political science from Cuba, a nationally renowned professor of anthropology, and also a nationally renowned social welfare historian who had approved but couldn't be present. The Dean opened the meeting by asking me a few questions, which I answered; however, an impassioned debate began between the chair and the Cuban professor on the issue of "socialism" in developing countries, with Dr. Eaton arguing that it was communism. Suddenly my dissertation defense became a heated argument between two people, and a few others joined. They argued for a long time, and eventually the Dean dismissed me so that the committee could vote. I sweated for about 20 minutes. Finally, the Dean called me in and announced approval!

I received my PhD in April 1969, three years after my marriage to a fine gentleman and the birth of my two children. How did I do it? It was with discipline, determination, and great encouragement from Ted, who asked me constantly how many pages and paragraphs I had written on my dissertation. He wouldn't permit me to give up.

After I was awarded my PhD, my husband took me on a cruise of the Pittsburgh Three Rivers (see Figure 8.2: Photograph of Mildred, University of Pittsburgh graduation, 1969). This was Ted's way of congratulating me for having completed my dissertation and recognizing my birthday.

Community Engagement

Mildred was a pioneer in social work. In a field often dominated by White men in the 1960s, Mildred pushed the boundaries of race, gender, and class in a field that she truly understood to be about understanding and helping those most vulnerable and marginalized in society. Her passion for teaching students to truly understand poverty began at Pitt when, as a faculty member, Mildred conceived a radical idea for the social work department to expose students to issues of race and class. The project involved students living with Black and White families on public assistance for a weekend. Mildred noted the following in her article about the project[12]:

> *College and university students are increasingly demanding relevant education, interaction with society, and involvement in the design of their learning experience. If one accepts this as a fact and deems it essential, then methods and approaches must be devised to achieve these objectives more effectively. One approach to this end is presented in this paper. This approach, while specifically designed for social work students, is considered to be applicable to students of other professions.*

Mildred describes the project[13]*:*

I proposed a course that would get students out into several of the main poverty and distinct ethnic communities to get knowledge about how poor and ethnic minority people lived. When I first proposed this at a faculty meeting, the Dean questioned whether or not poverty existed in Pittsburgh. He resided in an upper-middle-class community where there were few, if any, poor people or ethnic minorities. I developed a detailed course proposal that included these ethnic and economically poor communities. I included two of the predominantly African-American poor communities. I selected four or five communities: the Hill District—an all-Black community where most poor Blacks lived; Homewood/Brushton, a Jewish community; a Polish/German community; and another ethnic community.

The Dean approved the course, and it was interesting and revealing to observe the graduate social work students' reactions to their observations of life in these communities. One student's reaction was to the Hill District and she described her experience and said that she stood on the street on a day when it was raining. She said she was pleased that it rained because she could cover her White face with her umbrella so that she couldn't see the Black people staring at her. Whites almost never went to that area.

Not everyone thought this community laboratory was a good idea. The Council on Schools of Social Work, which accredited Schools of Social Work, seriously questioned the appropriate nature of the course on the basis of content before accepting it. In 1969, I submitted an article about the course to a prominent journal and it was rejected. Two years later, I submitted the same article to the same journal and it was accepted. My explanation? The passage of time.

Assassination and Activism

While Mildred was at Pitt, Dr. Martin Luther King, Jr., was assassinated. Mildred shares memories about activism at the School of Social Work in response to his assassination[14]*:*

Ted was at Hampton when Dr. Martin Luther King was assassinated on April 4, 1968. I had two children and was teaching and working on my PhD at Pittsburgh. I had arranged for the babysitter to stay with the children while I went to a faculty meeting. I was getting dressed to go and I was also listening to the radio. I heard a report that Martin Luther King Jr. had been assassinated. Angry and in disbelief, I told myself I would not attend the meeting. I called my friend Mary Page, a Black faculty member at the University of Pitt School of Social Work. We were two of only three Black faculty at the school. We began to plan a strategy for reacting to Dr. King's assassination. We arranged for a meeting of all-Black students and faculty to decide how to constructively respond to Dr. King's death. We made many phone calls to plan strategies.

In our faculty meetings, I had decided that I would make a demand for more Black graduate students and faculty. The refrain we had heard in faculty meetings was that "none are qualified." Even many of the so-called liberal Whites also took this position. Nevertheless, I kept up my one-woman campaign by repeatedly asking, "What have you done to find some?"

One guilty so-called liberal faculty said she had a Black student who wrote a horrible paper and asked me how she should grade her. I replied, "How would you grade her if you did not know if she was Black?" She said, "D," and I said, "You have your answer." During this time when we had several meetings between Black students and faculty, we learned that one Black male student was using "White faculty guilt" to get money to buy fancy clothes. We gave this student the "what for."

Once our group had our act together, we called for a meeting with the Dean of the School of Social Work, Dr. Samuel McCullough, to make our demands. We had arranged for a Black professor and administrator from another department to be our spokesperson. We were now a group of about 10: three of us Black social work faculty, our graduate students, and the other department faculty. We were all settled at the table in our seats, prepared to demand more Black faculty and students in the School of Social Work. The Black professor was a tall, handsome Black man with a long beard and dashiki.[15] When he arose in all his dignity, he barely got three words out like, "We are here to discuss" from his mouth when the Dean yelled at him loudly saying, "Boy!"

Shocked and angry at this unanticipated reaction, each of the members (except an Uncle Tom professor in the School of Social Work) arose as if planned and moved to the office door to leave. It was not anticipated by any of us that the Dean would refer to our spokesman in this way manner. This was humiliation. Before we could meet and react to what had happened, the Dean called me asking to meet with my friend Mary and me. Incidentally, his wife had died and he was now remarried to a beautiful student from Chile. We had lunch with him. He brought his new wife with him and paid for our lunch. He wanted to know why we all left the room after the professor got up to speak. We told him and he was surprised.

We discussed the situation—educating him about why we walked out. Mary and I told him about slavery and how the Jim Crow system relegated Black adults to be regarded as children, and African-Americans had learned to hate that term. We told him that Black men had historically been called "Boy" in the South, irrespective of their age.[16] I also told him that the accomplished psychiatrist Dr. Alvin Poussaint, when he traveled to the South, experienced being called "Boy." It was clear that the Dean's young, lovely South American wife had been trying to educate him about the history of African-Americans. He was about 65 [years old] and had lived in White neighborhoods most of his life. He agreed to work on the problem. We had a very successful meeting. The Dean and his wife became friends with my husband and me and invited us to dinner several times.

Following that, the Black faculty began recruiting undergraduate students at the University of Pittsburgh to apply for the Master's program in Social Work. I did not remain long to benefit from this change, but Black faculty were hired and more Black students were admitted. On the whole, most of the top positions went mainly to Black men and White men. Two Black men have been Deans. I learned recently that one of the Black students we had recruited for the Pitt School of Social Work is now the president of one of the numerous small colleges in Eastern Pennsylvania. My son, Awadagin, was directing a festival of classical music in small colleges in that area. He called to inform me that he had met one of our recruits. She told my son that she was one of the students I had recruited for the Pitt School of Social Work.[17]

Francine McNairy was that student and she shared her recollection of Mildred's impact on her life.[18]

Your mother came into my life as an angel who got me on my way and never had contact again. If she had not come into my life, I don't know where I would be. I was not the most productive student. I lived my first and second year in the community cafeteria! My third and fourth years were more serious. I was rejected from graduate school of education and I was graduating in a few weeks. A woman appeared from nowhere with her hair on top of her head like a little bun in a gray dress. She walked into the commuter cafeteria to the section with Black students and said, "I am Dr. Mildred Pratt, Professor in Social Work and we are looking to recruit BS [Bachelor of Science] students into the graduate program. Who is interested?" I raised my hand. She said, "I want you to fill out an application." She said that it was so late that all the fellowships were gone. But I could take the state civil service test and pass with 60 or higher, and the state would pay for graduate school. I got a 65. I was admitted to the School of Social Work.

I promised her and my parents that I would be serious and not trifling as I was as an undergraduate. Mildred appeared as an angel. That was what she was to me. Mildred took a gamble without knowing. I believe Mildred was placed on earth to give a kick and boost to give direction in my life. She wanted to change the composition of the graduate program. She was bold; she dared to be a different drum. She came in person and stated, "I am looking for graduate students." There was no fear, only determination.

Francine completed her degree and went on to become the President of Millersville University in Pennsylvania.

Mildred's time in Pittsburgh came to an end as she and her husband, Ted, decided to move to Illinois to accept appointments at Illinois State University. She shares the transition to Illinois State University in Normal:

At this time, my husband had decided to leave Hampton. The Dean had arranged a reception in a university lounge for us, recognizing our leave from the city. Yet, Ted and I had planned a going away party too. We both had accepted positions at Illinois State University since Ted had always wanted to live in the Midwest. He suggested that we give a big party and invite everyone, friend and foe. My dissertation chairperson came and ate and drank like a pig! Ted had insisted that I invite him. We selected professors from the Physics Department at Carnegie Mellon and from the Pittsburgh School of Social Work. Ted had many of his friends from Africa and India there. It was a great party with lots of food from both Sierra Leone and the United States. We had a jolly time.

Key Lessons

1. *Mildred had to balance family and career very early in her academic career. She met her husband at the beginning of her doctorate career and had two children shortly thereafter. She attributes her completion to her husband's support and encouragement. Mildred, however, carried much of the childcare load due to Ted's desire to teach at Hampton and give back to the institution that created the opportunity for him to pursue his physics career.*

2. *Mildred was a trailblazer in the social work field. She pushed the boundaries of curriculum and experiential learning to truly help her students appreciate issues of class and poverty. Her experiential learning course foreshadows her subsequent work on the Bloomington-Normal Black History Project.*

3. *Activism remained an important part of Mildred's life. She challenged discrimination with her son by writing to the administrator at the local clinic about the clinic's request for racial information; she challenged segregated placement decisions for social work students; she protested after King's assassination; and she sought to diversify the doctoral program at Pitt by single-handedly identifying a student for the program. Her determination, conviction, intensity, goal-oriented approach, and righteous indignation became guiding values for her activism.*

Photos

Figure 8.1: Ted and Mildred Pratt, Pittsburgh, 1964
Source: M. Pratt.

Figure 8.2: Mildred Pratt, University of Pittsburgh graduation, 1969
Source: M. Pratt.

Notes

1. (M. Pratt, personal communication, n.d.).
2. (Pratt & Pratt-Clarke, 2002). Reprinted with permission from Heartland Publishing, received May 10, 2017.
3. (M. Pratt, personal communication, n.d.).
4. (M. Pratt, personal communication, n.d.).
5. (M. Pratt, personal communication, n.d.).
6. (M. Pratt, personal communication, n.d.).
7. (M. Pratt, personal communication, n.d.).
8. Dr. Joseph Eaton, described as a "committed Zionist," was the chair of the School of Social Work's doctoral program from 1962 to 1966. See Barlow (2012) and Tabachnick (2012).
9. (Pratt, 1969).
10. (M. Pratt, personal communication, n.d.).
11. (M. Pratt, personal communication, n.d.).
12. See Page and Pratt (1973).
13. (M. Pratt, personal communication, n.d.).
14. (M. Pratt, personal communication, n.d.).

15. Dr. Mary Page suggests that the gentleman may have been Dr. Lloyd Bell (M. Page, personal communication, July 8, 2013). Mildred's notes indicated that he was in the Psychology Department and was an administrator (M. Pratt, personal communication, n.d.). See "Community Tribute" (2009) for a summary of Lloyd Bell's life.
16. See Beeth and Wintz (1992, p. 176) and Andrews (1990, p. 62).
17. This was a time of Black activism at Pitt. The activities of Mildred mirrored the activities of the Black Action Society in 1968 and 1969. See "Black Action Society" (2010) and Alberts (2013). See also Daniel (2009): "Looking back, January through July 1969 seems to have been the fastest-paced, most intense, nerve-racking period of my life. It was a time when reason often gave way to threats and acts of violence, a time when revolutionary 'brothers and sisters' first threatened those considered to be the White racist opposition and, sooner than later, focused on 'dealing with Negroes' they perceived to be 'counter revolutionaries,' 'Uncle Toms,' and 'old-fashioned Negroes.'"
18. (F. McNairy, personal communication, October 15, 2015). Permission received May 31, 2017.

References

Alberts, R. (2013). *Pitt: The story of the University of Pittsburgh*. Retrieved from http://digital.library.pitt.edu/cgi-bin/t/text/pageviewer-idx?idno=00c50130m;c=pittmiscpubs;cc=pittmiscpubs;rgn=full%20text;didno=00c50130m;view=image;seq=411;node=00c50130m%3A1.10.5;page=root;size=s;frm=frameset

Andrews, R. (1990). *The last radio baby: A memoir*. Atlanta, GA: Peachtree Publishers.

Barlow, K. K. (2012, October 25). *Obituary: Joseph W. Eaton*. Retrieved from www.utimes.pitt.edu/?p=23131

Beeth, H., & Wintz, C. D. (1992). *Black Dixie: Afro-Texan history and sulture in Houston*. College Station, TX: Texas A&M University Press.

Black Action Society. (2010, May 2). *University of Pittsburgh*. Retrieved from http://www.pitt.edu/~sorc/bas/history.html

Community tribute to Lloyd Bell. (2009, August 21). *New Pittsburgh Courier, City Edition*. Retrieved from http://courier-pittsburgh.vlex.com/vid/community-tribute-to-lloyd-bell-64160191

Daniel, J. (2009, October 19). The African American experience at Pitt: 1969–2009. *Pitt Chronicle*. Retrieved from http://www.chronicle.pitt.edu/story/african-american-experience-pitt-1969-2009

Page, M., & Pratt, M. (1973). Community laboratory: An innovation in higher education. *Journal of Education for Social Work, 9*(3), 45–50.

Pratt, M. (1969). *A study of the development of social welfare in a selected group of African countries: Ghana, Sierra Leone, Kenya, and Tanzania*. (Unpublished doctoral dissertation). University of Pittsburgh, Pittsburgh, PA.

Pratt, M., & Pratt-Clarke, M. (2002). *A tribute to love: Forty-six personal love stories of romance and marriage.* Bloomington, IL: Heartland Publishing.

Tabachnick, T. (2012, October 16). Joseph Eaton was professor of social work, committed Zionist. *Jewish Chronicle.* Retrieved from http://thejewishchronicle.net/view/full_story/20509332/article-Joseph-Eaton-was-professor-of-social-work--committed-Zionist?instance=news_special_coverage_right_column

CHAPTER NINE

Normal University Racism

Like most Black people in this "sea of White," I have had to learn with my fellow brothers and sisters that life in America is a constant diet of struggle for justice. Being competent is not a passport in this "White sea" but is a symbol for "stand back further," because a competent Black threatens the secure feeling of the racist in his myth that "all Blacks are inferior." —Mildred Pratt, 1972[1]

In general, anything a White faculty member does is good in the department. If I do the same thing, then it is not good quality. …Within this society, it is easy to accept that a Black man cannot be competent in the area of physics. —Theodore Pratt, 1974[2]

Ted and Mildred had a very difficult time at Illinois State University as they began their academic careers and raised their children in Normal, Illinois. Mildred's and Ted's transition to being faculty members at Illinois State University was not smooth; at the beginning they had to fight to hold the positions they had been offered. These initial issues would foreshadow more substantive issues that would arise once they began their appointments.

Normal, Illinois

Mildred describes her experiences with Ted getting settled and adjusted to Normal, Illinois in 1969[3]:

Prior to our arrival in Normal, our contacts in Normal had arranged for Ted, myself, and our two children to live in one of the professor's homes until we found a house. A few realtors solicited our business but we decided to deal with Adeline Adams. She was a fine agent who did a great job of helping us find a home that suited our budget and our family size. Our agent, who also later became a great friend, showed us any house that we wanted to see in Bloomington and Normal and didn't hesitate to inform us if racial discrimination was being practiced.

Adeline was careful to check with some of the White residents who would potentially be our neighbors gauging how they felt about having a Black family in their neighborhood. Adeline told us that one resident told her that they didn't know how this would work out, as they had never had Black neighbors, to which Adeline said, "You probably never had two PhDs as neighbors either, have you?" Their answer, "No." Most were shocked when they received this information. The fact was that our credentials exceeded that of any possible neighbors especially since only a few of them even had a Bachelor's degree.

She eventually found a house for us in Normal which we bought. Ted was very frugal and had saved his scholarship money and I had some savings. Together, we had enough to put a down payment on a house at 1405 West Hovey. Fortunately, the neighbors presented no major problems and exhibited no unkind behavior.

Nevertheless, when we moved to Normal, child care became a major problem. We learned that it wasn't possible to get a babysitter to care for children during the day while parents worked. We learned, however, that there were child care centers available. The one named La Petite Academy was perfect for us. Our children loved it and eagerly looked forward to the experience.

Ted was determined to live in a small American town, and Illinois State University was the offer that he accepted because for some reason he also wanted to live in the Midwest. I wasn't excited about the Midwest and definitely had reservations about relocating there. I was particularly concerned that the Midwest would not be the most a desirable region for Ted, who spoke with an accent (British and Krio) and wasn't a person who compromised. While we were called for an interview, neither of us was offered a position commensurate with our experience.

Ted's Faculty Journey

Ted had a difficult and painful experience at Illinois State University. In the spring of 1969, Ted signed a contract as an Assistant Professor of Physics eligible for tenure in 1976. His status was changed from "continuing" to "temporary" due to "failing a medical exam." After discussion with the Dean of Faculty over his 1970–1971 contract, he was again appointed as a continuing faculty member eligible for tenure in 1976.

In the fall of 1971, Ted applied for a leave of absence to teach graduate students in Rio de Janeiro, Brazil, since he hadn't been assigned any graduate students at Illinois State. In March 1972, he gave a public presentation to the Board of Regents criticizing the appointment, promotion, and tenure process, especially the lack of fairness and the absence of Blacks and minorities on promotion and tenure committees. He was granted a leave of absence from 1972 to 1973 to teach in Brazil.

Mildred shares her experience with Ted in Brazil from 1972 to 1973[4]:

We took a leave of absence from Illinois State University to Brazil. A friend of Ted's cajoled us to go to Rio de Janeiro, Brazil, where Ted got a position in the Physics Department as an Assistant Professor. I had the two children to take care of, but managed to balance their care with some professional activities of my own, which included teaching two seminar classes, conducting social welfare research and writing a book of my lectures, which was translated into Portuguese. Everyone in our family enjoyed it there. We had learned the language.

We also were generally very pleased with the school that the children attended (private and within walking distance from our apartment). Fortunately, the children first entered grade school in Rio De Janeiro, Brazil. Among the advantages were discipline, focus on learning, challenging academic curricula, and lack of racial problems. The children were all upper and middle class and many different colors. In fact, the school was so good that when we returned to the United States (Normal, Illinois), we were able to enroll each of them in a grade above their level. They each graduated from high school at the age of 16.

Ted was offered a permanent position at the University of Brazil. However, following our discussion of the offer in terms of what was best for the children, Ted wanted them to study musical instruments and get tennis lessons. Ted said we should go back because children should learn music. Since we were on a leave of absence, we went back. When we came back from Brazil, my husband's contract was not renewed. Mine barely was.

While in Brazil, Illinois State University sent Ted a notification of terminal contract for the year 1973–1974, though his tenure year was 1976. In his complaint of discrimination based on race and national origin, dated June 10, 1974, he states the following[5]:

In summary, I have provided evidence to substantiate my claim that at no time was there a positive climate in the Physics Department for accepting me as a competent faculty member with all of the rights and privileges of the other faculty members (all White). I further claim that this evidence clearly is primarily attributable to my race and national origin. …If further proof is needed to bear out my theory that at ISU [Illinois State University] only "Black bodies" are wanted…not strong competent scholarly Black faculty, indeed one may listen to a tape of a recent Black faculty-staff meeting with the Dean of Faculty and the President of the university. The whole attitude of the President and the Dean was one which said to the faculty that if they did not like the conditions of their employment, they could leave.

Ted's allegations against the university were extensive. He mentions the refusal of White faculty members to collaborate with him; the promotion of White faculty members with no publications and less visible accomplishment than him; the unwillingness of the department to appoint him to any leadership positions on committees; the lack of assignment of graduate students to work with him; his inability to select the courses he wanted to teach, though White faculty members had the choice; a deliberate under-evaluation by the department in the areas of scholarship, teaching, and service; the failure to report his publications and accomplishments in the university journal while reporting lesser accomplishments of Whites; and nonpayment of his travel expenses to conferences while paying for those of White faculty members.[6] He filed suit in May 1974 with the Equal Employment Opportunity Commission. Ted engaged the law firm of Chapin and Chapin in Springfield, Illinois, to help him in the charge he filed with the Fair Employment Practices Commission. The firm's letter dated March 26, 1975, states[7]:

I have reviewed the file and the evidence in the above matter at the request of Dr. Pratt. It appears to me that there is substantial evidence of racial discrimination against this man from the first year of his employment at Illinois State University right down to the date of his termination while he was on sabbatical leave in Brazil. The petty put-downs and humiliations that have been visited on this talented man are really quite shocking. In most cases of alleged discrimination, the evidence is quite subjective and difficulty to identify. Here it is so fragrant that it seems your commission would welcome it with open arms instead of moving it on to the back burner.

Ted attempted to seek employment for a period of two years, applying for various positions across the country. His papers include a letter to the Institute for Service to Education in Washington, D.C. dated March 31, 1976, indicating that he was "actively seeking a teaching position in physics in a university."[8] Unsuccessful in securing another job in his field, Ted, a 39-year-old Black PhD physicist, married with two children, was forced to redefine his career and his life.

Mildred reflects on Ted's short physics career[9]:

I really wanted to leave when my husband didn't get renewed. I don't know why he didn't want to leave. He applied for some positions, but during that time, White institutions just didn't hire Black people. We knew that when we left Pittsburgh. I even knew that we shouldn't have gone to this small town. He didn't understand racism in this country. The point is that Ted didn't understand the university, and I kept telling him we shouldn't come to the Midwest. But, he wanted to see other parts of the country. When he came to the United States, he was in Pittsburgh and then the small Black college of Hampton. I knew we weren't supposed to go to the Midwest. I knew that discrimination was bad, and it was generally difficult for Black people to get university-level positions.

I think he wanted to go to Illinois because he was looking forward to doing a lot of research, and when we got here, what they wanted us to do was to be advisors to students. So at that point, I wanted to tell him that we needed to leave this place. I didn't know where we would go. The department was racist. When White people come from other countries and can barely speak English, all they do is latch on to believing that Black people are stupid. Theodore studied at St. Cuthbert's Society in Fourah Bay in Sierra Leone, Hampton College, and Carnegie Institute of Technology. Ted had more publications than anyone there, and his White colleagues were jealous. During his all-too-brief academic career as a professor at Hampton, Federal University Rio de Janeiro in Brazil, and Illinois State University, he had 12 research journal publications that were requested by over 80 people in 24 countries, presentations at the American Physical Society, and a term as a reviewer for the *American Journal of Physics* (see Appendix A for Theodore Pratt's Curriculum Vitae).[10]

He applied to so many places, but they said you had to be a citizen and he was not. I think the fact that he was not a citizen affected his opportunities. He felt Illinois was a good community to raise children. He didn't think it was a good idea to move children around, so he decided to buy rental property and make money from that.

We bought 4 Larry Court[11] first. He had never done property management work before, and he had many problems with the tenants. Some student tenants didn't want to pay their rent, and he hadn't anticipated that. We had to plead for people to pay rent. It [the building] paid for itself, but that was about it. I was still teaching. …[and] somehow managed. Much of the work we did ourselves. We had to keep the lawns mowed, and if something broke, we had to try to fix it or pay someone to do the repairs. Before we could rent a place, we would clean up everything and then paint the whole place, because they would leave it in a real mess. I didn't like doing the work, cleaning the apartments and going to show the apartments, and it was a mess. The long and short of it is that when he died, there wasn't much money left.

Mildred's Faculty Journey

While supporting her husband in apartment ownership and maintenance, Mildred continued to pursue her scholarly career. Mildred's journey was also difficult from the beginning. Like Ted, she was offered a different position once she arrived on campus. She was expected to be a part-time faculty member and a part-time counselor in the Black HPS [High Potential Student] program. Mildred shares about her experience[12]:

I applied for and was offered the position of Assistant Professor in Social Work at Illinois State University. I had been promoted to Assistant Professor at Pittsburgh. However, when I came to Illinois State University, they didn't want me to serve in my teaching position. They had a "special office" for Black students who weren't doing well academically, and, that was the position they assigned me—to be a counselor for Black students. I was shocked when it happened. It wasn't the position I had been originally offered.

A Black guy who taught in the Math Department but was in charge of the program informed me that I had to counsel Black students. He was in charge of minority student affairs and responsible for distributing assignments to Black faculty. In other words, he was the one who was supposed to take charge of "Niggers." All Negroes who came, he decided what they were going to do. Like slavery, they had Blacks in charge, and that was what he was.

I went to the Dean and showed him the document with the offer. He rattled on and on, saying he would check on it only when I threatened to call a special office to discuss discrimination. At first the Dean didn't want to give me the name of the office. He eventually did, and I called the Equal Employment Opportunity Commission. A few days lapsed, and they put me in a cubicle in Social Work. I said, "If you don't clean this up, it will go way beyond this university." I was the only one with a PhD, and they were jealous. They quickly cleaned the mess up, and the Dean gave me the position to which I'd been originally assigned. It was fortunate that I had the letter that said "Assistant Professor." When they cleaned the mess up, they gave me an office in the main building. I wanted to sue because my dander was up, but my husband disagreed. I should have sued!

Mildred remembers a publicly disrespectful incident that happened during a faculty meeting at ISU shortly after her arrival[13]:

In the spring semester of 1970, there was an issue raised by Black students demanding a statue or some such representation honoring Malcolm X. Students were demonstrating and protesting on the campus, and the university arranged for a meeting of all faculty to discuss and vote on the issue of whether or not to erect a monument in honor of the recent assassination of Malcolm X.[14]

Following a very limited discussion, the issue was brought to a vote. There were very few Black faculty in the university, and of course there were very few people in this audience who stood up to vote for the memorial. Among those who voted for the memorial were my husband and me. The liberal Whites didn't even support affirmative action.

As soon as the vote was over, we were all dismissed. As my husband and I were leaving the hall, an old White lady grabbed me and in a heavy German accent said, "You are a student. Only faculty are to be here and vote." Her accusation humiliated me, and I responded by calling her "a little Hitler." My husband told me to leave the matter alone, but as I exited, I asked several faculty for the lady's name. Most who observed the incident ignored me. But, I finally found a [faculty] member for whom I'd delivered a guest lecture who provided her name. She taught in the Geography Department.

A correspondence from Mildred to President Samuel Braden dated February 19, 1970, describes this incident[15]:

> Dear President:
> Sir, at the end of the faculty meeting on Thursday, February 18, 1970, I was accosted rudely by a woman who inquired about my identity…asked about my status in the university, and said, among other things, "I saw you writing; you are a student, and a student is not supposed to vote. Show me your identification card." Completely stunned, I called my husband's help. The tone of the woman's voice was very infuriating, insulting, and, to say the least, provoking. My husband identified me to her, and at that time he was immediately asked also to identify himself. He did and asked her to identify herself. She refused and insisted that I was not a member of the faculty and that my husband was a liar. She never did identify herself; however, she was later identified as Dr. Schmitt [Schmidt] of the Geography Department. Sir, I demand a public apology for the insult heaped on me and my husband since the insult was made in public.
> Sincerely yours,
> (Dr.) Mildred Pratt, Assistant Professor, Sociology Anthropology Department

President Braden responded on February 26, 1970, acknowledging receipt of Mildred's letter. He indicated that he had investigated the matter and provided a summary of his investigation and Dr. Schmidt's response. He concluded his letter by indicating his willingness to conduct a similar inquiry in future situations.[16]

Mildred was not done communicating with university presidents. Her concerns about her promotion and tenure process led her to write to a different president in 1972, President David Berlo. Below is her handwritten draft[17]:

> April 26, 1972
> Dear Mr. President,
> My attention is directed to you for the following reason:
> 1. In May 1969, I was told by telephone by Dr. Sherman prior to being hired that my credentials qualified me for appointment at the Associate Professor level. I was not so appointed.

2. I was appointed to the position Assistant Professor in Sociology, Anthropology Department.[18] Having signed the contract to that effect, I received a subsequent letter informing me that I would teach part-time in SoA [Sociology–Anthropology] and serve as a counselor part-time in HPS [High Potential Students].

3. Upon arrival at ISU [Illinois State University], I was so assigned.

4. In November 1969, I was asked by Mr. Paul Wisdon to assist in recruitment of Black faculty. I immediately wrote him a letter citing the breach of contract as outlined above, asserting that I could not in good conscience encourage a Black person to come here. Mr. Wisdon immediately contacted me in utter surprise. In our conference he looked into my folder, read the contract, and agreed that there had been such a breach of contract. He promised to correct the problem. I was soon called in by Dr. [Shailer] Thomas, who had been informed to rectify the situation.

5. In the interim, I continued to perform my functions at a high level of excellence and remained Assistant Professor.

6. I was also to be insulted [and] literally accosted by a full professor at the university in a public (AAUP [American Association of University Professors]) meeting and told to show my ID card, as I "was not on faculty but a student." I wrote a letter to the then President Braden demanding a public apology.

7. In January 1972, you, Dr. Berlo, held a meeting with Black faculty in Fairchild Hall. Among other things, you admitted that you were "racist" because you have grown up in such a society, but you would do your best to demonstrate your commitment to assuring fair treatment of Blacks at ISU.

8. I have found myself since early April caught up in an entanglement regarding my department's recommendation that I be appointed to the position Associate Professor. As I have been struggling through the maze of what you described as inefficiency, my intellectual struggle to understand led me to conceptualize the situation as "institutional racism." This term, incidentally, is considered by Whites as necessary and unnecessary bureaucracy. When I informed Dr. Thomas, SOA [Sociology–Anthropology] Department chairman, that I was sure racism was a factor in my case, he denied it. You must know, Mr. President, how I was at pains to restrain myself from telling him how you had admitted that you were a "racist."

9. Now, Dr. Berlo, I am not a lawyer, but like most Black people in this "sea of White," I have had to learn with my fellow brothers and sisters that life in America is a constant diet of struggle for justice. Being competent is not a passport in this "White sea" but is a symbol for "stand back further," because a competent Black threatens the secure feeling of the racist in his myth that "all Blacks are inferior."

In simple language, I have been compelled to assert…"It is impossible for a Black to get justice" in this ISU community. I have then decided that the appointment process in this university community is filled with deliberately built-in stumbling blocks. Let me provide a brief summary of some of the many inconsistencies which I have encountered. Since you have the final decision-making responsibility here on campus, I am placing the facts in your hands. I refuse to be insulted by a system which is obviously "inefficient." You yourself said so.

The President's response, dated May 7, 1972, indicates that her concerns would be addressed by the Faculty Status Committee.[19] *Mildred was awarded tenure in 1974 after a difficult process*[20]:

My worst experience was trying to get promoted. The Director of the Social Work Program had no publications, and other faculty resented me tremendously because they hadn't conducted any scholarly research. They resented me for my degrees. Most only had a Master's degree. The Director of Social Work had a PhD from some little known college. I did not have good relationships with them, and I just went about doing my business.

There was a major faculty meeting about tenure. Something came up in the meeting about tenure, and it had to do with me. I was being considered and several people got up and made negative comments, and then this large man who wrote a lot of publications got up and said negative stuff. He had never spoken to me. The Department Head said, "He doesn't think any women are competent." There were several people up for tenure, and the faculty was supposed to vote. Everybody voted for me except the big, fat guy who never spoke to me.

I had made several speeches at conferences about the Black History Project, and that project, with presentations and written materials, is what helped me get tenure. No one on the committee was from Social Work. The department was Sociology, Anthropology, and Social Work.[21] The biggest problems with getting tenure were the three areas and the major emphasis on publications. They did not want to accept my work with the Black History Project as consideration for tenure. I did not have a mentor, but I did know a Dean in the College of Arts and Sciences. We had a good relationship, and she was instrumental in helping me.

To get promoted to Full Professor, I had to attend a meeting and present statements about myself. What I remember is that at the end of the meeting when I was called in, the Associate Dean told me that I was approved for tenure. I had a half-time position in Arts and Sciences and a half-time position in Social Work. I was responsible for research and administration and working with the Black History Project. It was a lonely experience. I retired as soon as I could.[22]

Despite being a full professor, Mildred was still seen as a Black body. She remembers an incident that happened in the neighborhood when she was asked to be a maid[23]:

One day I was walking to Jewel's [grocery store] about two blocks from our house in Normal. About halfway to Jewel's, a white lady waved and beckoned me to her from across the street. I was informally dressed with a Brazilian-tied scarf on my head because I hadn't yet combed my hair. This neighbor said, "I have a brother who is ill and needs someone to cook, clean, and help him dress." I was shocked that she assumed that because I was a Black lady, with a scarf on my head, that I'd be a perfect maid. Livid, I struggled within myself to respond appropriately. I carefully took a breath and decided to teach her a lesson. I said, "I am a full professor at Illinois State University and have a PhD, and I don't think

I'd make a good maid for your brother." She turned beet red and went back into her house. I've not seen her since.[24]

Mildred realized the importance of being an advocate and mentoring, counseling, and advising others. She remembers advocating for another Black woman related to an issue involving her appointment[25]:

I later found myself advocating for another Black female who was being similarly treated. This lady had earned a degree from the University of Pittsburgh in Social Work. She applied to and was being interviewed by Illinois State University in the Social Work Department. Some people within the department worked as field instructors. They held Master's degrees in Social Work and were also teaching classes. That degree was the only credential that they had. At the time this lady applied, there were only two of us with PhDs: the director and me. The woman came in to be interviewed, but they offered her a position as field instructor. I knew the position was for an Assistant Professor.

When I found out what they were manipulating, I called the Associate Dean of Arts and Sciences and told her what they were trying to do with this lady. She intervened and told them that the position was for an Assistant Professor. She had been assigned an office and was about to start when I found out. The Dean held a meeting with all the faculty. She told them what the position was and that was the opened position. The Dean insisted the lady get the position for which she had applied. By that time, the woman was so disgusted that she started contacting other universities for jobs, which she got, and she went back to the University of Pittsburgh. This was the most interesting example of how their racism was hurting the university. A candidate being interviewed for a teaching position at the university once asked, "Is there discrimination in the community?" I answered, "It exists in some form everywhere. Each of us has a responsibility to get rid of it."

Mildred was not only an advocate for African-Americans. She was also an advocate for other faculty, even the man who didn't vote for her to be tenured:

There was another incident involving the big, fat man. This same man was a national expert in juvenile delinquency and had written a couple of articles and books. There was a faculty meeting called, and one of the things to be discussed was giving this man a special title as a distinguished national scholar in his field. This man was not there. I always kept a copy of the university and department bylaws, so I knew when they said this man shouldn't get the title that they were wrong. I was the only one who voted for him, and reminded them that he met all the criteria. I said it was against university policy. No other faculty said anything. After some silence, the Department Head said we'd discuss it some other time.

The Department Head asked to speak with me as I was going to my office. He said that they were going to change the policy. He said, "Mildred, this was not aimed at you." I said, "I didn't think so." He was surprised that I would support this man who had never spoken to me and had treated me like dirt. But it was wrong.

Now, that man never knew I voted for him. You needed a certain number of votes to get a position. He eventually got the position.

Mildred shares some of her advice to faculty colleagues[26]:

There were several areas in which I mentored faculty who had to cope with problems associated with promotion, tenure, sexual harassment, etc. When I was Acting Director of Social Work for a year, I was clear in informing Black males and other males to be careful of sexual harassment and to avoid the possibility of accusation—to avoid the appearance of evil. I told them, "Don't not take students to your home, or in your office in the evenings when most faculty are gone, and keep your office door open while in conference with a student." I also arranged for faculty to co-author a publication with me.

> I gave people suggestions about the best ways to get tenure:
> Be sure to carefully read the policies and practices (like you would your Bible) to protect yourself and survive in the system.
> Keep abreast of policy and practice changes.
> Try to contact the appropriate source if you have questions.
> Be careful about gossiping.
> Try to get on committees as a way of getting points.
> Learn the informal structures and procedures of a complicated bureaucracy.

If I were giving advice to women, I would encourage them to get a doctorate degree in something. I would let them know that if they want to get a position and get promoted, they have to write papers and go to conferences. If you are a woman, you should expect that you are going to have some problems getting positions, tenure, and promotions, because men think that women should not have these positions. While I was getting a PhD, one professor said it out in the open: "If you are a woman, you have no business being a professor and most certainly not having tenure." He was blatant about it. You need to be prepared for the fact that some people don't want you to have experiences because you are Black.

Motherhood

In addition to her academic career, Mildred was very engaged as a mother to her two children, Awadagin and Menah. Mildred shares some challenges and experiences raising children in the 1970s and 1980s in an environment of racism[27]:

It was tough being a wife and mother and getting tenure. What I remember is that I had to get out in time to pick the kids from school. Sometimes Ted did. Most children walked home from school, but we stopped since we didn't think it was safe. I frequently walked to Illinois State University or rode my bike, and on one such occasion, some young White boys passed me in a car and yelled, "Nigger, get off the street!" I was shocked, but not too shocked to recognize that one of them was the son of an Illinois State professor. I'd seen him at a faculty picnic. After this incident, I both stopped walking or riding my bike to school.

It was difficult being a mother, wife, and professor. What I did was cook food on the weekends and freeze it so I didn't have to cook every day. Laundry wasn't a problem because I also did it on the weekends. We found that raising children in Normal had some major disadvantages. When the children entered grade school in Normal, there were very few African-Americans. Most of the African-Americans lived in Bloomington. When the children were attending grade school in Normal and were called "Nigger," they told us. When the children were in Rio de Janeiro, they didn't have to worry about that. Color was never an issue. However, when we returned to the United States from Brazil, we did have to be concerned.

Our concerns were raised shortly after we returned to Normal, when we decided to enroll both of the children in an advanced class. We simply told the school administration what grade the children should be in because we knew they were advanced. We showed them the grade reports, but it was all in Portuguese and the staff couldn't read it. The children spoke Portuguese fluently and of course when they spoke English, it was with a Portuguese accent. They'd been in school one week when I received an urgent call to come to the school to discuss some problem with our then five-year-old daughter, Menah. The teacher informed me that they would have to put her in a remedial program, because if she planned to live in the Midwest she needed to learn to speak "Midwestern." I thought this was very dumb. Anyway, I insisted that I wouldn't allow that and that was the end of that!

The next problem that the children had in school was when Menah was denied admission to an advanced math class. Menah came home crying because the teacher didn't enroll her in the advanced math class. I took the children to school and spoke to the teacher about this. The teacher said the class was filled and that she was sorry. I told her that Menah would be in the class. I went and spoke to the principal, who supported the teacher. I insisted that Menah had a right to be in the class. When I didn't relent, he said he would see what he could do. I waited, and he returned shortly to tell me that she could be in the class.

Menah has a personality very much like Mama Pratt [Theodore's mother]. She is very organized, and that is perhaps one of the reasons why she decided to study law. There is one comment that she made around the dinner table when she was in grade school. We were discussing issues related to what men could do and women could not. Interestingly enough, she had just studied President Lincoln's Gettysburg Address, and she presented her support of women's rights by quoting

"All men are created equal." When Ted and Awadagin both remarked that it did not refer to women, she became angry.

Mildred shares another experience with racism involving her daughter, Menah, and a national tennis tournament in 1981 in Birmingham, Alabama[28]:

When our children were around age 10 and 12, we (the family) drove to Birmingham, Alabama, for our daughter, Menah, to participate in the United States Tennis Association 14-and-under girls' tournament. In route, we drove up to a service station in the Deep South. The service station employee asked, "What can I do for you, sir?" and was very courteous throughout the incident.

In the early evening, we stopped at a small buffet-style restaurant for dinner. As we entered the room, angry-looking men immediately fixed their angry eyes on us. Ted asked for something, and the waiter said, "Nigger" something. We quietly sat down to eat, again smothered by the White men's angry stares. We quickly ate and left.

We stopped at a motel for the night. When we awoke the following morning, I told Ted that I'd barely slept because I was so afraid that some White men would crash in on us. Ted also confessed to having the same fear. When we arrived in Birmingham and settled in our hotel, we went to the outdoor tennis courts for Menah to practice for the tournament. We saw only one other Black girl practicing. Before we finished, it began to rain. The tournament director announced that if it was raining the following day practice would be in the tennis club, but that Blacks were not allowed there. We returned to our hotel and Ted called the United States Tennis Association, informing them of the local tennis organization's decision to hold tennis practice in a facility that did not accept Blacks. Negotiations continued throughout the night until the local tennis association found a public facility that the children could use.

Mildred also shares some reflections about racism experienced by her son, Awadagin[29]:

The children did well as undergraduates in college and reported no racial problems. However, when Awadagin entered the Peabody School of Music, he experienced some racial problems in Baltimore, Maryland. Awadagin breathed and lived for his music. He was devoted to it. He practiced all the time. I recall visiting him once and staying at his small apartment. His entire life consisted of his job as a waiter, music practice (violin and piano), and his music classes.

Awadagin's devotion to his craft also meant that he wasn't concerned about his clothes as long as they were clean. He dressed informally, as he does now. He'd spend a few hours at home and then take his violin to Peabody to practice at all hours of the night. He had tremendous support from the Peabody faculty, including the President. He was even given a key to the facility so that he could practice whenever he wished. I don't know when he ever rested because he'd stay at the Peabody until early morning, go home and eat, maybe take a shower, and then return to school.

I recall one trip when I was in Baltimore for a conference. Awadagin shared my hotel room so that we could spend more time together. I observed his hair design which just had chunks of hair twisted [dreadlocks]. I knew that he expected me to say that I thought his hairstyle was horrible. He tested me, asking: "Mom, how do you like my hair?" I carefully looked him over, and then shocked him by saying, "Well, it looks interesting." He shyly laughed, surprised that I didn't not take the bait.

Awadagin always marched to his own drumbeat. He has a wry sense of humor. Following one performance when Awadagin's dress included a pair of black dress pants and a plain cotton maroon T-shirt, his former piano teacher said as she congratulated him, "It seems someone forgot to dress," to which Awadagin retorted, "Why Leslie, you look fine."

On a less humorous note, there was an incident involving Awadagin's dreadlocks and the police. Early one morning when he was on his way home with his dreadlocks down and violin over his shoulder, the police arrested him for the crime of "being Black with long braids and looking strange." Fortunately, he had great friends, and "surrogate parents" in the Peabody School of Music who resolved the matter. When I visited Awadagin, he took me to meet his professors. The Dean brought out all of the staff, introducing them to me as "Awadagin's supporters." In truth, they nourished him as their son.

Unfortunately, there was another encounter with the police when Awadagin was walking through the train station with his music, violin, dreadlocks, jeans, and piano stool. The police stopped him and searched him. This time, he'd taken the train for one of his many performances. He was stopped by the police for, as they say, "being Black in the wrong place."

Mildred often wrote handwritten letters to her children. Two of those letters that she wrote to her daughter are below. Her letters to Menah reflect not only the depth of her love, but also her understanding of the importance of preparing a Black daughter for life in a world full of racism and sexism. She did this by instilling pride and self-confidence. Mildred's first letter to her 13-year-old daughter on December 18, 1980, is below[30]:

Dear Menah:

I think this is the first letter I have ever written to you. I wanted to write this letter because it has occurred to me that you will be graduating from high school in about three years and leaving home. These three years are very important to you and us—your family.

You are 13, a big girl now—a teenager. But I still remember the morning when you were born and how happy your father and I were to see and welcome you. You were just as special to us as Awadagin and just as special to us then as you are now.

You are not only special to us, your family, but also to your Grandmother Pratt, your aunts and uncles, and all of our White and Black friends, who, like us, want the best for you.

You are special—you are a Pratt. You are African—part of one of the oldest cultures in the world. Remember that and never take a *back seat* to anyone. You are *somebody special.*

You are special because you are very *bright.* You are strong. You want to be the best. You have a nice smile, a sense of humor, and you are a lovely young lady. Aspire to be the best that is in you to be. Don't let anyone set *low* goals for you, and don't set them for yourself.

Menah, when I think of you, I think of myself growing up. I was *strong* and *determined* to *achieve*—even though there was no "women's lib" then (smiles).

I know things are not easy for you. You may sometimes think us too demanding. I am sure that I sometimes had such thoughts when I grew up, but deep down inside I'm glad they helped and disciplined me, because I know I could not have managed to get to where I am now. I know a lot of the girls with whom I grew up did not even go to college, let alone get a PhD.

You are somebody!

We love you very much. We want you to be happy. We want you to be the best so that you can like and be proud of yourself.

Your mother

Mildred reaffirmed her commitment and love in August of 1984[31]*:*

My dear daughter, Menah:

Let me first say that *I love you* unconditionally. I want you to be happy. I think you are a lovely young lady, attractive in many ways—not the least of which is your delightful laugh and sense of humor. You are also a highly intelligent young lady with tremendous potential.

I hope you will be able to fulfill your highest dreams and potential for *you,* to make you happy and feel good about yourself. You are also a kind, sensitive person with great writing talent.

Don't give up on yourself. I will not; and, will help you all I can.

Whenever you want just to talk to pour out your thoughts and feelings, I am here for you.

Sweet dreams…

Mom

Key Lessons

1. *Black faculty suffered racism and discrimination as they sought to contribute to the educational mission of higher education. They were vulnerable to changing contract terms, discrimination, disrespect, and termination. Ted and Mildred began their faculty careers on unequal footing, fighting for the positions that they had been offered. Ted's contract was eventually not renewed, even before formally being considered for tenure. Mildred, too, had to fight for the Assistant Professor position which she had been offered. Both had been initially offered tenure-track positions. Upon arrival, they were offered different positions and that set the tone for their experiences at ISU as each step of their journey was a battle.*

2. *Ted and Mildred were outspoken activists and advocates for justice. They both fought for their positions. Ted filed a lawsuit and documented the discrimination that he experienced. Mildred, likewise, wrote letters to the president of the university on two occasions, documenting injustice and asking for redress. Mildred's advocacy reflected her self-advocacy, voice, self-confidence, and conviction that she belonged in the academy and deserved to be treated fairly and with respect and dignity.*

3. *Mildred was a powerful advocate for her family—her children and her husband. She was particularly sensitive to the experiences of Black girls and sought to reaffirm, reassure, and validate her daughter, perhaps with a sensitivity to her own childhood and the validation that she never received. She also was sensitive to her son, as a Black man, and the challenges that she knew he would experience, given her own experience with her husband. Mildred also supported her husband. She was an equal partner in the real estate work and the maintenance of the apartments. She was a traditional wife in many ways. As reflected in the first chapter, she cooked every meal; she did all the laundry; she mowed yards; she maintained a garden; and she transported the children to music lessons. Yet, she also pursued her own professional career.*

4. *Mildred's achievement of tenure and promotion to full professor was rare and remains rare. In 1989, Black women were only 0.7 percent of full professors and only 2.1% of full-time faculty (Benjamin, 1997, p. 9). Black women full professors were and are an anomaly in the academy (Holmes, 1999, pp. 32–33).*

5. *Mildred had a strong moral compass and sense of justice. Her advocacy was regardless of race. She was a strong voice for Black women in the academy, but also the lone advocate for the White male faculty member who had voted against her for tenure.*

Notes

1.   (M. Pratt, personal communication, April 26, 1972).
2. (T. Pratt, personal communication, n.d.).
3. (M. Pratt, personal communication, n.d.).
4. (M. Pratt, personal communication, n.d.).
5. (T. Pratt, personal communication, n.d.).
6. (T. Pratt, personal communication, n.d.).
7. (M. Pratt, personal communication, n.d.).
8. (M. Pratt, personal communication, n.d.).
9. (M. Pratt, personal communication, n.d.).
10. (M. Pratt, personal communication, n.d.).
11. Larry Court was a six-unit townhouse in Normal. They subsequently purchased 104 Shelbourne in Normal, an eight-unit building, and 606 East Taylor Street, a three-unit converted house in Bloomington.
12. (M. Pratt, personal communication, n.d.).
13. (M. Pratt, personal communication, n.d.).
14. Malcolm X was assassinated on February 21, 1965.
15. (M. Pratt, personal communication, n.d.).
16. (M. Pratt, personal communication, n.d.).
17. (M. Pratt, personal communication, n.d.).
18. Apparently, Mildred was the second faculty member and first full-time faculty member hired to teach social work in the Department of Sociology, Anthropology. There was no social work department when Mildred was hired. The Bachelor of Social Work program was not established until 1979 ("Illinois State University School of Social Work," December 13, 2013).
19. (M. Pratt, personal communication, n.d.).
20. (M. Pratt, personal communication, n.d.).
21. (M. Pratt, personal communication, n.d.).
22. Mildred was promoted to Associate Professor on August 21, 1974; to Professor on August 16, 1979; and she retired on July 31, 1993 (M. Pratt-Clarke, personal communication, n.d.).
23. (M. Pratt, personal communication, n.d.).
24. Mildred describes a similar incident that happened years later, in February 2012, at Canterbury Ridge (an assisted living facility) in Urbana, Illinois: "Today I was in the washroom of my apartment building, putting my clothes in the washing machine. An elderly woman walked up to me and asked if I would wash her clothes for her. Shocked that she would ask me to wash her clothes, I got myself together and asked her why she would ask me to wash her clothes. She could barely speak but said, 'I just asked you,' to which I replied, 'Would you just ask anyone in the washroom to wash your clothes?' She was mum, unable to speak. Would she have asked any White woman this question? I told her that I had three advanced degrees—two master's degrees and a PhD—and I did not wash clothes for people. She turned red and was unable to speak. In the year 2012, I must say that I was shocked to have been asked to wash her clothes. Yes, racism still exists" (M. Pratt, personal communication, n.d.).

25. (M. Pratt, personal communication, n.d.).
26. (M. Pratt, personal communication, May 4, 2012).
27. (M. Pratt, personal communication, n.d.).
28. (M. Pratt, personal communication, n.d.).
29. (M. Pratt, personal communication, n.d.).
30. (M. Pratt-Clarke, personal communication, n.d.).
31. (M. Pratt-Clarke, personal communication, n.d.).

References

Benjamin, L. (Ed.). (1997). *Black women in the academy: Promises and perils*. Gainesville, FL: University Press of Florida.

Holmes, S. (1999). *Black women academicians speak out: Race, class, and gender in narratives of higher education* (Dissertation Iowa State University). Retrieved from http://lib.dr.iastate.edu/cgi/viewcontent.cgi?article=13458&context=rtd

Illinois State University School of Social Work: *Accreditation*. (2013, December 13). Retrieved from http://socialwork.illinoisstate.edu/about/accreditation.shtml

CHAPTER TEN

Black History Project

I wish to coin the term "threeness" to describe the sense in which to truly be human, one must be connected to the past, the present, and future. One must know those past experiences of generations which were noble and those which were base. Both help us to survive in the present and enable us to leave a legacy for the future.—Mildred Pratt, January 14, 1989[1]

Dear Friends, I am writing to each of you with a request that you start searching for and saving anything that has to do with your family. We are fast losing our history because we do not think of or recognize the value of our possessions or artifacts. There are those small things that we think have no value, but they are historical and a part of our Black Heritage. Our older family members are dying out—those who could tell us a story or give us a picture or documents. We go through attics and dresser drawers and throw away many a paper without as much as a glance at it. Younger members consider some of these objects, manuscripts, photographs, and reminiscences of no use, but these mementos should be evaluated and preserved by the McLean County Historical Society. Please consider donating items that all may see and appreciate them and know that they are a part of our Black History.—Kathryn P. Dean, Acquisitions Committee[2]

The Bloomington-Normal Black History Project has been the brightest spot in my career. The warm camaraderie that characterizes all of our formal and informal contacts has enriched my life and made all of the efforts worthwhile. It is a delight to know that together we have actively changed the concept of what is history both in the local community as well as society at large. The human emotion and achievements generated by the project will continue regardless of who replaces me, because the momentum among the membership will sustain it.—Mildred Pratt, 1993[3]

The Vision

The Bloomington-Normal Black History Project played an important role in Mildred's life during her tenure at Illinois State University. The project was the culmination of many of Mildred's interests. Most profoundly it was about valuing individuals, in particular, African-Americans, who had been undervalued by society. Her friend and co-director of the project, Dr. Pam Muirhead, retired professor of English at Illinois Wesleyan University, provides the vision for the project and Mildred's seminal role[4]:

The Bloomington-Normal Black History Project is a community group dedicated to documenting the presence of African-Americans in McLean County. It was formally organized in the mid-1980s and eventually became an affiliate of the McLean County Museum of History. But before the project became official, before Oscar Waddell slapped his dollar dues down on the table and said, "Let's do this," there was Mildred Pratt's singular work as an interviewer and community organizer. Before all you amateur and professional historians start squirming in your pews, let me say that Mildred's efforts were not the first, but they were the most sustained. In the late 1960s and early 1970s, and…again around 1975, there had been efforts by others, most short-lived, to gather news clippings and search official records for evidence of African-Americans' lives in the twin cities.

Mildred's first interviews had a clear, small goal that gave her work great power. To teach her Social Work students at ISU [Illinois State University] how to conduct oral interviews, she sent them out to tape elderly Black residents of Bloomington-Normal talking about folk medicinal practices. What these residents also had to say about their migration to this region and about family and work and struggle and joy led Mildred to set out herself to interview every senior Black community member who would talk with her. One person recommended the next, and so on.

At that point in the 1980s and even today, Black History was all about who was the first this or that—who were the overlooked heroes, heroines, and achievers. Mildred was interested in this Black History Month calendar stuff, but the value and power of her work lay in her fundamental respect for the effort that we all bring to living in a community, particularly when that community makes your efforts to belong a daily struggle. She just admired the perseverance, creativity, and determination of everyday folks.

The more than 90 transcribed interviews that form the lasting core of the Black History Project are housed in the archives of the McLean County Museum of History. These interviews caught—just in time—the stories of people who were born as early as the 1890s and those who had lived through the Great Depression, two World Wars, and several cycles of the Civil Rights Movement. And these interviews—along with the letters, photographs, clothing, tools, furniture, and household objects,…even handmade kitchen cabinets, that families and individuals have donated to the Museum of History—make this county's Black History collection one of the most extensive and remarkable in—I'll be conservative here—the Midwest. And it's growing.

As many of you…know, Mildred did not do this work singlehandedly. Mildred's mantra was, "Should we form a committee?" It was worded like a question, but you knew it wasn't. All kinds of people said yes to Mildred's committees. Dean Virginia Owen at ISU; Caribel Washington, a community member and first president of the project; and Greg Koos, Executive Director of the Museum of History, were among Mildred's earliest supporters. Illinois State University, Illinois Wesleyan University, the David Davis Mansion, the McLean County Arts Center, and the McLean County Historical Society were members of a consortium of not-for-profit institutions that provided venues, expertise, supplies, and access to grants for art shows, one-day family artifact exhibits, speakers, archaeology digs at a home and a church, theater and music performances, talks, panels, and workshops for the Black History Project.

Mildred even took project members on the road to conferences in South Carolina and Missouri, to do workshops for struggling Black History groups in other towns, and to do research in Tennessee and Kentucky. I loved traveling with Mildred. She was a joyful road warrior who loved energetic talk, food, poetry, laughter, and driving. Almost every time she traveled to do research, she rode with some mix of her entourage of community members, academics, men and women, the elderly and the youngish, and White, Black, and tan folks. Sometimes in those early days when our group flowed into a small-town library, I could see a moment of confusion on the face of the person behind the desk who might have wondered if we planned some bizarre kind of sit-in.

And I don't want it to be forgotten that Mildred, an honored and much-published full professor, faced down an academic establishment that quietly believed that researching the everyday lives of Black citizens in McLean County was second-class work.

The grants ran their course. We have fewer programs now. Most of the original Black History Project interviewees have died. But the research continues. The Black History Project has even become a model for documenting the presence, pride, and passion of other more recently arrived McLean County communities. The playwright and actress Anna Deaveare Smith said of her own interviews in search of American character, "I'm always looking at something that is at the essence of an individual, but ultimately at the essence of a community."[5] The Black History Project that Mildred inspired expresses the essence of this community.

Pam shares a bit more about the relationship between the Black History Project and the Consortium and Mildred's leadership style[6]:

There's not much time between the founding of the Black History Project (1989) and the effort to organize the Consortium that started about 1990. The Project quickly became an affiliate of the History Museum. The Consortium [ISU, IWU, McLean County Museum of History, David Davis Mansion, McLean Co. Arts Center] was the essential conduit for grants and funding, but the activities were generated by the Project. The Project has never had an independent nonprofit tax designation. The day-to-day funding of postage, paper, office space, storage, publicity, secretarial help, and event management was handled by ISU and IWU. Eventually, ISU gave Mildred "course credit" for co-directing the Consortium/Project; I was IWU's co-director with funding coming directly from IWU Dean of Faculty's budget, and the secretarial work was assigned to the IWU English Department. The Consortium gave the members official access to the Black History Project, which gave the local organizations an important stamp of approval for their publicity and grant applications.

Your Mom was determined, absolutely determined as a matter of moral and professional principle, that the elderly members of the Black community who had contributed their life histories be included in, even better—be at the center of, the exhibits, performances, talks, that formed the core of the collected Black History Project material. The push for Black and feminist studies in the late 1980s and early 1990s helped enormously when it came to making a case for the Project. Not that it was easy. At the time, talk often exceeded action. But, Mildred had a talent for identifying like-minded people. Virginia Owen, Dean of Liberal Arts at ISU, had a direct hand in arranging funding when the Project and Consortium started. Greg Koos at the Historical Society, and Marcia Young (at the ISU Museum and later site supervisor for David Davis Mansion) pulled together resources from a number of pots. At that time, ISU wasn't worried about Mildred including non-academic community people (elderly Black folks) on her research trips, and she fostered a wonderful we're-all-in-this-together spirit. It wasn't just the professors/ professionals who were authorities. No doctorate would ever outrank Caribel Washington's [President of the Black History Project] life experience.

Mildred also was wonderfully savvy about race and power. She knew who needed to see Black faces, who would respond to a White male, and who needed to know that she had a PhD. The fun of it was that we all knew which strategy was being employed and we enjoyed playing our assigned roles. I vividly remember one research trip to Kentucky that sprang our biracial, multigenerational, town-gown crew on a small public library. Once they got over their surprise, the staff seemed delighted.

Empowerment

The unique nature of the Bloomington-Normal Black History Project is reflected by its integration of key social work concepts: community organizing, preserving history, ensuring institutionalization of the Project, and empowerment. With its focus on empowerment, Mildred consciously sought to engage the participants as equal partners with scholars. Mildred recognized the abusive history of research on African-Americans and sought to create a different model. Whereas early scholars portrayed Blacks as victims, and focused on weakness and negativity, Mildred sought to focus on the positive qualities that African-Americans possessed. In 1993, Mildred created a document called "A Statement Prepared: Bloomington-Normal Black History and Culture Consortium and Bloomington-Normal Black History Project" in which she summarizes the history of the project and the consortium[7]:

Sociologists, urbanologists, and cultural anthropologists were ravaging and raping Black urban communities in the urban inner cities for data. …The focus was on measuring and attempting to prove or disprove negative assumptions, views, …hypotheses, and theories based on their data-gathering instruments. They seemed careless and insensitive to the fact they were dealing with human beings. In the late 1960s, Black communities grew tired and angry with the proven and precedent, perceiving both the research proof and product to be briared. In their own ways, the Black communities began to cry out loud and clear, "Don't come to our neighborhoods."

The genius of this project and the hundreds like it all over the country is that those who made the history are involved as researchers along with the university scholars. Those who made the history experience the human encounters together with the scholars—[a] "give and take"—in a reciprocal relationship. This project in truth empowers our Black elderly who bore the pangs and arrows of segregation and overt racism. …[T]his project empowers the elderly Blacks in Bloomington-Normal to conduct their social history and present it to the public. It is this basic ideology which has served as the guiding force for this project. It can be said that the elderly Blacks were attracted to the project initially because of this ideology, and the subsequent cohesion has been sustained by it.

This social history effort is a history of masses of ordinary people. It examines and documents the Black community of interest—their migration to the area, urbanization, industrialization, family and neighborhood formation, social networks, how [they] acquired jobs and housing, formed churches and businesses, and coped in a dominant White community. It is essentially a holistic story told by the people themselves of how they worked to control their fate and to influence the character of the nation. While this social history effort is like many other local histories,[8] it differs in the sense that it includes artifact collection, historical archaeology, genealogy, and community programs where the elderly Blacks share their stories with the community.

The program is a multidisciplinary, multiracial, and multicultural humanitarian system that includes the active participation of academic and nonacademic people working together as colleagues. Another important characteristic of this program is that it includes elderly Blacks, the majority of whom completed no higher than a high school education. ...[T]he overall purpose of the project...is to chronicle the history of people of African descent in the towns of Bloomington-Normal since the first Blacks, two people of African descent, were brought to the area as "slaves" (indentured servants) in 1837.

In presenting the description and analysis of this social history effort, the organizing concepts utilized are empowerment and institutionalization. Empowerment is defined by [Barbara] Solomon as a "process whereby persons who belong to a stigmatized social category throughout their lives [can be assisted to develop and] increase skills in the exercise of interpersonal influence and the performance of valued social roles."[9] In their model for institution building, [Milton] Esman and [Fred] Bruhn defined institutionalization as the "process by which normative relationships and action patterns are established."[10] It is "concerned with purposes and values which extend beyond the immediate task at hand, with the spreading of norms which affect participants and clientele beyond the functional and productive specialization of institutions."[11] The people connected with the project were concerned that the project achieve its goals and that it develop formal structure in order to acquire the kind of support critical to its survival and goal attainment.

[A] Black local social history program...has and can be used as a system for helping to provide survival and effective socialization lessons for contemporary Black families. ...Values such as hard work, frugality, dignity, family, struggle, self-reliance, sharing, and perseverance helped the Bloomington-Normal elderly Blacks function, survive with dignity, and contribute to the Black "community of interest" and to society. The information aggregated about the experiences of the elderly Blacks is shared with the younger generations through local Black expositions, reminiscence sessions, [and] lectures by elderly Blacks to public schools and college students as well as at public libraries and in publication. Telling their stories in their own words is helping to build a bridge between the…older and younger [Black] generations, creating mutual support and understanding.

An organization such as the one described [here] requires many components and characteristics to be successful. Among intangibles are enthusiasm, commitment to the values and purposes, good working relationships, innovation, [and] organizational maintenance. The tangibles include people who represent several disciplines, age groups, social and ethnic groups, …institutions, [and] organizations [as well as] financial support. Perhaps the most critical factor is the commitment of a heterogeneous group of people to put the group goal above individual interests and goals…[working] as colleagues seeing and using the strengths of the various units which comprise the system.

Mildred explained why the project's oral interviews were so important and therapeutic to the elderly African-American participants[12]:

The respondents were experiencing a sense of pride, self-esteem, and enjoyment from recalling their early experiences. They were anxious to share their knowledge as well as direct the interviewer to other respondents. …The interviewer [Mildred] observed that the respondents enjoyed talking about their past, remembering the goose grease rubbed on their chests and the hog hoof tea they drank as children. [They] also felt good with their roles as teachers.

In retrospect, the respondents' behavior can be understood in the context of the history of Afro-Americans in this country. These people grew up in a period [of] social systems in which they were accorded little or no respect [and] were viewed as being ignorant, low-status, passive, powerless people. …To be set up in the role of teacher with much valuable and relevant knowledge to share made them feel pride and self-esteem. They also found themselves in a situation where the medicinal knowledge and skills which they had learned from their own non-formally educated parents was…considered valuable. These elderly Afro-Americans were also in a situation in which this aspect of their culture was being viewed in a positive manner. They expressed this wellspring of good feeling by stretching their memories as far back as they could and telling the interviewer how pleased they were that she had asked them to help and giving her unsolicited names of other aged Blacks.

The best part of the *Bloomington-Normal Black History Project* was giving these people who settled and had been subject to discrimination the opportunity to talk about it and tell their story. Educated Blacks who began to move into the area for jobs in the university and firms looked down on the uneducated Blacks. Older Blacks were aware of this and told me so when I conducted about 80 oral histories. They said the educated forgot the people upon whose backs they rode. I wanted them to tell their stories because it was their experience. I think they felt good about it. They looked forward to it.

They spoke eloquently and enthusiastically about religion, child-rearing, whippings, cooking, folk medicine, courtship, marriage, and how they learned to relate to Whites. They spoke with the kind of abandon and excitement that led me to recognize that for years they'd had this all bottled up inside, ready to explode. They also spoke about how their relatives and parents came to settle in the area and of how they found menial jobs, saved their money, bought and built homes, and endured and fought racism.

The value of oral history in working with elderly people was presented by Frederick Anderson. He said, "The very act of completing oral history with elderly persons reminds them that they are somebody, that they possess valuable information, and, in most instances, that their life is worth living."[13] This project has specifically empowered these elderly African-Americans:

1. [They are empowered by being involved] in this community project as planners and participants, researchers, historians, policy makers, [and] teachers.

2. They are empowered as teachers telling Blacks and Whites from professors to grade-school children about their culture, what they contributed, and how they were deprived of the basic resources guaranteed in the U.S. Constitution and the Bill of Rights.

3. They are empowered when they can tell how it was with their parents and grandparents who were in slavery to ones who intently and respectfully listen to them.

4. They are empowered when they are sought out by the largest newspaper in the area to tell their stories.

5. They are empowered by serving on committees, chairing committees, and making the critical decisions about the project, including telling me to "get Oprah Winfrey for our keynote speaker."

6. [They are empowered by serving] as equal members of committees with college and university professors.

7. They are empowered when they are able to convince the director of the museum that space and time be set aside for an African-American exhibit each year.

8. [They are empowered when they are] able to moderate a panel of [their] peers with great skill [and] confidence, and with the articulation of an English professor.

9. [They are empowered when] artifacts of their history are given a bona fide place along with other artifacts in the museum.

10. [They are empowered by serving] in roles as historical researchers about their own histories.

Two of the empowered community members were Caribel Washington and Reggie Wittaker. Mildred fondly remembers them and the joy of the work[14]:

Caribel was an inspirational person. She was very bright and the leader in the community of Blacks. Somehow Black people looked up to her as a leader. She didn't go to college, but she was a natural-born leader. She owned her own house. At a time when Black women couldn't be anything but maids, she got a job at

State Farm cleaning. Later she got a higher-up job as a secretary. She served as the President of the Black History Project.[15]

Reggie Whittaker was also a very inspirational individual who lived in Normal. At that time, almost all the Black people lived on one side of the town, many in public housing in Bloomington. He didn't. He was born blind and never married. He took care of himself in that house. He did his own cooking and everything. He didn't drive a car but managed with a cab.

We did a dig at Wayman AME church—Caribel's church. I will never forget that day. As we were getting near some really good stuff, we had to stop. Someone in archaeology worked with us at the dig. We found a few dishes and other things. We also went to a burial ground and cemetery in Tennessee. We put up a little marker for unmarked graves of slaves. It was fun. Pam [Muirhead] and I had a great time and took many wonderful trips together.

The Stories

The Bloomington-Normal Black History Project revealed the phenomenal nature of early African-Americans in Bloomington-Normal. The stories reflect the grit, determination, pride, and resilience of African-Americans. Excerpts from a few of the narratives are below[16]:

As a humanities activity, the Bloomington-Normal Black History Project tells how Blacks settled in the area. They are real-life stories of finding housing; courtship; marriage; childbirth and rearing; fighting for their country; fighting for individual freedom to work, eat at restaurants, [and] swim in swimming pools; and just surviving. Their stories of refusing to be denied jobs link them with the work of humanity struggling to be free, survive, and fully express their potential and self-hood.

These people came into a relatively hostile environment, carved out a life for themselves in a system of mutual support, found jobs, developed their own institutions, and eventually wove themselves into the total fabric of the two towns and contributed to its [their] development and that of the entire society.

Essentially what has been learned about Blacks in Bloomington-Normal is that between 1830 and 1960 they formed a "community of interest." Blacks in each town knew each other [and] shared a strong sense of racial and ethnic identity. Many were either friends or relatives or both. A strong mutual aid system developed which still exists among the elderly Blacks. Three women's clubs organized in the early 1900s still function.

Kin and nonkin adults disciplined the children, much like Miriam Makeba described in her book [on] growing up in South Africa. "Our neighborhood," she said, "is a large extended family. Every adult is every child's parent. …What this means is that if I do something wrong, any adult has the right to spank me…and if I am foolish enough to go home and complain to Grandmother…she will demand to know why and then spank me again."[17] Blacks who entered the area as hobos or strangers were "taken in." Orphaned children were cared for by relatives, friends, and neighbors of the "community of interest."

In short, these early pioneers seem to have been imbued with a strong value of self-help, self-reliance, frugality, work, saving, and discipline. While they valued education, they did not perceive a college education to be functional, because Blacks were not permitted into either white-collar or blue-collar jobs until the 1960s.

Blacks worked hard for low wages, saved their money, bought and built homes, set up businesses, and lived in quiet dignity with hope that their children would be educated and enter professions. The Blacks in Bloomington and Normal were also talented and skilled. Whether working for themselves or others, they applied their skills as tree planters, landscapers, bricklayers, tailors, cleaners, housecleaners, carpenters, engineers, barbers, dressmakers, beauticians, midwives, brewers, fire knockers, cooks, musicians, blacksmiths, coppers, undertakers, dentists, physicians, and common laborers. While forbidden by custom to work in the factories until around the 1950s, they took whatever jobs were available and made the most of them.

Reverend George Hoagland, for example, invented a mixture of oils for floors to which he gave the name "Oil of Gladness." This invention was patented in his name, and he is reported to have earned $50,000 a year.[18] Carter Harris, born a slave, was a delegate to the 1884 Republican National Convention. Though a common laborer and hired as a janitor at ISU [Illinois State University] in 1897 (where he worked 27 years), he was a student, teacher, and politician.[19] John White, who could not read or write and never attended school, was a skilled bricklayer in Bloomington.[20] Simone B. Malone, who legend has it came to Normal in chains as a runaway slave, constructed his own house in 1865.[21]

While Blacks who settled in Bloomington-Normal in the early days were much like the people of European descent who settled here; they were different in significant ways. They were Negro, colored, and mulatto, and therefore they were generally denied the full development, utilization, and benefit of their talents, skills, and intelligence. They were also denied the full of use of basic resources and facilities of these two towns. The steps they climbed were no "crystal stairs." In their own way, they helped to pave the way for their children's children and those of the race who would follow.

Bloomington-Normal Blacks were creative, resourceful, and hardworking. They developed their own businesses, social clubs, entertainment, civic and political organizations, churches, and social welfare. They also contributed their men to serve in the Spanish-American War, Civil War, and World Wars I and II. The women organized their own service corps to serve their men in the military. When Illinois State University would not permit Black students to live in the dormitories, Black people in Bloomington-Normal opened their homes to these students as part of the extended family system.

Denied full participation as citizens of the United States and in Bloomington-Normal, Blacks did "not go quietly into their oppression." In their own way, they joined their ancestors before them in efforts to be full participating Americans. While they fought in the Revolutionary War at Concord, Bunker Hill, [and] Lexington, and with George Washington at Valley Forge in the Civil War, the phrases "We the People" and "We hold these truths to be self-evident, that all men are created equal" did not include them.[22]

Unlike most other immigrants who came to these shores seeking freedom, most Blacks came in slavery. While the Irish, Italian, and other Americans might regard their forbearers' country of origin with pride, it was not until the 1960s that Black Americans identified with "African culture." They had been carefully and deliberately taught to abhor Africa and Africans as a land of jungles and savages.[23]

Blacks in Bloomington-Normal, individually and in groups, acted to realize full citizenship and to be a part of "We the People." They remembered how they did it. One woman held her own one-woman "sit-in" when denied a job as a factory worker. One man threatened to knock an usher over the banister when told he had to sit in the "crow's nest" in the movie theater. A mulatto mother, after being told by a waitress that she could sit and have a drink but the colored children (her son and daughter) could not, told the children, "Sit and drink." Ms. Posey, an ISU student, was told if she indicated on her job application form that she was Puerto Rican and not Negro, she could have a secretarial job. Straining to hold back the tears, she refused.

Ms. Murray was working as a maid one Sunday morning and, while cleaning up after breakfast, said one guest excitedly announced, "It's time to go hear the Darkies [Wings over Jordan Choir]." Ms. Murray angrily mounted the stairs and demanded, "Give me my money or else," and left the job. When Mrs. Williams' father became ill with tuberculosis, the family refused to have him remain at the Fairview Sanatorium because Negroes were admitted in a separate building. It was a shack in the back of the main building.[24]

Ms. Posey remembered how, when she was told that she could not swim in the swimming pool at Miller Park but must swim in the "hole,"…her mother stood up to "Big Al" and said, "I pay taxes, and she will swim in the pool." And she did. Ms. Hosea, working as a janitress in a local restaurant one day, had her daughters come in to eat, and when her daughters were refused, she left the job.

Now a Catholic nun, Sister Antona told of applying to the Catholic School of Nursing in Bloomington for training and being denied because "I'm not sure the other nuns would receive you." Sister Antona later entered St. Louis Infirmary for Blacks and was the famous nun who marched with Dr. Martin Luther King at Selma, Alabama.

Oscar Waddell served his country in the armed forces during World War II and recounted his experiences at a public park in Bloomington where Blacks were forced to swim in a dirty swimming hole separated from the White children. His elder friend Willie Stearles said to him, "Go along with it and one of these days it will be all right." When Oscar was preparing to leave to serve his country in World War II, he was looking for a place for his wife to live. When he found a place, he was initially refused by the White owner. Oscar said he was going to fight for his country and should be able to rent the house. Eventually, the owner relented and rented Oscar the house.

Like most Black males in Bloomington and Normal who held low-level jobs even if they worked in factories, Oscar found himself employed as a janitor. It was only when the manager threatened to close the factory down one evening because a critical machinist became ill that the manager, with tongue-in-cheek, asked Oscar if he could operate the machine. Oscar said he could and operated the machine superbly, because as he mopped the floors he had observed the operation of the machine.

In general, Blacks experienced second-class citizenship in most aspects of their lives in Bloomington-Normal until the early 1960s. Blacks who had served their country in World War II in support of freedom and the democratic way of life returned to towns which had changed little for Blacks. Many felt that they had experienced more civil rights in the armed services after the legislative and executive actions than they now enjoyed. Those who had served in the armed services and those who had benefited from the changes in the war industries were not content with things as they were. The "winds of change" were in the air, and a variety of civil rights groups were mobilized to declare war on racism in all of its forms. These winds touched Bloomington and Normal individuals who mobilized to protest discrimination in housing, employment, education, and other areas of life.

The NAACP [National Association for the Advancement of Colored People], under the leadership of Merlin Kennedy, mobilized, for example, to demand their rights to have a Black Santa Claus in their Christmas parade. Dr. Martin Luther King was invited to Illinois Wesleyan University to speak and lent his considerable moral and religious weight on behalf of civil rights in Bloomington-Normal. The institutions of higher education's students and faculty also engaged in various protest activities demanding Black faculty and students, buildings to be named for Blacks, and Black studies, courses, and programs. At least one church under the initiative of Luvada Hunter expressed its support of fair housing by asking its members to sign pledge cards.

Ms. Luvada Hunter's (an elderly Bloomington Black woman) life as [the] wife of a janitor is typical of those of many Black women in the area. A hat and dressmaker who worked out of her home, she cooked, cleaned, and looked after the children while her husband worked as a janitor at a local university. In the evenings and on weekends by mutual agreement with her husband, she attended and worked actively in social and civic organizations while her husband looked after the children. It was in this role that she spearheaded a drive in her church (a White church where she was one of the few Black members) to get open housing for Blacks. Around 80 years of age now with major health problems, she continues to be active and one of the most generous with giving time and energy to the Bloomington-Normal Black History Project.

Mildred summarizes the progress made and the work remaining in the 1980s[25]:

In summary, it can be said that by the 1980s Bloomington and Normal had made significant progress in moving to a more just society with respect to Blacks. That is, the institutions of higher learning had increased the number of Black faculty and students; Blacks were employed in professional positions in city government, factories, industries, and public schools; and restaurants and places of entertainment were open to Blacks on a nondiscriminatory basis. Housing was more open to Blacks. As social, political, and economic changes began to take place all over the nation for Blacks, they were also changing in Bloomington-Normal. Aided by the various civil rights groups, including the NAACP [National Association for the Advancement of Colored People], opportunities began to open up for Blacks. In Bloomington-Normal, the NAACP, various churches, civil rights groups, and individuals all contributed to the restaurants opening their doors, employers hiring Blacks in workplaces, and occupations [and recreation facilities] previously closed to them...opening their doors. Blacks also became more involved in the political process. The late Eva Jones was the first Black person elected to the Bloomington City Council.[26]

Despite these significant changes with respect to racism, it would be a gross error to assume that racism has been eradicated in these two towns, for it has not. It is important to highlight the fact that each of the two cities has a Human Relations Commission and individuals and groups dedicated to preventing racism and taking active steps to eradicate it. Perhaps the most significant project in this respect is the Not in Our Town program initiated by Marc and Darlene Miller, which has held at least three successful rallies and marches against racism. The town of Bloomington's Human Relations Commission's staff was very actively involved in working with the program, and its police department wore Not in Our Town buttons. This multiracial, multiethnic, and interfaith organization is performing a significant role in assuring that racism will not go unprotested in the area.

The Impact

The Bloomington-Normal Black History project was selected for the Bloomington-Normal Human Relations Commissions Award on January 14, 1989. Mildred's acceptance speech reflects her perceptions about the importance of the project in preserving and promoting humanity and human dignity[27]:

I am honored to be seated with one of the giants in the interest of preserving our humanism—Reverend Ralph Abernathy—and to be the recipient of an award named for giant Dr. Martin Luther King. No nation produces more than a few such persons. That is why it is so critical that we honor them and maximize the use of their wisdom. Reverend Abernathy, what you and those who worked so closely with you did was not just to free Blacks to vote and have access to public accommodations (as important as that was), but you injected a vaccine against the disease of human beings' inhumanity to each other. It is the task of those of us here and around the world to continue injecting that vaccine to weaken and eventually kill forever that debilitating disease. …While I accept this award with honor, I salute those who lived the lives which I have been privileged to unveil so that they may be shared.

Dr. W.E.B. DuBois coined the concept "twoness" to describe the dilemma which Blacks experience in America. He said, "One ever feels the sense of twoness." I wish to coin the term "threeness" to describe the sense in which to truly be human, one must be connected to the past, the present, and future. One must know those past experiences of generations which were noble and those which were base. Both help us to survive in the present and enable us to leave a legacy for the future.

As I began this project, I approached it with this "threeness" concept. I was sure that we would find both *noble* and *base* aspects of…past human experiences. Each must be uncovered. Among the noble values which guided early Blacks were *self-help, work ethic,* and *mutual aid.* They took the menial jobs available to them; saved their money; bought land, homes, and businesses; and did what they could [to] fight racist indignities to humanity, themselves, and those of us who would come after them. There were also brave Whites in those early years, predating civil rights acts, who affirmatively fought racism.

The base human actions uncovered—such as requiring Blacks to swim in a swimming hole rather than in the pool, and telling a mulatto mother that she could sit at the restaurant and eat, but not her darker-skinned children—must forever remind us that they shall not be sanctioned by civilized society.

This prestigious award is a tribute to many individuals, organizations, and systems both in and outside this community who support the project which the award honors. The 60 or more individuals from this community have become my friends, colleagues, and teachers. I am most indebted to the early Black settlers in this community who preserved their rich heritage, passed it [on] through families, and so enable us to gain from their wisdom, suffering, and joys. Greg Koos is especially applauded for his tenacious commitment to this effort to preserve the life histories and artifacts of Black people in this community.

I wish to close my remarks with a reference from Alex Haley. He said, "What *Roots* really deals with is the fact that everyone has family, has ancestors. We have become so involved with separating ourselves from each other that we overlook the common denominator of humanity that binds us all."[28] His new book, *A Different Kind of Christmas*,[29] is a novella about a young White man who grew up in the South—the son of a slave master. Like most such White children of that era, he was suckled and reared by women, then called "Black mammies."

These children developed closer ties with these Black women than with their own mothers. This affinity which the central character, Fletcher Randall, developed with such "house slaves" was confused by the negative attitudes which he developed about other Blacks. This dissonance remained with him until he found a resolution by becoming an active participant in the Underground Railroad. In sum, Alex Haley says what his book is about…"let us, if we will, go on with our anti-this, anti-that, and anti-the-other, but in the final analysis, if we don't learn to be brothers [and sisters], we will all share the same terrible fate."[30] His is the dramatic plea of a writer for humanism.

The actions of the Bloomington-Normal Human Relations Commissions today are their pleas for the preservation of humanism which binds us to each other now, to our brothers and sisters of the past, and to those who will come after us—if we do our jobs well today. This plaque is for all who, from one generation to the other, take the thread of humanity and help to weave the tapestry of many colors, textures, and designs which keep us able to refer to ourselves as a part of the human family.

Greg Koos Executive Director, McLean County Museum of History, summarizes Mildred's impact and the impact of the Black History Project[31]:

My core observation is that Mildred clearly understood how to organize communities. Her ability to identify, recruit, and empower people of the Bloomington/Normal African-American Community was the foundation for a successful project that spanned over 20 years of work. There really aren't many Black History projects that were as long lasting, as well directed and as productive as ours.

Key Lessons

1. *The project was, in fact, a success and created a legacy for future generations. The community responded to Kathryn Dean's request for contributions.*[32] *Documents and artifacts include a document prepared on a house constructed by a Black carpenter in the late 1800s and major holdings from the famous Duff family in Normal. The Duff family contributions include an original letter written by a slave and a complete bride's outfit worn by a slave at her wedding. Several relics from World Wars I and II were donated by another famous family, the Bartons. The Bartons descended from a full-blooded Cherokee Indian (a part of the "Trail of Tears") who was recruited by the founder of Illinois State University to plant trees in Normal. The project and the oral histories of almost 100 African-Americans in the Twin Cities are available online through the McLean County Museum of History website.*[33]

2. *The Black History Project was the synthesis of core values that reflected Mildred's background in both religion and social work: advocating for human dignity and humanity; providing voice to the voiceless; empowering those who have been disempowered; and preserving the past and history of those who are often overlooked. One Black History Project member shared that so many people were eager to work with Mildred because she was always so kind and considerate of the feelings of others, and was always speaking words of praise in public for the effort someone else made.*

3. *Mildred had a unique ability to build bridges across divides. She, in fact, bridged worlds that were often separate. Through the Bloomington-Normal Black History Consortium, she merged the academic world with the nonacademic world. She merged the White academy with the Black community. She merged Illinois State University in Normal with Illinois Wesleyan in Bloomington. In doing this, she exemplified the power of integration. She was able to be part of the Black community—and at home with many of the project members who did not have a college degree—and also part of the largely White community at the University. Her role in the Black History Project allowed her to mitigate the isolation of the academy and the Whiteness which was part of her professional life. It allowed her to return to be part of a community that was so familiar and comfortable to her from her childhood.*

4. *In addition to empowerment, the importance of institutionalization was critical to Mildred. She did not want the work to lose value. The work, the memories, and the artifacts needed to be preserved for future generations. She used the McLean County Historical Society as the institutional base and partner.*

5. *Mildred exemplified the work of many Black women activists and scholars who were able to use their education to help advance the community. Black women activists, community organizers, and feminists had their feet in two worlds. They were able to use and apply scholarship and educational training to advance community needs. The project benefited Mildred as part of her tenure and promotion journey; but it was not at the expense of the community. The community also benefited, as well. Mildred's role in the academy gave her power and the ability to use institutional resources and influence to transform the lives of African-Americans. More than that, her visionary work also preserved the stories to help transform others, including those in McLean County and all future visitors to the museum who will learn about the power and presence of African-Americans in Bloomington-Normal. Her project exemplified the motto of the National Association of Colored Women, "lifting as we climb," as she truly sought to uplift the Black community as she uplifted herself through the tenure and promotion process at Illinois State University.*

Notes

1. (M. Pratt, personal communication, January 14, 1989).
2. (M. Pratt, personal communication, n.d.).
3. (M. Pratt, personal communication, 1993).
4. (P. Muirhead, personal communication, August 19, 2012).
5. (A. Smith, interview on Great Performances, "Let Me Down Easy," WILL-TV, August 17, 2012).
6. (P. Muirhead, personal communication, April 1, 2013). Permission received May 28, 2017.
7. (M. Pratt, personal communication, 1993; Pratt & Muirhead, 1991).
8. (Bodnar, Simon, & Weber, 1982; Gottlieb, 1987; Trotter, 1984; Yans-McLaughlin, 1981).
9. (Solomon, 1976, p. 6).
10. (Esman & Bruhns, 1966, pp. 318–343).
11. (Esman & Bruhns, 1966, pp. 318–343).
12. (Pratt, 1985, 1988).
13. (Anderson, n.d.).
14. (M. Pratt, personal communication, May 7 and 12, 2012).
15. (Caribel Washington, 2012; Ford, 2011; McLean County Museum of History, 2008). Permission received from McLean County Museum of History, June 5, 2017.
16. (Pratt, 1987, 1988, 1999; Pratt & Muirhead, 1991).
17. (Makeba, 1987).

18. ("George Hoagland Returned," 1941; Steinbacher-Kemp, 2007).
19. ("Carter Harris," 1924). Ironically, though Carter Harris traveled to the 1884 Republican National Convention as a delegate, the obituary only mentions his role as a janitor. See Harbour (2008, p. 50) and Summers (2007).
20. ("Bricklayer's Legacy," 1970).
21. (Harbour, 2008, p. 50).
22. (Cummings & Wise, 1974, p. 149).
23. (Cummings & Wise, 1974, p. 148).
24. (LeBaron, 1879, p. 324).
25. (Pratt, 1999).
26. (Pratt, 1987).
27. (M. Pratt, personal communication, n.d.).
28. (Mabe, 1992).
29. (Haley, 1988).
30. (Petersen, 1989).
31. (G. Koos, personal communication, September 1, 2013).
32. (Muirhead, Hartzold, & Cobb, 2008).
33. (Bloomington-Normal Black History Project Collection, n.d.; Broderick, 2002; and Wyman, n.d.).

References

Anderson, F. (n.d.). *Oral history research with minority elders: Its potential for heritage retention, self-esteem, and program coherence in minority specific projects.* Paper presented to Arizona State University Workshop: Coming of Age in Arizona, Multidisciplinary Coordinating Committee on Aging, Tempe, AZ.

Bodnar, J., Weber, M., & Simon, R. (1982). *Lives of their own: Blacks, Italians, and Poles in Pittsburgh, 1900–1960.* Urbana, IL: University of Illinois Press.

Bricklayer's legacy to the city recorded by wife, friends. (1970, May 13). *Pantagraph.*

Broderick, S. (2002, December). Bloomington-Normal's Black History Project goes online. *Twin City Community News.*

Caribel Washington. (2012, January 3). *Pantagraph.* Retrieved from http://www.pantagraph.com/news/local/obituaries/caribel-washington/article_e764b4d6-3592-11e1-8178-001871e3ce6c.html

Carter Harris, born slave has been janitor for 27 Years. (1924, June 30). *Pantagraph.*

Cummings, Jr., M., & Wise, D. (1974). *Democracy under pressure: An introduction to the American political system.* New York, NY: Harcourt Brace Jovanovich.

Esman, M. J., & Bruhns, F. C. (1966). Institution building in national development: An approach to induced social change in transitional societies. In Hollis W. Peter (Ed.), *Comparative theories of social change* (pp. 318–342). Ann Arbor, MI: Foundation for Research on Human Behavior University of Michigan.

Ford, M. (2011, December 27). Local civil rights leader Caribel Washington dies. *Pantagraph*. Retrieved from http://www.pantagraph.com/news/local/local-civil-rights-leader-caribel-washington-dies/article_42308e62-30e3-11e1-80da-0019bb29

George Hoagland returned to Bloomington after 27 years. (1941, July 6). *Pantagraph*.

Gottlieb, P. (1987). *Making their own way: Southern Blacks' migration to Pittsburgh, 1916–30*. Urbana, IL: University of Illinois Press.

Haley, A. (1988). *A different kind of Christmas*. New York, NY: Random House.

Harbour, J. R. (2008). *Bury me in a free land: African-American political culture and the Settlement Movement in the Antebellum and Wartime Midwest*. Iowa City, IA: University of Iowa.

LeBaron, W. (1879). *The history of McLean County, Illinois: Portraits of early settlers and prominent men*. Retrieved September 1, 2013 from http://archive.org/details/historyofmcleanc00lebarich

Mabe, C. (1992, February 11). Storyteller Alex Haley dies at 70. *Sun Sentinel*. Retrieved from http://articles.sun-sentinel.com/1992-02-11/news/9201080096_1_mr-haley-roots-chicken-george

Makeba, M. (1987). *Makeba: My story*. New York, NY: New American Library.

McLean County Museum of History. (2008, March 10). Caribel Washington [Flickr]. Retrieved from https://www.flickr.com/photos/mcleancountymuseumofhistory/9689350202

McLean County Museum of History. (n.d.). Bloomington-Normal Black History Project Collection. Retrieved August 5, 2013 from http://www.mchistory.org/BNBHP_Collection_Finding_Aid.html

Muirhead, J. W., Hartzold, S., & Cobb, R. (2008). *Presence, pride and passion: A history of African Americans in Mclean County*. Bloomington, IL: McLean County Historical Society.

Petersen, C. (1989, January 1). Trying to make love sell: Alex Haley roots out the common denominator. *Chicago Tribune*.

Pratt, M. (1985). *Oral history: Teaching its use for social work practice*. Paper presented at Education for Practice Workshop, Washington, DC.

Pratt, M. (Ed.). (1987). *We the people tell our story*. Normal, IL: Bloomington-Normal Black History Project.

Pratt, M. (1988). *An innovative social work practice approach: Use of local Black history project to empower elderly Blacks*. Paper presented at National Association of Social Workers Conference, Philadelphia, PA.

Pratt, M. (1999). Turning points in African American history in Bloomington-Normal, Illinois. Retrieved from http://www.lib.niu.edu/1999/iht719930.html

Pratt, M., & Muirhead, P. (1991, March 20). *The Black family: Learning survival from lessons of the past*. Paper presented at the National Black Family Summit, University of South Carolina, SC.

Solomon, B. B. (1976). *Black empowerment: Social work in oppressed communities*. New York, NY: Columbia University Press.

Steinbacher-Kemp, B. (2007, February 3). George Hoagland: Pictures from our past. *Pantagraph*. Retrieved from http://www.pantagraph.com/news/pictures-from-our-past/article_5edaafaa-f8f8-5911-b803-e423b17bf1c0.html

Summers, C. (2007). *Carter Harris (1856–1944)*. Retrieved from http://www.mchistory.org/popups/CemWalk%20Bios/Harris_Carter.html

Trotter, J. (1984). *Black Milwaukee: The making of an industrial proletariat, 1915–45. Blacks in the New World Series*. Urbana, IL: University of Illinois Press.

Wyman, M. (n.d.). *Origins of the Bloomington-Normal Black History Project*. Retrieved September 1, 2013 from http://mchistory.org/research/resources/blackhistory/origins.php

Yans-McLaughlin, V. (1981). *Family and community: Italian immigrants in Buffalo, 1880–1930*. Urbana, IL: University of Illinois Press.

Part III Sunset

I have had a good life. I love you and your children dearly. Please continue to be good people, honest and fair, and helpful to people.—Mildred Pratt, August 10, 1999

I wish you, your family, friends, and all on planet earth peace and meaningful lives.—Mildred Pratt, 2009

CHAPTER ELEVEN

A Legacy

I have never forgotten the roots and soil which gave me sustenance to cope and weather the many storms to which, as an African-American, I have been, am, and always will be an heir. I only hope that mine have been shoulders on which, at least, some whose lives I have touched have stood, and will stand.—Mildred Pratt, 1993[1]

In our system, you have influenced at least 1,500 students. That is quite a legacy to leave the world. Your energy and caring has planted seeds for much social change. In teaching history, you have greatly influenced the future.—Mary Cunningham, Department Chair, 1993[2]

Mildred's life was guided by deeply held core values that she exemplified: service; empowering others; respecting human dignity; social justice; and civil rights. As a scholar, professor, community activist, and community organizer, she lived her beliefs in every aspect of her life. Her colleagues and friends saw her values daily in their interactions with her as reflected in their letters to her upon her retirement from ISU as professor emerita. Though her journey from cotton picking to the academy was often bumpy, students and colleagues recognized her impact on the academy, the community, and the field of social work.

"We Shall Overcome"

As an active participant in the Civil Rights Movement, Mildred was deeply committed to continuing the work and legacy of Dr. Martin Luther King, Jr. She delivered a speech for the Celebration of Dr. Martin Luther King Jr. Day on January 21, 1991, at Illinois Wesleyan University entitled, "Go Tell It on the Mountain: We Shall Overcome." The speech epitomizes her beliefs about social justice and equality and the collective responsibility to continue the work of the Civil Rights Movement by improving the life experiences of all people. Mildred's excerpted remarks are below[3]:

It is perhaps presumptive of me to say this, but I'd like to believe that Dr. King would, if he could, smile approvingly on this gathering here today. It is a gathering of us common, ordinary people called together to celebrate the life of a common, ordinary human being who, in his fight to liberate the human soul, became an extraordinary, common person.

Dr. King liked the "common touch," and expressed it in his desire for a "common funeral." If we would really celebrate his birth, we ought to do so in a common celebration open to all and available to all. Dr. King, on the other hand, would be in dismay that the leaders of the world have not yet learned the lessons of peaceful ways of dealing with conflicts. When will we ever learn?

And so I applaud you…for bringing these people together to honor Dr. King and the host of those who went before who struggled, suffered as brave warriors, and faced battles which make us squirm to read of them. Today I try to feel their pain, sorrow, and redemptive love for peace and freedom. Today and every day we must know that there is no such thing as a "free ride." We all have got to "go tell it on the mountain: We shall overcome." We must take the torch from those who went before us and carry it to the next generation. If we do not, who will?

It was started by Rosa Parks and Dr. King and the Civil Rights Movement. Before King's untimely death, some civil rights laws were passed, but we have been too content with the little we have. We have lulled ourselves to sleep as a few of us got through the gates—and the host of others fell at the gateway. Vincent Harding said, "There is no 'renewed racism.' It really never died. We just stopped weeding the garden and permitted racism to thrive."

Those who truly make history are the ones who regard history as a *sacred trust* to be "passed on." Lerone Bennett Jr., in his foreword to Vincent Harding's most recent book, *Hope and History*,[4] said, "Before the 300,000 could march on Washington, before Martin Luther King, Jr., could climb the mountain top…history had to take the form and color of a guerilla band of great teachers who…when there was no rain and the laborers few—prepared the ground for the harvest many of them would never see." I would add that many nameless brave men, living and dead, plowed in non-fertile ground reaping scant harvest until, eventually, drop by small drop, there was enough moisture to reap a harvest.

The Movement which Bennett insists must be capitalized upon was not a Black movement, not even a regional or national movement—it was a *human* movement with the aim of helping to purify humanity, to bring out the dormant good in all people for all times. It had no geographical boundaries. The Movement is not dead, it will not die—you cannot kill it by disparaging its founders. It is a movement to free the *human spirit* to be all that it can be and that the *Creator* intended it to be.

You cannot kill it by vetoing civil rights laws. You cannot kill it by institutionalizing the campaign slogan that affirmative action is taking jobs from Whites, or by asserting that Blacks and Hispanics are lazier, less intelligent, and less patriotic than Whites (*Chicago Tribune*, January 9, 1991). It cannot be killed by failure to recognize Dr. Martin Luther King's holiday—Martin's body is dead, but his spirit lives all over the world. The soul keeps marching on. Some Black men and White men and Black women and White women, Jews, Gentiles, Russians, White South Africans, and homosapiens all over the world keep the movement alive and sing the song he made popular, "We Shall Overcome."

Lerone Bennett said, "The case can and ought to be made that the movement freed more White people than Black people."[5] It freed White people from the cancer of raw hate—to use their energy in more creative, useful ways than yelling, beating, killing, lynching Blacks, frightening them with their White gowns, dogs, and water hoses.

It freed those Whites of "good will" who just went along with the program to protest to now socialize with Blacks—learn from them, laugh with them, be "brothers and sisters," [and] do the "high five." It liberated them to become *human beings*. John Henrik Clarke said that there is no such thing as *Black History;* it is rather the lost chapter of world history.[6]

The Movement will not be killed by those who refuse to accept the thread of "common humanity" which runs through the veins of each of us regardless of our station in life, the color of our skin, texture of our hair, or size of our lips. In his poem *Creation*, James Weldon Johnson said, "He breathed into him the breath of life and became a living soul."[7]

The Movement epitomizes the essence of what it means to be human—that it is to "breathe free." And so it will not die as long as there are human beings. Quoting a Soviet scholar, William Buckley, Jr., "when there is even one crack in cement, a blade of grass will grow."[8]

The Movement will not die because among us [some] believe we are free because we are "young, urban, Black professionals [who wear] Madison Avenue suits and have the latest most prestigious credit cards"—and hence do not need the Movement. You see, we know that even Supreme Court Justice Thurgood Marshall cannot enjoy all of the perks of his office because he has the green, but not the "White." Michael Tyson, who also has the green, but not the "White," said, when asked if he believed in God, "No, because if there is a God he must hate Black people."

The Movement cannot and must not die because we have too many Black men in prison, depressed, unemployed, too many who must sign up for military service because civilian life offers them too few opportunities. The Movement must not die because there are too many distinguished Black professors leaving prestigious, predominantly White universities for smaller, less prestigious ones because they are harassed by their White professors of lesser academic stature. The Movement will not die because many young college students and drum majors for peace have taken the torch as they "sit in" and protest racial harassment and brutality, and … the killing of human beings. The Movement must continue because we have not yet learned how to solve world problems through peaceful means.

The Movement is alive. Though the bell does not ring as loudly or the torch shine as brightly as it did in the 1960s, as long as there is a sound (ever so faint) or a torch (ever so dim), the Movement shall live on.

The Movement cannot, must not, die when research [is] conducted in 1988 among Black preschool children and 65 percent of them still choose White cabbage patch dolls over Black ones "because the Black dolls look bad."[9] The Movement cannot and must not die when one of every 1,000 Black males age 15 to 24 dies of homicide. The Movement cannot and must not die when we have a mayor in Bradley, Illinois, who is so myopic as to say, "We as a city do not need to declare Dr. Martin Luther King's birthday a holiday and celebrate it because there are only a handful of Blacks in the town."[10]

All the more reason why they ought to celebrate it, because their souls need cleansing. They need the Movement to humanize them. So do many other sections of our society. Those Whites in the Movement can truly sing, "Every time I feel the spirit, I will pray." The Black brothers and sisters can truly say of them, "Do you call them a brother or sister?" "Yes! Yes!" Then, don't scandalize *His name*.

We need the Movement because we have too many Black academicians who have positions as distinguished professors who delude themselves into believing that they "got there" on their own merit—and can now maintain that status by advocating that *we do not need affirmative action laws*, because *merit*, not *color*, is the only criterion which counts. As one such young professor was told by another eminent older Black panelist, "You would not even be in that position to be speaking if there had been no Civil Rights Movement and affirmative action laws to demand that Blacks *also* be accepted on their merits." What that professor and those of his type need to know is that if they leave that "ivory tower," shed [their] Madison Avenue suits and replace [them] with "dreadlocks" and shabby clothes, and walk through an "all-White" neighborhood, [they are] likely to be treated like any of us (a "nigger"). It happened to me in Normal—a White woman in my neighborhood asked me if I'd be a maid for her brother. My sister-in-law, whose husband was Minister of Finance for his country, was solicited at one of the local supermarkets to be a maid too.

The difference between you, "Mr. Professor," and many of us other Blacks who know our *reality,* is that we know we need the Movement and have a responsibility to nourish it.

Any person living in the United States in 1991 is truly unaware of the real world—[if they do] not to know that, in Vincent Harding's words, "the ties between Birmingham and the Berlin Wall (and may I add Vaclav Havel [Czechoslovakia]) and Martin Luther King are central to that sense of common ground on which our humanity is built."[11] Vincent goes on, "When seen as far more than a contest for legal rights, when understood as a Black-led, multi-racial quest for democracy in America, for the healing of the nation, for the freeing of all our spirits, then the story belongs to everyone in this country" [and] around the world.[12]

Go tell it on the mountain: We shall overcome.

And so, Mayor Kenneth Hayes of Bradley, Illinois, the Movement is alive, for you apologized to Reverend William Copeland and proclaimed that the village will celebrate Dr. King's birthday.[13] Reverend Copeland's protest is a testament that the Movement goes marching on—and it does so with velocity in some sectors of the world and with [a] snail's pace in others. I applaud you, Mayor Hayes, and all the small, predominantly White towns in our nation (including Bloomington) who proclaim this *day* a legal holiday by releasing its employees to celebrate it.

We need the Movement so that, like the wise, old Black slave women who said, "I was born a slave, but I ain't never been no slave,"[14] we can say, "I was born *Black*, but I ain't never been nobody's nigger." We need the Movement so that every state in this nation will, like the state of Illinois, pass legislation mandating that African-American and Hispanic history and culture be taught in public schools. I wish the legislation had included higher education.

The Movement must go on, for that surge of energy of the young Blacks in the 1960s whom Dr. King said abandoned middle-class values and careers to cheerfully become jailbirds [and] troublemakers, took their Brooks Brothers attire off and put on overalls to work in isolated rural areas, is still pushing at the door to again be unleashed. If unleashed, it will cause our young Black and Whites today to give up the expensive leather jackets, Nike shoes, Seiko watches, parties, etc., to take up the torch for human freedom and carry it. To do so will not only transform them but all those around them[15]. One 90-year-old Black woman said of these young people of the 1960s, "They helped me be a brave woman."[16]

Martin said…when the history books are written…somebody will have to say, "There lived a race of people, Black people, fleecy locks and Black complexion people, who had the moral courage to stand up for their rights, and thereby they injected a new meaning into the veins of history and of civilization…"[17]

Let us keep this Movement going—let us keep purifying our *spirits* by remembering those Black and Whites, Jews and Gentiles, Muslims, and those true *humanists*—many whose names we know, and a host of others whom we do not know—…who helped to make life better for us. Let their names be read in Sunday schools, in sermons, in schools; let monuments be erected to them; let them be immortalized in poetry, song, dance, painting, sculpture, and most of all in our behavior toward our fellow humans. Let us keep telling the story of how "The Strong Men (Women) Keep Coming"[18]:

We must not only see that this story is told and told over and over again, but we, our children, and their children must be the story tellers—we must assure that the story is told "like it was and is."

Our young African-American children must grow up knowing who they are, where they came from, who they came from—who suffered, died, was humiliated—so that they can be where they are. They must know on whose back they were carried.

So, young Blacks, lest you forget those Blacks who went before us. Slaves (field and house), janitors, maids, washerwomen, chauffeurs,…common laborers, sharecroppers, cotton choppers, and pickers were always ladies and gentlemen—though not recognized by their master and employers as such. No, we disparage and dishonor ourselves and our race when we fail to recognize that these people "ran the interference" for us so that we can get college educations, white-collar jobs, etc.

As Paul Lawrence Dunbar said, they masked their "personhood" to survive and pave the way for us. He writes in "We Wear the Mask": "We wear the mask that grins and lies…But let the world dream otherwise, We wear the mask!"[19]

We must keep on improving and validating our story and telling it to young Blacks. We must broaden their shoulders so that they can say to future Blacks, "He ain't heavy—he's my brother." Our young Blacks must know they are Black, not be ashamed of it. We must all know that if we forget our Blackness, we make it easy for others to forget our humanity.

On Sunday, December 1, 1990, on a news report, Garrick Utley asked a reporter why young, professional middle-class Blacks support conservative Republicanism and oppose affirmative action laws and policies.[20] How can they support a Republican party which considers appointing [William J.] Bennett to head the Republican Party when he supports tactics such as those employed by Senator [Jesse] Helms to defeat a Black candidate for senator? In a desperate, last-minute move to avoid defeat, Helms asked working-class Whites if they wanted to lose their jobs to Blacks as a result of affirmative action laws. The reporter's response was that most of these young, middle-class professionals do not know why these laws are necessary—they have little or no knowledge of the Civil Rights Movement.

If they are age 25 now, they were born in 1965, so by 1970 (the bottoming out of the Civil Rights Movement), they were age five. If they were enrolled in northern schools, they learned next to nothing about Africa [or] African-American history, culture, and struggle. It is not unusual to ask Black students about prominent African-Americans whom all should know and they do not. Even when they raise their hands to indicate they know Martin Luther King, they are unable to say what he did.

You see, it is all right to recite Dr. Martin Luther King's creative genius in his prose, but I would argue that if you would recite it that you have an obligation to know what motivated it. It was out of his years of humiliation and that of his fellow human beings that he wrote. That prose was born out of suffering.

Shelby Foote said before the Civil War [that] Americans said the United States "*are*." After the war, [they said] the United States "is." He said we came to think of ourselves as "one people."[21] What Dr. King and those active in the Movement did was to save the *soul* of the United States just as surely as Abraham Lincoln saved the *body* of the United States.

To do what those people did required an uncommon courage.

I remember that when Dr. King was shot, I was scheduled the following day to attend a faculty meeting and I simply decided I would not go. The Black students and faculty organized to demand Black faculty and students. In a negotiating session with the Dean who [called] our Vice President (our spokesperson), "Boy," we immediately all got up and left *except one man*. He was a Black man, but I will not call him an "Uncle Tom." You see, the original Uncle Tom referenced in Harriet Beecher Stowe's classic *Uncle Tom's Cabin* was Josiah Henson.[22] Josiah Henson spent 30 years on a plantation owned by Isaac Riley in Montgomery County, Maryland. Escaping slavery and moving to Canada, he became a Methodist minister, businessman, [and] leader in the abolitionist movement, and helped 118 slaves escape. He began a cooperative colony of former slaves in Canada, published three sets of his memoirs, visited England and met Queen Victoria, and, 50 years after his escape from slavery…was invited to the White House by President Rutherford B. Hayes. Later when he visited the surviving wife of his slave master, Mathilda Riley, she did not recognize him. She asked to feel his arm broken in his youth by a neighborhood gang. Now convinced it was Josiah Henson, she said, "Why sir, you are a gentleman," to which Josiah replied, "I was always a gentleman, madam."[23]

We must tell our young people about the Movement so that they will keep it going. A part of telling includes hearing the wisdom of our brothers and sisters who were slaves. A former slave woman described the dilemma of African-Americans: "Slavery was a bad thing, and freedom of the kind we got with nothing to live on was bad. Two snakes full of poison. One lying with his head pointing North, and the other with his pointing South. Their names was slavery and freedom. The snake called slavery lay with head pointed South. The snake called freedom lay with head pointed North. Both bit the nigger, and they was both bad."[24]

And the telling also must indicate having them know that the Movement is universal and not bound by time or space. They need the perspective of C.T. Vivian rising from the sidewalk facing the sheriff who had knocked him down, blood streaming from his face as he, Vivian, said, "We are willing to be beaten for democracy."[25] This reverberated on the other side of the world when the young fasting Chinese student in Tiananmen Square [said], "We are willing to starve for democracy."[26]

If we are to keep the Movement alive, we need dreamers. We need people who see things as they are but who can dream of how they ought to be and, like all *good* poets and artists—like James Weldon Johnson, Leonard Bernstein, Vaclav Havel, Martin Luther King, Gwendolyn Brooks, Nina Simone, and Langston Hughes—actually work to make the *dream reality*.

James Weldon Johnson's words, [Let not] "that for which millions prayed and sighed, That for which tens of thousands fought, For which so many freely died… come to naught,"[27] but like Langston Hughes, "Dream a world where all men shall know sweet freedom's way."[28]

Go tell it on the mountain: We shall overcome.

Mildred was awarded the Town of Normal's Martin Luther King Award for her contribution to the community. Paul Harmon, former Mayor of Normal, comments about an incident involving the award. His comments reflect on the depth of Mildred's integrity and commitment to her values[29]:

Public office can have its ups and downs. Among the ups is when you can recognize a person for their meaningful contributions to the community. My first important encounter with Mildred was when she was recognized with the town of Normal's Martin Luther King Jr. Award. This up, however, was followed by a down. A few years later, Mildred returned the award to the town because Martin Luther King Jr. Day was not declared an official town holiday by the town council. But this down was followed by an up in that Normal now officially recognizes Martin Luther King Jr. Day. This resulted in current Mayor Chris Koos and I being able to again recognize Mildred and re-present the award a couple of years ago.

Retirement[30]

Mildred retired in 1993 and the McLean County Community News announced the retirement reception that was held on April 23, 1993[31]:

> *Pratt, who has her PhD from the University of Pittsburgh Graduate School of Social Work, joined Illinois State's social work faculty in 1969. …In addition to her 24 years as an educator, Pratt may be best known recently in the community for her work as Co-Director of the Bloomington-Normal Black History and Culture Consortium and creation of the Black History Project. … Pratt spearheaded the accreditation process for Illinois State's Social Work program, which last year attained department status. The author of two books, nine journal articles, and 25 papers presented at scholarly meetings, Pratt was the 1989 recipient of the Martin Luther King Jr. Award from the Normal Human Relations Committee.*

Mildred's retirement speech is below[32]:

Thanks to my long-term friend, Art Lewis, who prepared me to relax and accept this ritual. He reminded me that part of being human is to participate in the rituals of life. Indeed it is a symbol of being part of the human community. Thanks, Art. My heartiest thanks to my dear colleagues in Social Work: Professors Mary Cunningham, Jeanne Howard, Mary Campbell, and the entire Social Work department, who just would not let me go quietly into that good retirement. And to my colleagues throughout the university, I thank you. And to the students who suffered through my 221 Class and "lived to tell about it" and be here. You have all made my outgoing immensely more festive and humane than the incoming. It is like the Black folks in Texas used to say, "I may come to world in a Model T but I want to leave it in a Cadillac." You are sending me out in a Cadillac. And, so my social work colleagues, "I owe you one."

A very special thanks to my colleagues from outside the ivy-encrusted halls of the university, whom I truly regard as my friends,…who have helped keep me aware of the many upon whose shoulders I rode on my journey, and who said, "She ain't heavy—she's my sister." I have never forgotten the roots and soil which gave me sustenance to cope and weather the many storms to which, as an African-American, I have been, am, and always will be heir. I only hope that mine have been shoulders on which at least some whose lives I have touched have stood, and will stand.

My deep appreciation to Dr. Virginia Owen and her staff, who have been so enormously supportive of the Black History Project and Consortium—not just with money, but your deep and abiding interest in seeing the project survive and thrive and indeed breathing life into the history of a people which has far too long been buried in their heads, basements, attics, trunks, and closets.

There is a wonder about being human—the lives we touch and are touched by never remain the same, but leave lasting marks as surely as do the waves which wash upon and kiss the pebbles and sand on the beaches. And so today I feel like a pebble which has been touched by you who have so generously come here to remind me of the endearing waves your lives have washed upon me, and like the pebbles washed upon the beaches, the reminders of our paths having met will forever be with me as I move to the next stage of my life—which is still a mystery to me, but that's good.

Like Thurgood Marshall, I am going to do a lot of sitting, and I know I will reflect on my life which may find itself visible in some way. On this same note, there is an old saying among African-Americans. It goes, "If White people ask you where you going, tell them where you been." Well, where I have been is very critical to where I am going. Like most Black women who were born and grew up poor in the South in the 1920s and 1930s, I have had to work since I was "knee high to a duck" to help our family eat and survive. It began before I entered grade school and continued through grade school, high school, bachelor's degree, two master's degrees, and a PhD up until now—so I am ready for some "doing what comes naturally."

Since I came here in 1969, I have had three different offices in the same building and offices in three different buildings. My office floors, chairs, desk, bookcases, window sills, cabinets and tops of cabinets and office doors will be most relieved to have the heavy weight at long last lifted from them—yes, perhaps that is why I decided to retire—I had no more space for stuff!

No, I don't have a compass for where I go next—and this is the first time I've ever had this luxury,…so I'll bask in it for a while.

Recognition

Mildred's Curriculum Vitae (Appendix B) demonstrates the extent of her professional achievement, but the letters below illustrate Mildred's personal impact. Many colleagues and students recognized Mildred's leadership. Their letters reference her role with the Black History Project, her unwavering commitment to mentoring faculty and students, and her core values.[33]

Dean Virginia Owen, who was so supportive of Mildred's career and the Bloom-ington-Normal Black History Project, wrote the following to her on April 22, 1993:

What an occasion it is to celebrate your career at Illinois State University! From the beginning of the Social Work Program, you have been a pillar of strength and commitment. Your energy, enthusiasm, and caring have been infectious. There is no better ambassador for your program, your profession, and for the university than you.

I cherish these last few years of working with you on the Black History Project most of all. It is in this project that I have seen your dedication and commitment bear fruit in a different arena from the university. You have done more to break down the barriers between the university and the local African-American community than anything else the university has ever been involved with. Without making efforts to preserve the remembrances of African-American residents of the Bloomington-Normal area, a significant chapter and legacy in the history of the community would have been lost.

Now that you are retiring, I know that your work will not cease. It will simply change arenas. I know, however, that the strength and perseverance that you represent will continue to serve as a role model and a beacon of encouragement for those with whom you associate.

My very best wishes for your retirement.

Mark Wyman, a colleague in the History Department, also commented about Mildred's impact through the Black History Project[34]:

What an energetic, wide-ranging approach to history you brought to the Bloomington-Normal Black History Project! And, I must add, what a lesson you gave to me on the importance of coming at a study of the past along many different avenues. By getting different fields of study involved and linking them immediately to the African-Americans of Bloomington and Normal, you guaranteed that this needed project would move forward with strength and vigor.

I learned something else about the importance of your work when I talked recently with the director of the county historical society about the current exhibits at the society. He told me quite bluntly that without all the activities of the past few years by you and your coworkers, they would have had very little to put on display about African-Americans in our community. This is history as empowerment. It means that your project does more than save precious memories from the past. It is also raising the importance of a large group of the population that has traditionally been excluded.

Somehow, within the makeup of Mildred Pratt, there are ideas that brought all this about. I want to rush to join the chorus of praise for all you have done, well aware that large numbers will benefit from your work and yet be totally unaware of your importance. But I will know of your work and will always sing your praises.

Mildred's faculty colleagues recognized not only Mildred's influence with the Black History Project, but Mildred's larger impact on them as faculty members. Jeanne Howard, a faculty colleague, saw Mildred as a role model and shared her admiration for her "intelligence, wisdom, dedication, enthusiasm, commitment to ideals, and integrity."[35] On April 19, 1993, Barbara Heyl, a faculty colleague in Sociology, wrote the following, noting in particular the power of Mildred's presence in the department[36]:

You have played a more important role in my 18 years here at ISU [Illinois State University] than you may realize because our paths have crossed in the hallways of Schroeder in such a quiet, professional manner. But I have treasured every contact. I have watched your commitment to your students and program, and I took it as a model. I know I was not alone in this. Your integrity, steadfastness, and wisdom helped all of us in the SASW [Sociology, Anthropology, Social Work] Department keep straight over the years about what the most important issues were in our mission with students and as a public university. Your contribution to the Social Work Program for all those years was a key pillar upon which it could grow and become ever stronger. Even though we did not chat often, just knowing you were there was a source of comfort, and now to contemplate your not being here feels like a genuine loss.

I want to mention especially my respect for your work in establishing the oral history project—for your wonderful vision of the project and your ability to bring this vision to reality. Your commitment empowered everyone involved in the project and enriched our whole community with the personal connections that were made. The remarkable life stories and historical details that have resulted from your work are now available for all of us to enjoy and appreciate for years to come, whereas without your efforts they might have gradually become irretrievable.

I will do all I can to keep this project alive and thriving. I will keep my students informed of opportunities open to them to participate in the project, and those of us in sociology, anthropology, and social work will collectively be sure that the next generation of students know that not only did our programs benefit from your labor of love in teaching and research, but so has the broader community of which we are all a part. Mildred, we know that we are all doing better because you have lived and worked here with us.

Mary Campbell, a faculty colleague in the Social Work department, also reflected similar sentiments[37]:

How difficult it is to express to you how you have inspired me as a social work educator over the years. Those early days in the Social Work house were so important as Jeanne and I struggled to learn about the program, to improve the curriculum, and to meet the needs of the students. Your leadership was invaluable and your vision became our vision.

Our community is so much richer because of your time with us, both the ISU [Illinois State University] community, the social service community, and the Bloomington/Normal community. Your simplicity of life, your deep commitment to stop injustices wherever you could, and your belief in the inherent value of all people has inspired me as I teach in the policy area. On those rare occasions when you have shared your personal awareness of the impact of discrimination I have grown tremendously in my understanding of life through the eyes of another. Thank you Mildred, you have inspired so many along the way....

Mary Cunningham, another faculty colleague in the Social Work department, also shared thoughts about Mildred's impact and her inspirational leadership[38]:

I'm sitting here wondering how a program replaces its foundation. You teach history so well and you have been present throughout the history of this program. As I prepare for this site visit, I find copies of old site visit reports and you are present in every one of them. I am thankful for all of the policies and procedures that you helped establish for this program. I remember too your involvement in helping to hire me and your strengths as a recruiter. Now you have been involved in helping to replace yourself, although you cannot be replaced.

There is an old saying that you can take the woman out of social work but not social work out of the woman. I have so often been reminded that you are the most gifted community organizer that I know. So many times you challenged us to take on tasks and find the resources for projects that seemed so far out of reach. Somehow, we have always found the energy and money.

In our system, you have influenced at least 1,500 students. That is quite a legacy to leave the world. Your energy and caring has planted seeds for much social change. In teaching history, you have greatly influenced the future....

In her personal condolence after Mildred's death on August 10, 2012, Mary Cunningham wrote the following: "I was her colleague at ISU [Illinois State University]. There I felt her strength, sense of ethics, loyalty, and social skills. Several times I stood outside her classroom and listened to her lectures.... I know that her sense of history and social justice rings throughout the lives of hundreds of students."

Carl Holland, a faculty colleague, wrote the following[39]:

The academic rite of passage called retirement forces us laborers who will remain to pause and reflect about the retiree's value. Your value to the profession, the University, our program, the reassignment of duties, the voids that must be bridged for student and faculty developments and adjustments in personal relationships are but a few things that come to my mind as I reflect on your departure as a daily colleague.

I will greatly miss you as a friend, a valued colleague, and as a vital part of the social work program. My current and selfish concerns are the replacement of your varied roles among us. I feel assured that you have assisted us in finding a replacement for content areas that you taught. I am less than convinced that we can find replacements of your disciplined advocacy roles for justice and equality in developing us as faculty. For examples, who can as forcefully intervene in faculty meetings when:

- Racial and sexual equality is threatened?
- Course content is being flaunted?
- Academic and/or practice pseudo-elitism raises its ugly head?
- Cultural and/or religious bias is revealed?
- Homophobia causes students or faculty to panic?
- The poor and developing peoples of the world are misunderstood?
- Programmatically, we as a faculty fail to "see the forest for the trees?"

These important faculty developmental roles have been enigmatically enhanced by you. Although we may stumble here and there, your abilities have prepared us to continue at a higher level of performance.

Mildred's impact was not limited to her faculty colleagues. She was also a tremendous influence on students, many of whom became senior administrators. Sandra Alcorn, a former student and Dean of Social Work at Aurora University, shared the following[40]:

I wanted to be sure to get a word of appreciation in on this significant occasion of your retirement. Every year at Aurora University when I speak to our field instructors at our Recognition Luncheon, I am thinking of you. I am talking about the value of field instructors as mentors in the lives of our students. As my field instructor, you did more than support me in my dream of becoming a social worker; you gave my amorphous dream a focus. You identified my strengths and turned my vision to social work education as a way of developing those strengths and finding personal satisfaction. How right you were!

For 10 years in social work education, I worked at trying to balance and integrate my personal and professional roles (there weren't too many mentors around for us then, but I was seeking and observing); thank goodness that came out well, not without a little bit of luck! And, then, you actually surfaced again in what I would call a midlife dream.

When I figured it out, the message was so clear...so long ago, you said I must get a doctorate and not be frivolous in this pursuit. Though it came later in life, I needed to accomplish that to take charge of my career. Now, after 30 years in social work and 23 years in social work education, I feel so rewarded and so grateful for the role you played in my development. I don't know if you heard this through the grapevine, but last year when Pitt called me to come "back home" as Distinguished Alumna of the Year, I had my chance to say thank you in the presence of the graduation class to the teachers who pointed me in the right direction and gave me what I needed to launch out into social work. I mentioned your name, though you were not present, so this is my time to acknowledge you personally.

Diane Zosky, Director of the Illinois State University Social Work Program and former student, shared the following reflections about Mildred in an email to Mildred's daughter, Menah, in 2013[41]*:*

I knew your mother. Although I am now the Director of the School, I was her student in the fledgling ISU [Illinois State University] BSW [Bachelor's of Social Work] Program in 1978. I was in her social policy class. May I tell you of a few personal experiences I had with your mother? Although I was a good student all my life, mostly "A" work with an occasional "B" grade, I was fairly introverted and not particularly confident in my college work as I felt that I came from a high school and family that did not particularly prepare me for higher education. I was the first in my family to go to college. Although my grades showed that I was capable of college-level work (I graduated with a 4.0 GPA [grade point average]), I don't think I really knew it inside. But a pivotal moment happened in your mother's social policy class. Your mother returned a paper to me with an A grade, and on the top she had written, "This is very scholarly work." You may know that your mother had very high standards and did not "suffer fools well."

Students were mostly in awe of her. I will never forget that, Menah. It was literally at that point that I remember thinking to myself that perhaps someday I would complete a PhD in Social Work like your mother. I held her in such high regard and truly [put her] on a pedestal. I never lost sight of that aspiration. I went on to receive my MSW [Master's of Social Work] degree from UIUC [University of Illinois at Urbana–Champaign] and worked for several years in medical social work and with domestic violence. When my daughters were two and four years old, I returned to school to complete my PhD from Loyola.

But one more story. Inspired by your mother's words to me, I eventually came back to ISU in 2001 after my PhD to join the School of Social Work, where my dream began. As I said, I had your mother on such a pedestal; she was such a large presence to me. Then when I came back to ISU and your mother was emeritus status, I was able to see her again at the graduation dinner. And... I was so stunned to see that she was really not a very large person but ... quite petite. You see, Menah, I had always literally and figuratively looked up to her that she seemed larger than life to me, and this illusion I could see later in reality as someone who was really "small but mighty."[42]

Key Lessons

1. *Mildred's life in the academy was undergirded by a foundation rooted in a deep appreciation for history. Her speech, "Go tell it on the Mountain," evidences her understanding of history and its role and connection to the present. She was widely read—from literature, to poetry, to newspapers, to books on multiple topics. She was passionate about the importance of generations understanding history so that they could help humanity. She recognized her own ability to help others and was willing to be "shoulders" upon which others could stand.*

2. *Mildred's commitment to empowerment and developing the potential of others can clearly be seen in the letters from faculty colleagues and former students. She had a tremendous impact on the department. Her impact was not limited to her role with the Black History Project. It expanded to being a role model, force, and presence in department meetings, being a moral compass, demonstrating integrity, and standing up for her core values with strength, determination, hard work, and dedication. At the same time, she was kind, caring, and sensitive, yet she had a firm belief in the importance of encouraging students to actualize their potential. The letters reference her wisdom, integrity, and steadfastness. They refer to her professionalism, constructive approach to problems, good will, and unfailing friendliness. These values did, indeed, define Mildred Pratt. Her colleagues recognized that Mildred Pratt made a difference.*

Notes

1. (M. Pratt, personal communication, n.d.).
2. (M. Pratt, personal communication, n.d.).
3. (M. Pratt, personal communication, January 21, 1991).
4. (Harding, 1990, p. ix).
5. (Darden, 2014, Introduction).
6. (Clarke, 1987).
7. (Johnson, 1922).
8. (Shlicta, 2011).
9. See Gopaul-McNicol (1988) and Bergner (2009) for a discussion of this work.
10. (Slansky & Sorkin, 2006, p. 217).
11. (Harding, 1990, pp. 6–7).
12. (Harding, 1990, pp. 6–7).
13. Revered William Copeland led a three week boycott that ended when the mayor agreed to celebrate the holiday ("King Organizers," 1990).
14. (S. Shaw, personal communication, 1990).
15. (Harding, 1990, pp. 67–68).

16. (Harding, 1990, p. 69).
17. (Harding, 1990, p. 126).
18. (Brown, 1990, pp. 56–58).
19. (Dunbar, 1993).
20. (Vanderbilt Television News Archive, 1990).
21. ("Remembering Civil War historian," 2005).
22. (Stowe, 1852). To learn more about Josiah Henson, see Henson (1849) and Williamson (n.d.).
23. ("Real Uncle Tom's cabin," 1977).
24. (Hurmence, 1984, p. 80).
25. (Democracy Now, 2015).
26. (Harding, 1990, p. 5).
27. ("Opinion," 1913, p. 173)
28. See *I dream a world,* a poem by Langston Hughes (Rampersad, 1994, p. 311).
29. (M. Pratt, personal communication, n.d.).
30. With respect to the retirement announcement, I want to share that the McLean County Community News, originally published this retirement announcement. The author did her best to find the copyright holder, but the newspaper is no longer in business.
31. (*McLean County Community News*, 1993, p. 2).
32. (M. Pratt, personal communication, n.d.).
33. (M. Pratt, personal communication, n.d.).
34. See also, Wyman (n.d.).
35. (M. Pratt, personal communication, n.d.).
36. (M. Pratt, personal communication, April 19, 1993).
37. (M. Pratt, personal communication, n.d.).
38. (M. Pratt, personal communication, n.d.).
39. (M. Pratt, personal communication, n.d.).
40. (M. Pratt, personal communication, April 21, 1993).
41. (D. Zosky, personal communication, June 19, 2013).
42. Jeanne Howard, a colleague at Illinois State University, shared a similar reflection about Mildred: "I joked at her retirement party that I worked with her for several years before I realized she was short! It's true—that's just how dynamic and energetic a person she was" (J. Howard, personal communication, August 8, 2012).

References

Bergner, G. (2009). Black children, White preference: Brown v. Board, the doll tests, and the politics of self-esteem. *American Quarterly, 61*(2), 299–332.

Brown, S. A. (1990). *The collected poems of Sterling A. Brown* (M. Harper, Ed.). Evanston, IL: Northwestern University Press.

Clarke, J. H. (1987, January). Why Africana history? *The Black Collegian.*

Darden, R. (2014). *Nothing but love in God's water: Black sacred music from the Civil War to the Civil Rights Movement.* University Park, PA: Pennsylvania State University Press.

Democracy Now! (2015, March 10). *Civil Rights Icon C.T. Vivian on nonviolence & hypocrisy of U.S. promoting democracy abroad.* Retrieved from https://www.democracynow.org/2015/3/10/civil_rights_icon_ct_vivian_on

Dunbar, P. L. (1993). *The collected poetry of Paul Laurence Dunbar* (J. M. Braxton Ed.). Charlottesville, VA: University Press of Virginia.

Gopaul-McNicol, S. (1988). Racial identification and racial preference of Black preschool children in New York and Trinidad. *Journal of Black Psychology, 14,* 65–68.

Harding, V. (1990). *Hope and history: Why we must share the story of the movement.* Maryknoll, NY: Orbis Books.

Henson, J. (1849). *The life of Josiah Henson, formerly a slave, now an inhabitant of Canada, as narrated by himself.* Boston, MA: A. D. Phelps.

Hurmence, B. (Ed.). (1984). *My folks don't want me to talk about slavery.* Winston-Salem, NC: John F. Blair.

Johnson, J. W. (Ed.). (1922). *The book of American Negro poetry.* Orlando, FL: Harcourt Brace & Company.

King organizers end boycott of stores. (1990, December 22). *Chicago Tribune,* p. 5.

McLean County Community News. (1993, April 14).

Opinion. (1913). *Crisis Magazine, 5*(4).

Rampersad, A. (Ed.). (1994). *The collected poems of Langston Hughes.* New York, NY: Alfred A. Knopf.

Real Uncle Tom's cabin yet stands. (1977, November 1). *Danville Register.* Retrieved from https://www.newspapers.com/newspage/30025156/

Remembering Civil War Historian Shelby Foote. (2005, June 29). *PBS Newshour.* Retrieved from http://www.pbs.org/newshour/bb/remember-jan-june05-foote_6-29/

Shlicta, P. (2011, February 27). William F. Buckley left us three years ago today. *Thinker.*

Slansky, P., & Sorkin, A. (2006). *My Bad: The apology anthology.* New York, NY: Bloomsbury.

Stowe, H. B. (1852). *Uncle Tom's cabin.* London: J. Cassell.

Vanderbilt Television News Archive. (1990, December 1). Focus (Blacks and the GOP). *NBC Evening News.* Retrieved from https://tvnews.vanderbilt.edu/broadcasts/572671

Williamson, J. (n.d.). *Documenting the South: Josiah Henson.* Retrieved May 21, 2017 from http://docsouth.unc.edu/neh/henson49/summary.html

Wyman, M. (n.d.). *Origins of the Bloomington-Normal Black History Project.* Retrieved September 1, 2013 from McLean County Museum of History: http://mchistory.org/research/resources/blackhistory/origins.php

CHAPTER TWELVE

Travel, Trials, and Triumph

"Escapade" by Mozelle Perry[1]

I saw a large and impressive cloud appear
High in the sky from my perch on a hill.
As I lay on folded hands and dreamily stared,
It settled right above me and began to whisper a story
Of wonders from on high.
It told of distances traveled throughout its venturous
life.
It told of lands it'd visited,
Then it sang a song of sorts.
It whispered, "Someday I'd [you'll] understand its song,"
But for now
I'll make you a picture and you can give
Names to these lofty works of art.
Much bemused, I stirred and gazed as this cloud
Began to change shapes as if a
Specter there in that still and unknowing sky.
I saw a pixie sleeping on a pillow of down,
Then, a panther who greeted me with a frown.
A baby lamb then frolicked across the sky.

Old Saint Nick flew up with Dancer close by.
Then I saw a great soft pillow that invited me to fly
away

Mildred's life after retirement was full and fulfilling. Her time with Ted was limited by his death, just three years after her retirement. A year after her retirement, Ted had a stroke and Mildred's time was devoted to his full-time care for two years before his death in 1996. As difficult as his death was for her, she committed herself to creating a legacy for him through the Pratt Music Foundation. The Pratt Music Foundation, founded by a group of family friends, provides music scholarships to youth with talent and need. In addition to the Pratt Music Foundation, Mildred rediscovered her independence and love of adventure.

She enjoyed traveling and loved riding Amtrak, going on Elderhostel trips, and meeting new friends. Mildred was friendly and enjoyed meeting new people. She remembers making lasting friendships by sharing breakfast, lunch, and dinner with other people and couples. She deeply believed in the importance of humanity and connecting with individuals on a personal and human level. Her life was accentuated by the people she met and the places she visited. Mildred saw Marian Anderson perform at Indianapolis, Indiana.[2] She and Ted met Pearl Bailey on an Amtrak train and never forgot how Mrs. Bailey graciously gave them an autographed photo of herself. Ted and Mildred often traveled to New York to watch the US [United States] Open Tennis Tournament. Mildred was so pleased to meet Richard Williams, Venus' and Serena's father, and remembered how gracious he was at the US Open. She and Menah travelled to Freetown, Sierra Leone in 1989 to spend time with Ted's family.

After Ted's death, Mildred became a globe-trotter. She visited England to watch Wimbledon; Eastern Europe, including Czechoslovakia, Hungary, and Poland through Elderhostel; the Bahamas for Menah's sweet sixteen wedding anniversary ceremony; and the Mediterranean on a cruise on which Awadagin was performing for her 80th birthday. On the Holland American cruise liner in the Mediterranean Sea in October 2008, Mildred reflected "on a life which I never dreamed possible."[3] She remembers walking "on grounds trod by Jesus and his disciples."[4] Most memorable, Mildred was fortunate to visit the White House on three occasions when Awadagin had the honor of performing—twice for President Clinton and once for President Obama. In this chapter, she shares her memories of those historic occasions, the challenges of Ted's illness and death, the joy of creating the memorial to Ted's life, and her preparation for her own funeral, including her decision to be recorded reciting poetry and singing spirituals.

The White House

In 1992, Awadagin won the Naumburg International Music competition and was the first African-American instrumentalist to win the award. The award launched his classical music career and he began performing across the country in major concert halls, including the Kennedy Center.[5] Vernon Jordan heard his performance and was instrumental in arranging for Awadagin to play at the White House. Awadagin was able to invite his mother and sister as his guests. Mildred was so excited and she contemporaneously wrote about her opportunity to visit the White House. On June 1, 1994, she wrote about the initial call[6]:

Our good friends from Pittsburgh, Pennsylvania, the Hammonds, were visiting us. I'd been out running errands, and upon my return Ted calmly said, "I got a call from the White House." I was not in shock because he joked with me in this way many times. He paused as I walked past him and assured me that this was no joke. We were to learn that the White House had arranged for Awadagin to perform there. We were all so ecstatic that we failed to get sufficient information and had to call back for details. We were to understand that Vernon Jordan, a high-powered African-American lawyer and friend of Clinton, had suggested that Awadagin be invited to the White House to perform.

Dagin detailed the sequence that had resulted in his invitation to perform. He said he'd had dinner at Vernon Jordan's home after they had heard him perform at the Kennedy Center. Impressed with the performance, they insisted he should perform at the White House. He said he was eventually told to appear at the southeast entrance to the White House, where he met the White House social secretary and was invited to perform on June 10th.

Dagin said he could invite one person to both the dinner and recital or two people to one event each. He said he would take his girlfriend and me. I hesitated that I should go. Dagin told me to notify him at his home when I decided. Ted insisted, and the following day I left a message on his phone that I'd go to the concert. He called me twice and I was not home. I called him later. He said he'd made reservations for me at his hotel, St. James, where the White House was housing him.

We had taken the Hammonds to Peoria for lunch at Stephanie's. When we arrived home, Linda Marder [Awadagin's agent] had left a message that the White House had arranged for two extra invitations for Ted and me to both events. She said, however, that she'd told them Ted would not want to come. Well, as soon as Ted heard this, he said, "Call Menah and invite her." I called Menah's office and left a message. Menah called Linda for details.

In the meantime, after Linda got the message, she called me regarding Menah's call. She said there was misunderstanding. Since Ted was not going, there was now only one extra invitation for me. She said she would call and try to get Menah included. In the meantime, Ted said, "Call Menah and have her proceed to get her plane ticket, etc., and plan to go, hoping for the best." Linda [later] said all things are go for Menah and she'd call to tell Dagin that now he'd have not two but three lovely ladies to escort to the White House. Finally, we were all set for this historical occasion.

Mildred wrote about that "historic occasion" of June 10, 1994[7]:

Today has been the most fantastic day. I left O'Hare at 12:14 p.m. and arrived in D.C. at National Airport at 2:55 p.m. Around 3:15 p.m. Menah arrived and we took the cab to Holly's house. We found her and her two lovely, active boys in their large old home with great character, which they are refurbishing. We spent about 30 minutes with Holly. It seemed that we were old friends as we chatted together. She brought us to Jack's apartment. Shortly thereafter, Awadagin called and came over with his girlfriend, and we chatted for a while. He took my hat in jest to assure that I would not wear it to the White House.

Menah called for a cab to pick us up at 7:10 p.m. We went downstairs to wait for the cab at 7:05. By 7:15, the cab had not arrived. Several cabs came by but refused to stop for us. They simply waved back at us. Around 7:20 p.m., a police car (from Georgetown University) stopped and looked around. We went to the male and female police in the car and informed them of our ordeal with the cabs and asked if they would call one for us. We said that we had to be at the White House by 7:30 p.m. Fortunately, they believed us and said they would take us. We had a delightful chat en route to the White House.

When we got to the southeast gate of the White House, we walked in. At the entrance to the White House, the guard checked his list for our names, found them, and requested verification. Upon receipt of the identification, we were given a name card with our seat number. Upon entering the White House guards checked our purses, and we were escorted up the stairs by an official White House escort. We were taken to the East Room of the White House, where other guests were assembled for drinks. We were told the schedule for the evening as we were escorted to the East Room. Shortly after we arrived, Dagin and his girlfriend arrived.

We mingled in the crowd. Among the people whom we identified in the crowd were Whoopi Goldberg and her fiancée, Lyle (an organizer of technical workers in the entertainment industry); Ann Landers; Marianne Edelman (Children's Defense Fund), who deliberately came over and spoke with us; Frank Gifford and Cathy Lee; Charles Kuralt; Colin Powell and his wife; Vernon Jordan and his wife; Brit Hume and his wife; and Bob Costas and his wife. We later met the President's National Security Advisor and Hillary's Chief of Staff.

After the assembly in the White House East Room, we were lined up to go into the adjoining room to meet the President (Bill Clinton and his wife, Hillary), Vice President (Al Gore and his wife). We were told that our names would be called out by one of the White House officials. My name was called out: "Dr. Mildred Pratt." When the President shook my hand, I told him I was honored to be there and that when I saw him on the campaign trail at Crown Center in Kansas City, I never thought I'd be meeting him here in the White House. As I shook the hand of his wife, Hillary, she said that ever since Dagin was scheduled to play at the White House, Patsy Bowles (her Bloomington friend) had been ringing the White House to sing her praises of what a fine person I was. I told her thanks and how honored I was to meet her. Menah chatted longer with the Gores about Nashville, etc.

After these introductions, we were all directed to the Rose Garden, where we were directed to our tables underneath the tent for dinner (see Figure 12.1: Photograph of the White House dinner menu, 1994). I sat with Whoopi Goldberg's fiancée, Lyle; the wife of the National Security Advisor; Bob Costas' wife; Mrs. Clinton's Chief of Staff; a Black gentleman who identified himself as Faith's husband (he was retired and lived in Sugar Hill in Harlem in an apartment he had bought from Diana Washington); another gentleman from Louisville; and another lady. I chatted with Lyle about union organizing. We were entertained by musicians the entire course of the dinner. Mr. and Mrs. Clinton, the Gores, and Hillary's mother sat among the invited guests. Following the dinner, we were directed back to the East Room for Awadagin's performance. Menah and I sat in the second row, where we could watch Dagin's hands.

The great surprise of the performance was that he played my favorite piece. When I heard the first few bars, I was ecstatic and almost cried. The crowd was generous in its applause and was certainly hoping for an encore. Awadagin bowed graciously to all, especially to the President and his wife and the Gores. The President joined Dagin on the stage and announced that people could go to the adjoining room to dance if they wished. He took Dagin's hand and said, "You were magnificent." When the President left Dagin, he came directly to me and said that Dagin was great and how proud I must be. I said, "Thank you, Mr. President." Many people turned to me and praised Dagin. An avalanche of people went up to congratulate Dagin. Among them were Ann Landers and her guest, Brit Hume, etc.

As I remember I met Colin Powell and told him that I'd read of an account in the *New York Times* where he admonished Black students that they had a responsibility to perform well because they were "riding on the backs of other Blacks." He said that the other part of his statement was that the students needed to do well so that they could be the "backs" for other Blacks to succeed.

I, of course, did not dance; few people did. We all stood around and chatted. Menah got autographs from the President, his wife, and the Gores. I got Hillary's, and Menah got the President's for me. The President did not leave until the last guests did. We were among them. He said last words to Dagin, shook his hand, etc. As the President was leaving the room, the social secretary told him the story of how Menah and I had been brought to the White House by the Georgetown police. The President said to get their names and [to] send them a personal note of thanks.

The most significant parts: the graciousness of the staff, the President and his wife's friendliness and real personal interest in the guests, Dagin's playing my piece, and how many people liked Dagin's playing.

Mildred wrote a thank you note to Honorable President Clinton and First Lady Hillary Clinton on June 13, 1994[8]:

Dear Mr. President and First Lady:

It was a joy to have spent an unforgettable evening in the White House on Friday 10th, 1994. I wish to express my gratitude to both of you for inviting my family to share the evening with you and your friends. Further, we deeply appreciate your generous invitation to Awadagin to perform for you, the Gores, and the invited guests.

I was impressed with the warmth and hospitality of the total White House staff. It is unfortunate that it is not possible for every United States citizen to have the experience we had at the White House. It would doubtless weaken the unwarranted and unrelenting criticism of almost every action in the White House.

My family joins me in wishing you and the Gores good health and a long tenure in the White House, doing good for the nation and its people.

Sincerely yours,

Mildred Pratt

Mildred describes her second visit to the White House[9]:

The second time that we visited the White House also occurred when Clinton was President. As I attended these various trips at the White House, I know that my husband, Dr. T.A.E.C. Pratt, and my son, Awadagin, made them possible. My husband insisted that we take the trips and not him. It was so much like him. He did so much for the children and me. The next time that I went to the White House when Awadagin was performing, Darlene and Marc Miller went with us, and Gellert Modos, too.[10] Awadagin performed in a large banquet room. We were not invited to the dinner, but we were able to sit in chairs in the same room to see Awadagin perform. We did have a chance to roam around in the White House until the dinner was over. The President had promised to take a photograph with us after the dinner. When he arrived to take the photograph. I remember him saying, "Hurry up with this because I have to go to the bathroom."

Mildred cherished her photo in the White House with First Lady Hillary Clinton, Marc Miller, Mildred Pratt, President Bill Clinton, and Menah Pratt-Clarke.[11] Mildred was also delighted to be invited to the White House to meet President Obama. Having been in Springfield, Illinois, when President Obama announced his candidacy, she was thrilled to be able to see him at the White House[12]:

I never expected to have the opportunity to go to the White House a third time. In early October 2009, Awadagin called to say that President Obama had requested him to perform at the White House in November. My son was invited to perform before a small group at the White House with other musicians.

This visit was made possible because President Obama had requested that children come to the White House to celebrate "Children's Music Day." They wanted some children to be present for a presentation at the White House. Awadagin and his friends were asked to give music lessons to a small group of children. For this trip, Awadagin had a conversation with Darlene and Marc Miller (President of the Pratt Music Foundation). They decided that they should negotiate a plan for taking some of the Pratt Music Foundation scholars to the White House for the event. When they got the approval from the White House, they began to plan for all of the scholars to go. The Millers solicited donations from the communities of Bloomington and Normal to pay expenses for all of the scholars to attend.

Fortunately, Menah was needed to handle the [music] sheets for Awadagin.[13] We also had an opportunity to be present at the reception, where there were many celebrities in the foyer. Menah also was fortunate to get President Obama's autograph!

Mildred was just delighted to have a photograph of her with the president and first lady. The photo includes First Lady Michelle Obama, Awadagin Pratt, President Barack Obama, Menah Pratt-Clarke, and Linda Marder [Awadagin's agent].[14]

Trials

Mildred devoted a significant part of her early retirement years to caring for her husband and her later years to working with her friends to create a legacy in his honor. Ted suffered a stroke in 1994 and died in 1996. While he was hospitalized in 1994, Mildred wrote "An Ode to My Husband, Dr. T.A.E.C. Pratt, of 30 Years".[15]

When we first met in August of 1964 in the cleaners and, a few days afterward, in the nearby restaurant in Pittsburgh, Pennsylvania, it never occurred to me that you would ask me to marry you and that 30 years later we would still be together with two grown children who had not done too badly with their lives. I am still happy that we met and are still together, albeit much older [with] gray hairs adorning our heads.

While each of us have our own health problems, if God pleases, I hope we will have many more years together. Since you have been in the hospital, I think of all our years together—the smiles, laughter, pains, hurt, good times, [and] joy. [The] goose bumps and joyful tears remind [me] that the smiles, laughter, good times, and joy have been in much greater supply than the pains and hurt. As I reflect, I have not been a perfect wife, but I have tried and have loved and cared for you— and I still do and will continue doing so till death do us part.

Today, I sorely miss your "Mildred," as you call me in your own way. And, most of all, I miss your hearty laughter, which from the first day I met you was for me your trademark. As I close this ode, I want you to know that I will not make the decision as to where you will or should go when you are released from the hospital. That is your decision to make. I just want you to know that wherever you are, I will care for you as best I can and with love. I love you.

Mildred remembers some precious moments during Ted's illness[16]:

Episode I

One particular touching and romantic event occurred about two weeks before Ted's death when we attended the Julliard String Quartet's performance at Illinois State University in 1996, which was the last live performance of classical music Ted attended. How much he enjoyed the music! He was so frail, in such great pain as he experienced the final phase of the dreaded disease—cancer. He was "skin and bone," except for his large swollen legs, feet, and hands, which were in excruciating pain. I tried to relive the pain by gently massaging them. To see Ted smile as he gestured that this helped relieve the pain made me feel good; he was in heaven, intensely enjoying the music. For both Ted and me, this was a precious, romantic moment—almost spiritual! This moment was the essence of our love.

Episode II

Ted was ill with a stroke and cancer for two years. On the occasion of our 32nd wedding anniversary, Ted was in the hospital when I was visited him as I did twice a day during his four weeks of hospitalization. On that particular visit he demonstrated another of his many denials that he needed to be in the hospital. (He did not know he had a stroke and could not move his left leg). He asked, "Did you bring the keys to the car and my clothes?" I said, "No." "Then, did you bring the pickup truck?" he asked. "Yes," I said. "Then drive it around to the nearest entrance to my bed," he said, "and then you can wrap me in the sheet and we can sneak out of the hospital." I knew he was serious, but also knew that he could not walk. I simply turned from him and let the welled up tears flow, unabashed. While I tried to conceal this sadness, he must have known the feeling—and said, "I guess that is not a good idea." When he left the hospital, we laughed about the incident—each of us obviously aware of what we would have looked like creeping out of the hospital sheeted all in white.

Episode III

Ted was eventually discharged from his Physical Therapy at the hospital, with orders not to drive until further improvement, more tests, and instructions to be careful not to fall. We were now home, ready to test my wheelchair driving and carpentry skills in arranging the wheelchair ramp. I struggled to push him up the ramp without the two of us falling onto the garage floor. Once we'd landed safely inside the house, Ted announced to this incompetent wheelchair driver, "I want you to take me to the store." I took a deep breath and out it came: "Do you really think we can manage that? Whatever you want I can go and collect it for you." "No," he said as loudly as his impaired speech could say the word. I took my best award-winning deep breath and bravely said, "OK, let's do it." To myself, I wondered what was so necessary for him to shop for that could not wait until at least another day. He negotiated the trip to the store with me who was convinced that we'd need to spend the night there—doubting I'd get him up that ramp again. He directed me to the jewelry case and asked me which of the bracelets I'd like. Tears welled up in my eyes as I selected one. He insisted I take two. Always the subtle romantic, he had done just what he did five years prior when he wanted me to have the diamond ring I never had. He got me to the jewelry store by saying he wanted to take me to the new restaurant in downtown Bloomington to have soup.

Episode IV

A week home from rehabilitation at the hospital and months before he was approved to drive, Ted informed me he'd drive himself to the outpatient rehabilitation clinic. I tried to discourage him, but to no avail, and now he was in his truck, backing across the street in heavy morning traffic at full speed, hitting the tree in the neighbor's yard across the street from us. In disbelief, I quickly got into my car and honked my horn at full blast hoping the traffic would stop, which it never did. I breathed heavily and followed Ted all the way to the clinic, and a few blocks from the clinic, I lost him. I pulled into the clinic and did not see him. I looked around in panic until I found him driving up from a different direction. We faced each other in panic, and he lovingly said, "Thank you for following me."…

When our spouses or lovers die, after a long illness, one is prone to only think of the pain in the loss, but for one's own sanity and coping, one should remember the precious moments even during the illness.

When Ted died, Mildred wrote a note to his mother, Mama Pratt, for her sister-in-law, Dorothea Amara-Bangali, to deliver to her in Sierra Leone. Dorothea was visiting the United States from Sierra Leone during Ted's illness. She agreed to personally deliver the letter to Mama Pratt in Freetown and share the news of her son's death. Mildred's letter to Ted's mother, written on October 30, 1996, is below[17]:

Dear Mom Pratt:

Your dear son never thought that his death would come so soon. Even though he was recovering nicely from the stroke he had in November of 1994, he developed cancer (or the doctors discovered it sometime in October [August] this year), and he simply could not recover from it. I think it was discovered too late. The fact is that he and I were playing tennis through August this year, even though he did not have complete use of his left arm and leg. He was looking forward to visiting his son in New Mexico and being in New York in late November to see him perform.

I have enclosed these copies of statements that the children and I wrote for his memory book for the October 13th celebration of his 60th birthday. At the time when we began planning the surprise birthday party in June this year, we had no idea of his impending death. The children and I thought we should have a grand celebration of his 60th. Now we are all so glad we held the celebration and honored him with and in the presence of his 30 or so close friends and relatives. He was both surprised and delighted. Those invited from out of town and unable to attend sent photographs, cards, and memory letters for the memory book which Menah and her husband prepared for the event. We were all so happy and honored that Dorothea could be present to sit at her brother's table.

When Dorothea called to inform us that she was in New York, we were so happy that we and immediately invited her down to spend some time with us. She was sad, as we all were, to see your dear son's health deteriorate so fast—but that is the way with late-diagnosed cancer. Each morning that Dorothea was here with us, she sat on the couch with her brother, read the Bible to him, and prayed. He looked forward to these inspirational sessions and believed in them. While they definitely helped his spirit, it's clear that God was ready for him to be relieved of his pain. Both his children were with him during the death process, and he cherished their presence. He listened to and gained comfort from his son's music (three CDs) as he lay in his bed.

The children join me in thanking you for your son. We're always keenly aware that he sacrificed life in his own country with you and his other relatives and friends for us. We shall always remember that. Our love for and gratitude to him is enduring. He had friends all over the country who adored him. On his deathbed, I assured him that I would do my best to assure that you were cared for—though at that time he was too weak to speak, his eyes told me that he understood and trusted me to do so.

We love you, Mildred, Awadagin, and Menah

Mildred's season's greetings in 1996 included her reflections on Ted's death[18]:

The Pratt Family enters this season of holidays without a person who has been a tremendous force in our lives, as well as many other people's. After his 1994 stroke, Ted was making a dramatic recovery through enormous work and determination on his part. Indeed, he stretched his endurance and human will to his very last breath. Suddenly, in late August, he began to lose weight and became quite weak. After seeing several medical personnel, he was diagnosed with terminal cancer. After a wonderful surprise birthday party for him on October 13, he died 17 days later at 1:08 a.m. on October 30, 1996.

Ted's impact of his 60 years of living both on people in the United States and Sierra Leone was enormous, beyond what he or either of us could have imagined. His skills and knowledge as a teacher live on in the students he taught in the United States, Brazil, and Sierra Leone, and perhaps more importantly in his children, Awadagin and Menah. He taught much by his own example, determination, discipline, and responsibility to use all one's talents and work hard.

When Ted died, Mildred, at her daughter's persuasion, decided to move to Nashville, Tennessee, where Menah was living. Mildred sold the family's house and the rental properties, and started a new life in Nashville. She spent time with her grandchildren: Emmanuel, who was born in 1997; Alexander, who was born in 1998; and Raebekkah, who was born in 1999. Mildred also taught at Tennessee State University before deciding to return to Bloomington-Normal. Mildred returned to Bloomington-Normal in 2001. She wanted to focus her energy and efforts on the Pratt Music Foundation.

Memories and Memorial

The Pratt Music Foundation was a very important project for Mildred. In a letter dated November 22, 1996, about a month after her husband's death, Mildred describes a memorial for him that arose from discussions with family friends at an afternoon remembrance lunch. Ted had not wanted a memorial or funeral, so in honor of his request, a few friends were invited to visit at the house. Conversations with dear friends—Marc and Darlene Miller, Jack and Patsy Bowles, and Pam and Jack Muirhead—ensued about ways to honor Ted's life. Mildred shares the background about the Pratt Music Foundation[19]:

Near the end of his life, Martin Luther King made a statement which should be a guiding principle for each of our lives. He said he'd like a long life—longevity has its place—but it is far better to die for something than live for nothing. Well, it happens that Martin Luther King not only lived and achieved much, but in death left a legacy of ideas and actions which live on unto this day. Dr. T.A.E.C.

Pratt's was a short life, but one which touched many lives, and with this Memorial Scholarship, sparked by his friends Jack and Patsy Bowles and Darlene and Marc Miller, will continue to do so.

"Ted," as many of us came to call him, was born a Creole on September 19, 1936, in Freetown, Sierra Leone, and christened Theodore Allatantu Emmanuel Cyril Pratt. His parents, Elizabeth Jane Horton Pratt and Daniel Gershon Pratt, were traders, and his father later became a government-employed accountant. Both valued education and, as middle-class people, sought the best schools in Sierra Leone for their bright son. Ted spent most of his early childhood [with] his mother's extended family [the Hortons] while his parents were in the up-country operating their business. The Hortons have had a long history in Sierra Leone as prominent government officials, professionals, and educators. Ted learned to love sacred and classical music while living with the Hortons, where the girls in the family were taught piano and the boys organ. In addition to learning music, he also learned soccer and taught himself tennis.

Ted's formal education was acquired on three continents—Africa, Europe, and North America. He received precollege education at the prestigious Prince of Wales School in Freetown, designed for the teaching of science. His post-secondary education was at Fourah Bay College in Sierra Leone, Durham University in Great Britain, Hampton Institute in Virginia, and Carnegie-Mellon Institute of Technology in Pittsburgh. He achieved his PhD in Nuclear Physics at Carnegie-Mellon and was admitted to the Sigma XI Honorary Society. He was the first person from Sierra Leone to earn a PhD in Nuclear Physics.

Born with the "wrong color" and residing in the wrong place at the wrong time caused his Nuclear Physics career to be short-lived. However, his six years in the career in higher education resulted in prolific publications. His one-year teaching in Rio de Janeiro, Brazil, was extremely productive, as he authored several papers and journal articles and directed a Master's thesis. His journal articles were requested by researchers and academics on every continent.

After leaving academia, Ted decided to devote his time to his family and remain in Normal, where, using his business acumen learned from his parents, [he] purchased and managed his own property, and in so doing found himself fairly proficient as his own attorney.

Dr. Pratt was a renaissance person. He was an avid reader and both loved and dabbled in poetry, classical music, soccer, tennis, chess, and music composition. He was a Sunday school teacher, assistant organist, and choir director for the Buxton Methodist Church and founded the Sierra Leone Lawn Tennis Association. ... He was a nuclear physicist who also loved classical music, particularly the piano and organ. He loved listening to opera on Saturday afternoons on public radio.

He enjoyed playing chess and tennis. He loved watching soccer and screaming "Goal!" at the top of his lungs every time one was made, regardless of the team. Most importantly, though, he loved his family and sacrificed so many parts of his life for them. His love of classical music and his generosity toward his family and children, Awadagin and Menah Pratt, are memorialized through the Pratt Music Foundation.

These interests were passed down to his children. Indeed, the first thing that was done upon waking was to turn the radio on to the public radio (classical music). He taught the children many skills, not because he had any illusion that they would excel in each, but [so] that they would at least excel in one and, further, would have a variety of interests to pass their time and enable them to live more interesting and fulfilled lives. He wanted them to be self-reliant and taught them to change oil and tires, mow, paint, save money, map trips for tennis tournaments, swim, [and] ride bikes. [He] was their first music teacher and only tennis instructor. He also taught them the importance of discipline, hard work, that "with rights go responsibility," and how to relate to people. He took the role of parent seriously. He lived to see his children well-established in their careers: Awadagin as a classical musician and Menah as a practicing attorney with a degree in Law and a PhD in Sociology.

Ted's life illustrates the virtues of discipline, hard work, determination, commitment, and exposure to opportunities and varied experiences—all the hallmarks of successful individuals. Although brilliant, he also had a wonderful spirit and personality. He had a great gift of laughter and the ability to relate to a wide range of people with great ease, from the garbage man to the snow shoveler to the mailman to judges and lawyers. It is the intention of this scholarship fund, in his memory, to create opportunities and experiences for young people who demonstrate the virtues exemplified by Ted's life.

The children (Awadagin and Menah) and I would like any memorial for Dr. Pratt to embrace the general principle that all children be introduced in their early years to science and music. There are three basic principles that we wish the memorial fund to include:

1. An emphasis on making the scholarship available to children who otherwise may not be able to financially afford the learning experience.
2. A focus on precollege (perhaps pre-secondary) children and providing them with a head start in science and music.
3. Structuring the memorial fund in an IWU [Illinois Wesleyan University] administrative system, which will assure the continuation of the funds and the guiding principles eventually developed for the fund.

Beginning in 1998, the Foundation named three scholars and has steadily increased that number to almost thirty annual scholarships. Since 1998 (through 2016), the Foundation has awarded over 200 annual scholarships and raised an endowment of over $600,000 to support the scholarships.[20]

Music Lessons

Although the Pratt Music Foundation was initially a tribute to Ted, Mildred, as a young child, in so many ways epitomized the type of student the Foundation sought to support—students with talent who, because of financial means, were not able to afford lessons. Although Mildred was not able to take lessons as a child or sing in the college choir at Jarvis, she decided to take lessons as an adult with the goal of recording a CD of poetry and spirituals to be played at her funeral. Mildred shares her recollection of that decision[21]:

My most daring act was to begin taking music lessons (the first success in my efforts to sing publicly). I remembered that I'd been kicked out of the choir in my college because a student said I sang alto sometimes and sometimes soprano. (What's interesting is that I did not know what alto and soprano meant!) Well, in the summer of 2008, I decided to take private singing lessons at Illinois Wesleyan University. I wanted to record my singing so that it could be put on a disk and played for my funeral. Dr. Carren Moham (at Illinois Wesleyan University, Marian Anderson's relative) accepted me. I took the singing lessons for about two or three months, at the end of which Dr. Moham taped my songs, which are to be played at my funeral. An unintended consequence of my desire to sing at my October 15, 2009, birthday party is that I've been asked to do my first gig in January 2010.

Dr. Carren Moham, professor of voice at Illinois Wesleyan University and Mildred's voice teacher, fondly remembers this season in Mildred's life and shares her amazement at Mildred's incredible character and fortitude[22]:

I came to Illinois Wesleyan University in August 1998 as Assistant Professor of Voice in the School of Music. I met Dr. Mildred Pratt soon after that, in November 1998, when she came to the first concert I did at IWU [Illinois Wesleyan University]. She introduced herself to me after that concert, and we hit it off immediately. After that, she rarely missed any of my performances on campus and was most often at programs I sang in the community. I could count on walking out onto the Westbrook Auditorium stage at IWU and seeing her on my right about halfway back, smiling that wonderful smile.

Each year, I organize and coordinate the Festival of Spirituals and Songs in Honor of Reverend Dr. Martin Luther King, Jr.[MLK] to commemorate the King

Holiday. This event is held at IWU's Evelyn Chapel. Again, Dr. Pratt was at the first one, sitting on my right in about row seven, and she came to every one until she was no longer able. After the program we would usually find time to sit and talk—about spirituals, about singing, about life. It was during one of these times, January 2008, that Dr. Pratt said to me, "Dr. Moham"—she always called me Dr. Moham no matter how many times I told her to call me Carren. She just smiled and repeated, "Dr. Moham"—"I have a project that I need your help with." I knew about the Pratt Foundation, so I assumed that the project had something to do with the Foundation.

I saw Dr. Pratt at several functions after that point, but she didn't mention the project. Then, in June 2008, she called me up and asked to meet with me about her project. We made an appointment for her to come by my office to discuss it. She came to the appointment, and after we talked for a while, she reached into her bag and took out a list of some of her favorite spirituals and songs and showed it to me. She told me that she wanted to do a DVD of her singing some of them to leave for her family as a remembrance after she was gone. She said that she had discussed the idea with members of her family, and some of them thought that it was weird. She asked me what I thought. I told her that I thought that it would be a very special gift and that I was sure that her family would come to think so as well.

I then asked her some questions about her singing background—had she ever sung before; had she ever taken voice lessons before—the usual questions. She smiled that wonderful smile of hers, giggled, looked up at me, and replied, "No." Naturally, I was thinking, *Oh, dear,* in my head, but didn't say it out loud. I could tell that this was something that was very important to Dr. Pratt, so I said to her, "Well, let's see what we can do." So we scheduled a voice lesson time and went to work—getting the vocal cords stretched out, getting the breath support going, learning the music, [and] figuring out which songs she really wanted to record— or, as she said, "the ones I sound the best on."

Dr. Pratt had at least one lesson per week for the next several weeks. One day after we had been working together for about four months (and I thought things were going pretty well), I was reading my email the day after her lesson. There was an email from Dr. Pratt's daughter, Menah, on Dr. Pratt's behalf.[23] It seemed that Dr. Pratt thought that things were taking too long, and she wanted to speed them along. She had envisioned this whole process taking only a couple of months. I couldn't help but smile. I emailed back and explained that I knew that the project was important to Dr. Pratt, and we wouldn't take any longer than was necessary to do it right and do it well. And, as I told Dr. Pratt at her next lesson, it was, after all, for posterity, and she wanted to sound her best!

Dr. Pratt was very determined; she practiced diligently, and she sounded pretty good—especially for someone who was about to turn 80 and had never really sung before! She was so proud of herself when she really got her breath support going, because as she said, "It really helps with my swimming!" We made two DVD recordings in July 2009. The first one was of Dr. Pratt singing 17 of the spirituals and songs from the list she brought in. The second was of her reading some of her favorite poems, including one that she wrote for her 80th birthday and gave me a copy of called, "A Quarrel Among Body Parts." She was so nervous and excited when we were making the DVDs—that giggle! She giggled at the end of the last song because she thought she had messed up. She didn't know it at the time, but I left that giggle on the recording.

Dr. Pratt really got into singing and performing. The next thing I knew, she was singing all over the community, giving short recitals in several venues around town. She often threw herself big birthday parties for which she cooked delicious foods. At the end of the meal on her 80th birthday celebration, she told us that she had a surprise for us. We adjourned to the clubhouse, where she treated us with a 30-minute recital of some of the songs that she and I had worked on and recorded. She dedicated the performance to me, and I was never so happy and so proud of one of my students! We often enjoyed the treat of hearing her sing for us at other parties after that. I told her that I thought we had discovered her "inner diva," to which she giggled and exclaimed, "I think we did!" I often refer to my voice students as "my kids," and Dr. Pratt was always very excited to tell people that she studied voice with me and that, she, too, was one of "my kids."

Dr. Pratt and I were talking after her lesson one day when she asked me about the portrait and the several likenesses of Marian Anderson that are hanging in my office. I explained that Marian Anderson was one of my idols; however, she was also a distant cousin of my maternal grandfather. At our next meeting she brought an original program of a concert she [had] attended given by Marian Anderson on March 7, 1954, at the Murat Theatre in Indianapolis, Indiana. That concert program now hangs in my office under the portrait of Marian Anderson.

Dr. Pratt told me that she wanted me to sing that program for her before she died. Marian Anderson was a contralto and I am a soprano, so I couldn't reproduce the program exactly. However, on February 27, 2011, I performed a program entitled "A Tribute to Marian Anderson," on which I sang many of the songs from the 1954 program and dedicated [them] to Dr. Pratt. I walked out onto the stage, and there was Dr. Pratt, on my right about halfway back.

I mentioned earlier the Festival of Spirituals and Songs in Honor of Reverend Dr. Martin Luther King, Jr. I always ended this program by singing my rendition of the spiritual, "Wade in the Water." One year I decided not to sing it, thinking that everyone was probably tired of hearing it. Unbeknownst to me, that was Dr. Pratt's favorite part of the program. She was not happy that I decided not to include it on the program that year. She didn't say anything right then and there. However, when I returned to my office, I received a call from her. She let me know in her very straightforward yet loving way that she didn't think it was a good idea for me to omit "Wade in the Water" from the program, and, while she wasn't trying to tell me what to do, she thought I should add it back to the program the next year.

I said okay, hung up the phone, and went to my colleague's office and told him, "Dr. Pratt just got on me for leaving 'Wade in the Water' off the MLK program." We both laughed out loud. I added it back the next year and have ended the MLK program with it since. Dr. Pratt came up to me that year and thanked me for putting "Wade in the Water" back on the program, and she told me then that she wanted me to sing it at her funeral. I asked her why she didn't include it on her DVD. She said, "Because I want to remember you singing it."

Amazing Grace

Mildred recorded her program in 2009. However, she continued to live a robust and full life after 2009. She travelled internationally, she attended her son Awadagin's concerts, and she even managed to sing at his wedding in December 2011. Unexpectedly in May of 2012, she was diagnosed with cancer. After a short round of chemotherapy in June, Mildred decided to meet death with the same passion and enthusiasm with which she had embraced life.

She participated in the family reunion on July 5th and 6th with relatives from Sierra Leone. She took morning wheelchair rides as long as she could to see the sunrise in the morning. However, she stopped eating on July 21st and was getting progressively weaker. Ten days before Mildred died, on July 27th, her wonderful friends from Bloomington—Pam Muirhead, Patsy Bowles, and Darlene Miller—came to visit her. Mildred was now living with her daughter, Menah, in Urbana. Everyone went into her bedroom. They talked and sang, but Mildred was unresponsive.

So after a bit, they left her room and went into the living room. Mildred's grandson, Emmanuel, stayed in the bedroom with Mildred so that she would not be alone. After a few minutes, Emmanuel came to the living room and said, "She wants you back." When asked how he knew this, he said that she said something about "those people." Emmanuel was Mildred's "little buddy," as she called him during her stay at the house. He spent hours with her as she was transitioning, and he'd had always had a special, patient, loving, and kind relationship with her. He understood her and knew that she wanted everyone back in the room.

So everyone went back into the bedroom, and Mama said, "Sing." After some discussion of what song to sing, Patsy, Darlene, and Pam decided on "Amazing Grace." They sang the first verse and then realized that they did not know the other verses. So Pam took out her iPod to find the other verses and began to line out the song for Patsy and Darlene in the style of the old Black church. Pam, an English professor, began by reading the first line in a dignified manner, like a true poet: "'Twas grace that taught my heart to fear." The group then repeated in song, "'Twas grace that taught my heart to fear." Pam continued, "And grace my fears relieved," and they repeated in song. All of a sudden, Mama said, "You all not too good."

Everyone was shocked. Mama hadn't not spoken at all during the entire visit. Everyone laughed, including Mama. They did sound terrible and they knew it. They promised Mama they would do better. Mama decided that she needed to help out and sing with them. She drank a little water and started to sing, "Through many dangers, toils, and snares I have already come." Too weak to continue, she allowed them to finish: "'Tis grace that brought me safe thus far and grace will lead me home."

Darlene, Patsy, and Pam sang the two remaining verses:
The Lord has promised good to me,
His Word my hope secures;
He will my shield and portion be,
As long as life endures.

Yea, when this flesh and heart shall fail,
And mortal life shall cease,
I shall possess within the veil,
A life of joy and peace.

As soon as they finished, Mama said, "Give yourselves a round of applause." She put her hands together and clapped and said, "Bless you, bless you all." It was truly amazing—amazing grace and an amazing gift. With all the grace in the world, Mildred transitioned to sing in the heavenly choir on August 6, 2012.

The Concert

Mildred's service was held on August 19, 2012, at Illinois Wesleyan University. I [Menah] spoke at the service. The program was entitled, "Mildred's message to the Universe." My [Menah's] remarks are below[24]:

Good evening. Awadagin and I are extremely grateful that each of you was willing to come and help celebrate and remember our mom's fabulous, full, and enriching life. For those of you who knew my mom well, you will appreciate that she had planned for this day for a long time. She was not afraid of death; she prepared for it and she prepared us for it. She got all her affairs in order—her will, her power of attorney, her health-care documents. She was deliberate about it. In fact, after one visit to her attorney, Frank Miles, she said to me, "Menah, I've decided I'm not going to die." I said, "What do you mean?" She said, "It's just too much work!" We laughed so much—like she had a choice over the inevitable! But, she put a lot of work into planning for dying. My brother and I were talking about how many letters we received from Mama about the end of her life journey. The first one I found was dated August 10, 1999, almost 14 years ago.

She wrote a letter to my brother and me. It said, "In the event of my death, please do the following…." It listed several things to do, and then she added the following note: "I have had a good life. I love you and your children dearly. Please continue to be good people, honest and fair, and helpful to people." I think those words reflect what she stood for—being a good person, being honest and fair, and being helpful to people.

What is fascinating is that at the age of 70, she was content with her journey, but she continued to live an even more amazing life. She traveled to Europe, Hungary, and Czechoslovakia with Elderhostel; she went to Albuquerque, New Mexico, to see hot air balloons through Elderhostel; she went on a Mediterranean cruise to see the Sistine Chapel in Italy; she went to the Bahamas to see me renew my wedding vows; she went to the White House to hear her son play in front of President and Mrs. Obama; and she spent a lot of time with her grandchildren, Alexander, Emmanuel, and Raebekkah. She also had gigantic home-cooked dinner parties at her home. But she also continued to think about this day.

On June 30, 2008 (almost four years ago), she wrote another letter to my brother and me. It said, "I will be taped singing and reciting my favorite poetry. The audio/video tape of me singing and reciting should be the program." So today is that day that she planned for several years ago. In the summer of 2008, at the age of 80, she took voice lessons with Dr. Carren Moham and poetry lessons with Dr. Pam Muirhead, faculty members at Illinois Wesleyan University. After a year of lessons, she recorded this concert in July of 2009.

She had written a little note that she wanted me to share about the program. The note reads:

Thank you all for being great friends to me and to my children and grandchildren. I hope that you will enjoy the music[25] and poetry.[26] Many of the songs…

are ones that as a child in rural Texas we sang and recited at night as we assembled around the potbelly wood-burning heater at bedtime. Many of the poems I selected are ones that I said in college in my first and only poetry recital. I was 16 years of age then and had memorized all of the poems. Sorry, at 80 my brain is a bit [too] lazy to memorize the poetry. The voice lessons, in particular, were so important to me because in college my professor told me that the children in the choir complained that I was an obstruction to them because I sang both alto and soprano. What none of them knew was that I did not know the difference between the two. As you listen to me sing, if you hear some of both, I hope you'll understand. I wish you, your family, friends, and all on planet earth peace and meaningful lives.

The program today is called "Mildred's Message to the Universe." Gerry Erley, a local Bloomington artist, created the cover program with that title (see Figure 12.2: Mildred Message to the Universe, 2012). So today is Mildred's message to us through song and poetry. It is a message of courage, perseverance, and triumph over obstacles. It is also about the power of the human spirit. It is about her experiences as a Black woman born to ancestors of slaves, surviving the Great Depression and sharecropping, achieving success, and giving back. It is about searching for meaning in the world, for understanding life and death.

Carren did indeed sing Wade in the Water at Mildred's service. In her death, Mildred not only left a gift of poetry and spirituals, but she also left a legacy of a life fully lived. Most importantly, she left a template of how she did it and how we can do it. Her journals, papers, and life story were left behind to inspire, encourage, and enlighten the world (see Figure 12.3: Photograph of Mildred's journals and writings, 2017). Thank you, Mama.

Photos

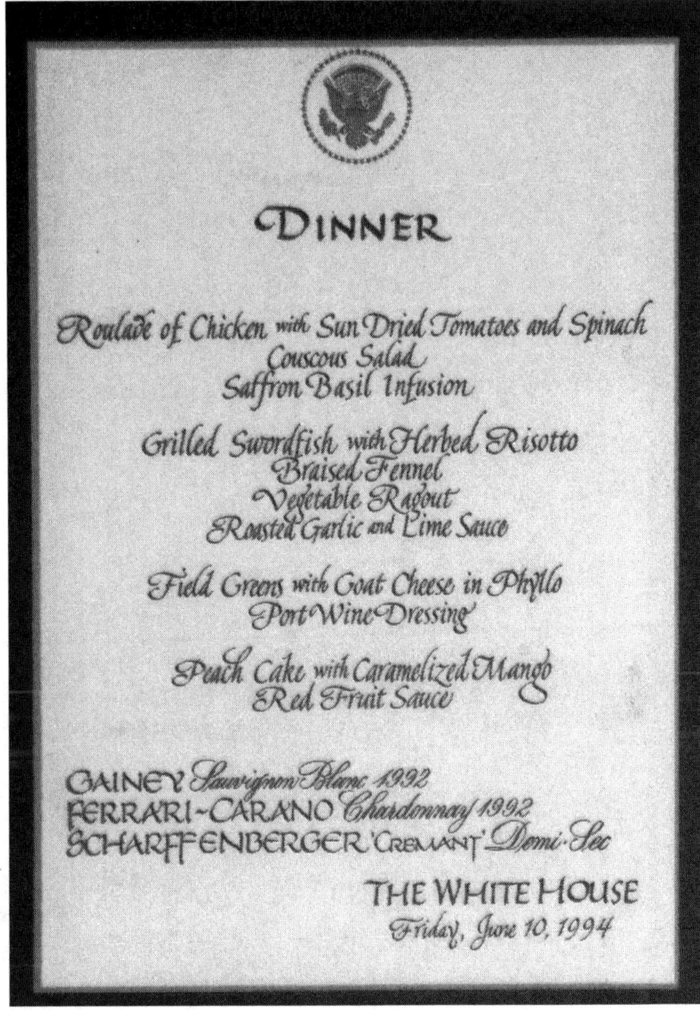

Figure 12.1: White House dinner menu, June 10, 1994.
Source: M. Pratt.

Figure 12.2: Mildred's message to the universe, 2012
Source: Gerard Erley, artist, with permission.

Figure 12.3: Mildred Pratt, journals and writings, 2017
Source: M. Pratt-Clarke.

Notes

1. (M. Perry, personal communication, n.d.).
2. Marian Anderson was well-known in the Black community. See Taulbert (1992, p. 35) and Andrews (1990, p. 214).
3. (M. Pratt, personal communication, n.d.).
4. (M. Pratt, personal communication).
5. For more about Awadagin's musical career, see Awadagin (n.d.); Easton (1992); and Wigler (1992).
6. (M. Pratt, personal communication, n.d.).
7. (M. Pratt, personal communication, June 10, 1994).
8. (M. Pratt, personal communication, June 13, 1994).
9. (M. Pratt, personal communication, n.d.).
10. Gellert Modos was an Illinois State University music professor and the piano teacher for Menah and Awadagin in Normal. See Bishop (1986).
11. (M. Pratt, personal communication, 1996).
12. (M. Pratt, personal communication, n.d.).
13. ("Awadagin Pratt Performs at the White House").
14. (M. Pratt, personal communication, 2009).
15. (M. Pratt, personal communication, n.d.).
16. (Pratt & Pratt-Clarke, 2002, pp. 73–75). Reprinted with permission from Heartland Publishing, May 10, 2017.
17. (M. Pratt, personal communication, n.d.).
18. (M. Pratt, personal communication, n.d.).
19. (M. Pratt, personal communication, n.d.).
20. ("Pratt Music Foundation").
21. (M. Pratt, personal communication, n.d.).
22. (C. Moham, personal communication, February 24, 2013).
23. I [Menah] remember that phone call. Mama called me and politely, but firmly, asked me to send an email to Dr. Moham gently reminding her of the deadline and urgency of the project. I told mama that I was sure she knew it was important. Mama insisted I send the email, which I did.
24. (M. Pratt-Clarke, personal communication, n.d.).
25. Mildred's sang the following songs: *Lord, How Come We Here; Jacob's Ladder; Amazing Grace; Sometimes I Feel Like a Motherless Child; Mother Is Standing by My Bedside Crying; Standin' in the Need of Prayer; Lonesome Valley; Honor, Honor; If I Had a Hammer; Last Night I Had the Strangest Dream; Kumbaya; Study War No More; We Shall Overcome; Swing Low, Sweet Chariot;* and *Ride On, King Jesus.*
26. Mildred recited the following poems: *The Creation,* James Weldon Johnson; *The Negro Mother,* Langston Hughes; *Mother to Son,* Langston Hughes; *We Wear the Mask,* Paul Lawrence Dunbar; *I Dream a World,* Langston Hughes; *Invictus,* William Ernest Henley; *Crossing the Bar,* Alfred Lord Tennyson; *Macbeth, Act 5, Scene 5, 19–28.* William Shakespeare; *Death,* Joyce Grenfell; *If I Should Die,* Thomas Gray; *A Late Lark Twitters,* William Henley; *Remember Me,* David Harkins; *To Those I Loved,* Isla Paschal Richardson; *Do Not Stand By My Grave and Weep,* Mary Frye; *Bed Ritual,* Mildred Pratt; *A Quarrel Between Body Parts,* Mildred Pratt.

References

Andrews, R. (1990). *The last radio baby: A memoir.* Atlanta, GA: Peachtree Publishers.

Awadagin. (n.d.) *Awadagin Pratt Biography.* Retrieved August 5, 2013 from http://www.awadagin.com/biography.htm

Awadagin Pratt performs at the White House: 2 of 8. *The White House.* Retrieved August 5, 2013 from http://www.whitehouse.gov/photos-and-video/video/awadagin-pratt-performs-white-house-2-8

Bishop, R. (1986, May 11). Hungarian pianist will perform Sunday. *The Times-News.*

Easton, T. (1992, May 13). Peabody pianist wins prestigious competition, Pratt is first Black Naumburg recipient. *Baltimore Sun.* Retrieved August 5, 2013 from http://articles.baltimoresun.com/1992-05-13/news/1992134056_1_awadagin-pratt-naumburg-pianist

Pratt, M., & Pratt-Clarke, M. (2002). *A tribute to love: Forty-six personal love stories of romance and marriage.* Bloomington, IL: Heartland Publishing.

Pratt Music Foundation. Retrieved September 1, 2013 from http://prattmusicfoundation.com

Taulbert, C. L. (1992). *The last train north.* New York, NY: Penguin Books.

Wigler, S. (1992, May 17). Pianist follows own path to excellence. *Baltimore Sun.* Retrieved from http://articles.baltimoresun.com/1992-05-17/features/1992138277_1_awadagin-dreadlocks-pianist

Appendix A: Theodore Pratt's Curriculum Vitae

Name
Theodore A.E.C. Pratt

Date of Birth
19 September 1936

Marital Status
Married with two children

Education
High School—Prince of Wales, Freetown, Sierra Leone, 1949–1954
University Education—Fourah Bay College, Freetown, Sierra Leone, 1954–1956
University Education—St. Cuthbertis Society, Durham, England, 1956–1957
University Education—Hampton Institute, Hampton, VA, 1961–1963 (BA '63)
University Education—Carnegie Institute of Technology, Pittsburgh, PA, 1963–
    1967 (MSc '65)
University Education—Carnegie Mellon University, Pittsburgh, PA, 1967–1968
    (PhD '68)

Teaching Employment
Prince of Wales School, Teacher, 1958–1961
Hampton Institute, Teaching Assistant, 1961–1963

Carnegie Institute of Technology, Teaching Assistant, 1963–1965

Hampton Institute, Assistant Professor, 1968–1969

Illinois State University, Assistant Professor, 1969–1974

Federal University of Rio de Janeiro (U.F.R.J.), Brazil, on leave of absence from ISU, working exclusively in administration, teaching, and research at the graduate level in physics, 1972–1973

Research Experience

Oak Ridge National Laboratory, Oak Ridge, TN, Summer 1962

Carnegie Institute of Technology, Research Assistant, 1965–1966

Carnegie Institute of Technology, Project Physicist, 1966–1968

Space Radiation Effects Laboratory, Newport News, VA, Guest Scientist, 1968–1969

Space Radiation Effects Laboratory, Newport News, VA, Visiting Scientist Privileges, 1969

Membership in Professional Societies

American Physical Society

Optical Society of America

American Association of Physics Teachers

American Association for the Advancement of Science

Membership in Honor Societies

Alpha Kappa Mu

Sigma Xi

Miscellaneous Honors

Winner of the Irene Codrington Memorial Prize at Hampton Institute as first graduate of the 1963 zone

Victorian Fellow, International Institute of Education, 1963–1965

Listed in "American Men and Women of Science, Tempe, Arizona"

Summary of Scholarly Productivity Experience

A. Publications concerned with pure and applied physics:
   1. "Muon Partial Capture Rates Using Si28, S32, and Ca40 as Targets and Ge-Li as Detector," *Il Nuovo Cimento* 61B, 119–130 (1969).
   2. "Muonic X-Ray Efficiency Calibration of Germanium–Lithium Drifted Detector," *Nuclear Instruments and Methods* 66, 348–350 (1968).
   3. "The Range Effect in the Gamma Neutrino Angular Correlation Experiment," *Nuclear Instruments and Methods* 66, 351–352 (1968).
   4. "The Resolution Effect in the Gamma Neutrino Angular Correlation Experiment," *Nuclear Instruments and Methods* 70, 213–217 (1969).

5. "The Muon Capture Mechanism in Light Complex Nuclei," *Il Nuovo Cimento* 68A, 477–496 (1970).
6. "A Study of Ge-Li Drifted Gamma Spectrum Shapes" (co-author: M.L. Luther), *Nuclear Instruments and Methods* 92, 317–323 (1971).
7. "The Resolution Effect in the Muon Neutrino Gamma Correlation Revisited," *Nuclear Instruments and Methods* 92, 413–417 (1971).
8. "Some Further Comments on the Muon Capture Mechanism," *Lettere Al Nuovo Cimento* 2(1), 1–6 (1971).
9. "The Background Subtraction Problem Connected with Ge-Li Detector Gamma Shapes," *Nuclear Instruments and Methods* 99, 205–216 (1972).

B. Publications concerned with the teaching of physics:
1. "Construction and Possible Uses of an Electron Linear Accelerator" (co-authors: D. Bamman and E. Lesniak), *American Journal of Physics* 40(11), 1628 (1972).
2. "Teaching Physics without In-Class Examinations," *Revista Brasileira de Fisica* 3(1), 173–180 (1973).
3. "A Study in Student-Teaching Grading Interaction Process" (co-author: M.I. Pratt), abstracted in "Research in Education" published in *Improving College and University Teaching,* Spring 1976.

Note: 170 requests for reprints have been received from 148 scientists in 23 countries.

C. Presentations at various professional meetings:
1. As a student, public presentations were made in 1962 and 1963 at the 16th and 17th Annual Eastern Science Conference at Raleigh, NC, and Boston, MA, respectively.
2. As a professional physicist, public presentations were made at American Physical Society Meetings, *Bulletin of the American Physical Society* 14, 1177 (1969), and *Bulletin of the American Physical Society* 15, 24 (1970); an American Association of Physics Teachers meeting, *American Journal of Physics,* Suppl. 1 40(19), 15 (1972); and the National Symposium on Physics Education, *Brazilian Physical Society, Simposio Nacional de Ensino de Fisica* III(1), 70 (1973).

Appendix B: Mildred Pratt's Curriculum Vitae

Name
Mildred Pratt

Marital Status
Married

Education

1951	BA, Jarvis Christian College, Hawkins, TX. Religion and Sociology.
1952	MA, Butler University, School of Religion, Indianapolis, IN. Psychology and Philosophy of Religion.
1955	MS, Indiana University, Department of Social Service, Bloomington, IN. Social Work.
1969	PhD, University of Pittsburgh, Graduate School of Social Work, Pittsburgh, PA. Community Work and Public Health.

Employment

1952–1954	Flanner House, Indianapolis, IN (Community Work).
1955–1956	All Peoples Church and Community Center, Los Angeles, CA (Girls Social Group Worker).
1956–1959	All Nations Foundation, Los Angeles, CA (Program Director and Camp Director).

1959–1962   Rouge-Ecorse United Community Centers, Ecorse, MI (Program Director and Field Work Supervisor for Wayne State University and University of Michigan Graduate School of Social Work).

1962–1969   University of Pittsburgh, Graduate School of Social Work, Pittsburgh, PA (Field Assistant Professor).

1964   U.S. Department of Health, Education, and Welfare, Agency for International Development (Professional Escort, three months).

1969–1993   Illinois State University, Department of Sociology, Anthropology and Social Work, Normal, IL (Professor).

1993-Present   Illinois State University, Normal, IL (Professor Emerita).

1997–1998   Tennessee State University, Nashville, TN (Adjunct Professor).

1972–1973   Universidade Federal de Rio de Janeiro, Department de Servico de Social, Rio de Janeiro Brasil, and Pontifica Universidade Catholico de Rio de Janeiro, Brasil (Special Lecturer).

Publications

A. Journals

1. Sirls (Pratt, Mildred, et al.), "Group Work Revisited: A Position Statement," *Jewish Social Welfare Forum*, Fall 1967, Vol. 4, No. 2.

2. Pratt, Mildred, "A Model for Social Welfare in National Development," *International Social Work*, 1970, Vol. XIII, No. 1.

3. Pratt, Mildred, "Partisan to the Disadvantaged," *Social Work*, July 1972, Vol. 17, No. 4, pp. 66–72.

4. Pratt, T.A.E.C., and Mildred Pratt, "A Study of Student Teacher Grading Interaction Process," *Journal of College and University Teaching*, Spring 1976.

5. Pratt, Mildred, "Effect of Mechanization on Migrant Farm Workers," *Social Casework*, February 1973, Vol. 54, No. 2, pp. 105–113. Abstract also published in *Social Work Abstracts*.

6. Pratt, Mildred, and Mary Page, "Innovation in Higher Education: Community Laboratory," *Journal of Education for Social Work*, Fall 1973, Vol. 9, No. 3.

7. Pratt, Mildred, "An Approach to Teaching Introductory Course in Social Welfare to Undergraduate Students," summarized in Fall 1973 news of Council on Social Work Education.

8. Pratt, Mildred, "The Social Welfare Institution and African-Americans," *The Journal of Afro-American Issues*, Fall/Summer 1975, Vol. II, No. 3/4, pp. 365–381.

9. Book review of James Montgomery's *Family Crisis* to appear in Fall 1984 *Journal of Comparative Family Studies*.

10. Pratt, Mildred, "Turning Points in African-American History in Bloomington-Normal, IL," *Illinois History Teacher*, 1999, Vol. 7, pp. 30.

B. Books
1. Pratt, Mildred, Cadernos da P.U.C., *Servica de Disenvolvimento,* Pontifica Universidade de Catholica de Rio de Janeiro, Brasil, Divisio de Inter Cambria E. Edicoes, 1973.
2. Pratt, Mildred, "Ida Wells-Barnett," in Trattner, Walter (ed.), *Biographical Dictionary of Social Welfare in America,* Westport, CT: Greenwood Press, 1986.
3. Pratt, Mildred (compiled and edited), *We the People Tell Our Story: Bloomington-Normal Black History Project,* Gummerman Printing, Bloomington, IL, October 3, 1987.
4. Pratt, Mildred, and Pamela Muirhead, "The Black Family: Learning Survival Lessons of the Past," in Rodgers, Augustus (ed.), *The National Black Family Summit* (pp. 349–368), Columbia, SC: College of Social Work, University of South Carolina, 1991.
5. Pratt, Mildred, "Saddler, Juanita," "Sanders, Maude," and "Smith, Celestine," in Hine, Darlene Clark (ed.), *Black Women in America: An Historical Encyclopedia,* Brooklyn: Carlson Publishing, Inc., 1993.

C. Presentations
1975, Pan-African Studies Second National Conference at University of Louisville, Louisville, KY, "The Institution of Social Welfare and African-Americans."
1977, workshop conducted for Department of Children and Family Services, "Knowledge About Ethnic Minorities Relevant to the Provision of Homemaker Services."
1977, paper presented at workshop on aging, "Aspects of Aging."
1983, discussant at the Illinois Child Care Association, Chicago, IL, "Socializing African-American Children in an Era of Renewed Racism."
1983, participant in a roundtable at the Annual Program Meeting of the Council on Social Work Education, Ft. Worth, TX, "Strategies to Maintain Student Enrollment in Bachelor's of Social Work Courses."
1984, participant in a roundtable at the Annual Program Meeting of the Council on Social Work Education, Detroit, MI, "Strategies for Faculty Development in Undergraduate Social Work Programs: Persisting Through 'Publish or Perish' Policies."
1984, presented a paper at the Regional Conference on Social Work Education, University of Wisconsin, Eau Claire, WI, "Multiple Approaches to Increasing and Retaining Student Enrollment."
1984, resource person for a symposium at the Annual Program Meeting of the Council on Social Work Education, Detroit, MI, entitled, "Doing More with Less: Maintaining Quality in Baccalaureate Social Work Education."

1985, presented a paper at the Annual Program Meeting of Council on Social Work Education, Washington, DC, "Oral History: Teaching Its Use for Social Work Practice."

1985, keynote speaker for Illinois Department of Children and Family Services First Intercultural Conference, Chicago, IL, "Providing a Framework for Working with Cultural Groups in Child Welfare."

1987, speaker for Illinois Department of Children and Family Services Conference, Chicago, IL, "Bridging Racial and Cultural Differences."

1987, speaker for Illinois Department of Children and Family Services, Chicago, IL, "Bridging Racial and Cultural Differences."

1987, speaker at Children's Memorial Hospital, Chicago, IL, "Relevance of Race and Ethnicity in Medical Social Work."

1987, presentation at the National Association of Black Social Workers, Boston, MA, "Social Support and African-American Families: Past Knowledge and Future Directions."

1987, program and exhibit, McLean County Historical Society and Museum, Bloomington, IL, "Bloomington-Normal Black History."

1988, presentation at the National Association of Black Social Workers, San Francisco, CA, "A Model for Using Local Black History Product and Process to Empower Elderly Blacks and Socialize Young Blacks for the Decade Ahead."

1988, presentation at the National Association of Social Workers, Philadelphia, PA, "An Innovative Social Work Practice Approach: Use of Local Black History Project to Empower Elderly Blacks."

1989, presentation at Council on Social Work Education Annual Meeting, Chicago, IL, "Local Social History of African-Americans: An Approach to Meeting Ethnic Identity Needs in a Complex Society."

1989, presentation at Afro-American Historical and Genealogical Society, Washington, DC, "A Case of Local Black History."

1989, keynote speaker at Banquet of the Central District Club of Women and Girls, Normal, IL, "A Look to the Past for Strength to Face the Future."

1989, presentation at the Logan County Correctional Center, Lincoln, IL, "The Bloomington-Normal Black History Project."

1989, presentation at Little Egypt Afro-American Historical and Genealogical Society, Southern Illinois University, Carbondale, IL, "We the People Tell Our Own Story."

1990, presentation at the 75th Annual Meeting of the Association for the Study of African-American Life and History, Chicago, IL, "Conceptualization of the Underground Railroad as Social Welfare."

1990, presentation at the Afro-American Historical and Genealogical Society, Washington, DC, "Institutionalizing Local Black History Projects."

1991, keynote speaker for the First Annual Dr. Martin Luther King Jr. Gospel Festival, "Go Tell It on the Mountain: We Shall Overcome."

1991, presentation at the Black Family Summit, Columbia, SC, "The Black Family: Learning Survival Lessons of the Past."

1991, presentation at the Illinois Department of Children and Family Service Adoption Conference, Schaumburg, IL, "Transracial Adoption: Is it in the Best Interest of the Child?"

1991, part of a panel at the Association for the Study of African-American History, Washington, DC, "Anatomy of a Local History Project: Blacks in Illinois, the Bloomington-Normal Experience."

1992, presentation at the Annual Regional Conference of Historic Preservation Commissions, Webster Groves, MO, "The Organization of the Bloomington-Normal Black History and Culture Consortium."

1992, presentation at Links, Inc. Bloomington, IL, "Cherishing the Best: Cultivating the Present, Creating the Future."

1993, presentation, Black Family Summit, University of South Carolina, School of Social Work, Columbia, SC, "Please Mamma, Don't Give Me No More Cowchip Tea: African-American Folk Remedies and Their Implications for Medical Care Personnel."

1993, presentation at Illinois State Department of Children and Family Services, Collinsville, IL, "Transracial Adoptions."

1993, presentation at the Afro-American Historical and Genealogical Society 16th Annual Conference, Carbondale, IL, "The Importance of Local Black History."

1993, presentation at the Illinois, Beginning with Women...: Histories and Cultures conference, University of Illinois, Women's Studies Program, Urbana, IL, "Maude Sanders: A Black Peoria Physician Against the Odds."

Other Scholarly Activities

1. A full page of my article published in the *Journal of Education for Social Work*, Fall 1973, was quoted in the book *Institution for Social Welfare* by Rex Skidmore and Milton Thackery (pp. 208–209).

2. My article published in *International Social Work*, Vol. XIII, No. 1, 1970, was quoted in the *Journal of Education for Social Work*, Fall 1978, by Laura Jamishida.

3. 1978, keynote speaker and resource person at the Springfield Chapter of the Association of Black Social Workers Conference.

4. 1978, the National Public Law Training Center in Washington, DC, requested a reprint of "Partisan the Disadvantaged" to use in their classes.
5. 1980, discussant at the National Association of Social Workers Illinois Chapter First Biennial Symposium for the presentation of a paper which I helped prepare titled "The BSW [Bachelor of Social Work], a Boom or Bust for Social Work Practice: A Report of the Joint School Survey of 1979 Baccalaureate Social Work Graduates."
6. 1980, reviewer for the *Human Organization Journal of the Society for Applied Anthropology.*
7. 1980, reader for manuscripts for the National Association of Social Workers Illinois Chapter Biennial Symposium.
8. 1983, reviewed a manuscript for the *Journal of Human Organization* entitled "The Rise and Fall of a Social Experiment."
9. June 3, 1985, speaker and workshop leader on "What Is Culture?" and "Black Culture" at a training program sponsored by the Illinois Coalition Against Sexual Assault in Starved Rock Park, IL.
10. June 3, 1985, workshop speaker on "Black Families" at the Ounce of Prevention Training Program in Bloomington, IL.
11. 1985, reviewed a manuscript for *Human Organization: Journal of the Society for Applied Anthropology.*
12. June 28–30, 1985, attended the Bertha C. Reynolds Centennial Conference with a partial scholarship from the sponsors of the conference for an essay which I entered in a contest honoring Frank Bancroft.
13. 1986, "The Underground Railroad: Conceptualized as a Social Welfare System," accepted for publication by *The Western Journal of Black Studies.*
14. April 1988, gave presentation on "Black History" at the Department of Children and Family Services Workshop on Cultural Awareness in Bloomington, IL.
15. January 1988, set up the Bloomington-Normal Black History Exhibit for Fest at University High School.
16. January 1988, set up the Bloomington-Normal Black History Exhibit for the Bloomington-Normal Human Relations Commission Awards Dinner.
17. October 30, 1990, speaker for professional staff on "How to Work With Ethnic Minorities," at McLean County Human Services in Bloomington, IL.
18. February 20, 1990, presented "History of Blacks in Bloomington-Normal" at ISU's Multi-Cultural Center in Normal, IL.
19. April 10, 1990, special guest panelist for panel discussion on "The Black Family: Coming Together Through Foster Care and Adoption" in Bloomington, IL.

20. February 23, 1990, speaker on "The Father of Black History: Carter G. Woodson, a Living Legacy" for the staff of the Springfield District of the Department of Internal Revenue in Bloomington, IL.
21. November 1990–June 1991, Member of the Illinois Department of Children and Family Services Ad Hoc Advisory Committee on Transracial Adoptions.
22. May 16, 1991, presented a speech on "Stewards of Our Heritage" at the Martin Luther King Community Center's Program, "Black Women: Achievements Against the Odds," in Rock Island, IL.
23. 1991–present, appointed by the Department of Children and Family Services' Director to the Roundtable for African-American Children and Families.
24. 1991–present, Member of the Minority Heritage Committee of the Illinois State Historical Society.
25. July 1991, presented a workshop on "How to Start a Local Black History Project" at the Little Egypt Afro-American Historical and Genealogical Society Meeting in Carbondale, IL.

Special Activities
A. 1972–1973, leave of absence activities in Brazil.
   1. Teaching activities (courses)
      a. "Some Group Work and Group Concepts Relevant to Community Development in Brazil," Department of Social Service, Pontifica Universidade de Catholica de Janeiro.
      b. "Group Work as a Method in Social Work," Department of Social Service, Pontifica Universidade de Catholico de Rio de Janeiro.
      c. "Group Theories in Community Work Practice," Department of Social Service, Pontifica Universidade de Catholico de Rio de Janeiro.
   2. Special lectures
      a. "Some Aspects of Community Work Practice," Department of Social Service, Universidade Federal de Rio de Janeiro.
      b. "Social Group Work in Community Development," main guest speaker for Social Work Month in Brazil (Victoria, Santos, and Dumont).
   3. Visitations
      a. I traveled to some (6) states in Brazil, learning about the cultural, social, and economic aspects of the country.
      b. I visited a wide variety of social welfare service agencies in Rio de Janeiro as well as a major Latin-American center for social research.

B. Grants

    1962–1963, U.S. Public Health Service Fellowship for PhD study at the University of Pittsburgh.

    1970, received two ISU [Illinois State University] faculty development grants, which totaled $1,314.

    1970, received $1,001 on an ISU research grant.

    1976, received an I.D.P. [Innovative Design Project] grant from ISU for the amount of $305.

    1985, received $437.90 from the Bloomington Human Relations Commission for the History of Blacks in Bloomington Project.

    1986, received a $620 grant from the Department of Sociology, Anthropology, and Social Work.

    1986, received a $1,000 grant from the Illinois Humanities Council and the National Endowment for the Humanities.

    1988, received a $4,500 grant from the Illinois Humanities Council and the National Endowment for the Humanities.

    1988, received $400 from the Illinois Humanities Council and National Endowment for the Humanities.

    1988, received $1,500 from the Alice and Fannie Fell Trust (ISU Foundation).

    1990, received $750 from the McLean County Arts Council.

    1991, received a $2,880 grant from the Illinois Arts Council.

    1992, received $2,550 from the Illinois Arts Council.

    1992, received $2,750 from the Illinois State Board of Education.

C. Service Activities in and outside of University Settings and Committees on which I Served at Illinois State University

1. Board Member of the McLean County Family Services Agency.

2. Member of the University Task Force for a School of Social Work.

3. Member of the Faculty Development Grant Committee.

4. Member of the University Child Care Task Force.

5. Member of the College of Arts and Science Committee to evaluate the Sociology-Anthropology Department.

6. Member of the Sociology-Anthropology Faculty Status Committee and Council.

7. Chairperson of the Committee to Design an Undergraduate Major in Social Work.

8. Member of the University to Redesign the Health, Physical Education, Recreation, and Dance Programs.

9. Member of the Academic Freedom Committee.

10. Member of the Human Relations Committee.
11. Member of ISU Graduate Council and Chairperson of the Admissions Committee.
12. Elected by ISU Academic Senate to the Panel of 10 (the committee from which search committee chairs are selected).

External Service Activities

1. Consultant to Pittsburgh Child Guidance Clinic.
2. Directed a workshop for the Illinois Department of Children and Family Services.
3. Member of subcommittee of McLean County Planning Commission.
4. Member of Illinois Interagency Committee on Migrant Affairs.
5. 1980–present, Member of McLean County Welfare Service Committee.
6. 1983 May, appointed to the Council on Social Work Education Task Force on Recruitment of Students into Social Work Education Programs.
7. 1983, appointed to the John Scott Center Board.
8. 1984 February, nominated for election to the Council on Social Work Education's House of Delegates representing Black educators.
9. 1985, Member of Council on Social Work Education Corresponding Committee.
10. 1988–1989, Member of Governor's Illinois Forum on Welfare Reform.
11. Member of the Board of McLean County Historical Society.
12. Member of the Advisory Committee for the development of an Illinois African-American Heritage Trail Guide, sponsored by the Illinois Department of Commerce and Committee Affairs, Bureau of Tourism, Illinois Historic Preservation Agency, DuSable Museum, and *Chicago Sun Times*.

Honors

1. Listed in the *World Who's Who of Women in Education*.
2. Listed in *Who's Who of American Women*.
3. 1981, selected to be a site visitor for Council on Social Work Education Accreditation of Undergraduate Social Work Programs.
4. Recipient of "Citizen of the Year" award from the Omega Psi Phi Fraternity, Inc.
5. 1988, recipient of "Award of Gratitude" from the Peoria Housing Authority.
6. 1989, recipient of the Town of Normal Martin Luther King Human Relations Award.
7. 1990, the Bloomington-Normal Black History Project (of which I am founder and co-director) received a superior rating from the Illinois Congress of Historical Societies and Museums.

8. 1990, recipient of a certificate from the YWCA in recognition of having been nominated as a "Woman of Distinction."

9. May 16, 1991, recipient of a Certificate of Appreciation at the Rock Island Martin Luther King Community Center Program, "Black Women: Achievements Against the Odds."

10. 1991, Martin Luther King Committee Center Award for Community Service, Rock Island, IL.

11. 1992, Martin Luther King Gospelfest Speaker Award, Bloomington, IL.

12. 1993, Sixth Annual African/Latin-American Recognition and Achievement event, Outstanding Faculty Award.

13. 1993, Baha'i Society Human Relations Award.

14. 1997, 14th Recognition Award for Bloomington-Normal Black History Project.

15. 1998, Award from Illinois State University Honors Program, Nashville, TN.

16. 2001, A Tribute to Black Women Award from the Black Graduate Students, Illinois State University, Normal, IL.

17. 2001, selected to be featured as an April 2002 Illinois State Scholar.

Index

S

ROCHELLE BROCK & CYNTHIA DILLARD
Executive Editors

Black Studies and Critical Thinking is an interdisciplinary series which examines the intellectual traditions of and cultural contributions made by people of African descent throughout the world. Whether it is in literature, art, music, science, or academics, these contributions are vast and far-reaching. As we work to stretch the boundaries of knowledge and understanding of issues critical to the Black experience, this series offers a unique opportunity to study the social, economic, and political forces that have shaped the historic experience of Black America, and that continue to determine our future. Black Studies and Critical Thinking is positioned at the forefront of research on the Black experience, and is the source for dynamic, innovative, and creative exploration of the most vital issues facing African Americans. The series invites contributions from all disciplines but is specially suited for cultural studies, anthropology, history, sociology, literature, art, and music.

Subjects of interest include (but are not limited to):

- EDUCATION
- SOCIOLOGY
- HISTORY
- MEDIA/COMMUNICATION
- RELIGION/THEOLOGY
- WOMEN'S STUDIES

- POLICY STUDIES
- ADVERTISING
- AFRICAN AMERICAN STUDIES
- POLITICAL SCIENCE
- LGBT STUDIES

For additional information about this series or for the submission of manuscripts, please contact Dr. Brock (University of North Carolina at Greensboro) at r_brock@uncg.edu or Dr. Dillard (University of Georgia) at cdillard@uga.com.

To order other books in this series, please contact our Customer Service Department:

(800) 770-LANG (within the U.S.)
(212) 647-7706 (outside the U.S.)
(212) 647-7707 FAX

Or browse online by series at www.peterlang.com.